PREACHING CHRIST

SEEING CHRIST THROUGHOUT THE BIBLE

DR. CHARLES VOGAN

RAVENBROOK PUBLISHERS

www.Ravenbrook.org

www.ShenBible.org

2

CONTENTS

PREFACE

I was not born a Christian; I became one. As a new believer, I had just had an encounter with the living Christ; but that didn't mean that I knew much about him. Like so many others before me, I had a chance to teach and preach about Christ right away as I was training for the ministry. But my lessons revealed a distinct lack of data about Jesus which no amount of inserting his name into my teaching could fix. I really didn't know what I was talking about.

Now it's forty years later and I feel that I'm finally in a position to talk about Jesus. I've done a lot of studying the Bible during that period of time, and the vision of Christ has become much clearer to me.

If you understand the problem that I'm talking about, and you're willing to admit that there is a problem in our churches, maybe you can see why so little of preaching today is really about Jesus. Ignorance about Jesus is impoverishing our modern sermons and Bible teaching. But is it also laziness? I believe that the information that we have in the Bible is open to all who are determined to dig it out; and, according to his promise, the Lord will give wisdom to all who ask for it.

We shouldn't assume that preaching Christ will be easy. It took faith to see him in his day, and it will take faith to dig through the Bible and preach him from every text. We will have more or less trouble seeing Jesus in many texts, Old and New Testaments, because we've been trained *not* to see him in those texts. But as Jesus faithfully taught his disciples to understand him and his ministry, he will do the same for us when we sit at his feet and are willing to listen and learn.

> And beginning with Moses and all the Prophets, he explained to them what was said in all the Scriptures concerning himself. (Luke 24:27)

We have a spiritual crisis in our time because the church isn't applying Christ to the wounds of the modern person. And yet we claim that we are! There are many reasons for the failure of the church to heal our culture and turn it from its mad rush into destruction; but one

5

reason is that nobody has much to say about the Christ. They can't find enough data. The models we are using to interpret the Bible actually dam up the spiritual river of life to a trickle, and people are starving on moralisms and empty promises.

That's what we're going to address in this work. It's time to open the floodgates of the Bible to let the Spirit of truth flow freely in the Church and reveal the fullness of the Son of God to us. The Prophets understood the Messiah, and the Apostles were masters at revealing him to the world. So let's follow their lead as they use the entire Bible to describe Jesus Christ to us.

INTRODUCTION

Just about every evangelical church in the country claims to preach Christ, to be God-centered in its ministry, to "hold up the name of Jesus" in their sermons and Bible lessons. You would be hard-pressed to find a church that didn't make that claim. And yet I've heard many a sermon that didn't do any such thing. The claim was an empty promise. It turned out that they centered on man, not God; they said little to nothing about Jesus; it was all about what we are supposed to do as Christians.

They dropped the name of Jesus all over their sermons and lessons, but always as the object of their actions – almost never as the Primary Mover of our faith, what Hebrews describes as the "author and finisher of our faith." I got the feeling that they actually knew very little about Jesus, which is probably why they didn't tell us much about him. One preacher in particular was trying to describe what life is like in the Trinity, and all he could think of was that Jesus submitted to his Father – leaving vast amounts of treasures unexamined about the Godhead. This in spite of the fact that the passage he was dealing with was full of revelation of the Trinity!

I'm not sure why people keep believing the false advertisement. Perhaps they're weary of church-hopping, of going from place to place looking for some food for their souls. Perhaps they have never heard a Christ-centered sermon and don't know what they're missing. Perhaps it's loyalty to the pastor that keeps them coming back for husks and chaff. But if everyone were honest about this situation, they would change the sign out in front of the church from "Christ-centered" to "man-centered," because that is in fact what's being offered in most churches today. Their claim to being Christ-centered is a lie at the worst, and deep ignorance at best.

Hymn writers, ironically, are better at pointing the way to God than the preachers are. Perhaps that's because the very heart of praise is singling something out in God and giving thanks for it. Why would we praise ourselves? Particularly the older hymns focus on and explain the many aspects of God and his works in Providence and Redemption. Many of the modern songwriters, however, are committing the same error that their counterparts in the pulpit commit – what's called in today's parlance "I love you, Mary" worship songs. They are no more than romance songs with the name switched from "Mary" to "Jesus." But the good songwriters are skillful at bringing us to the throne of God and showing us his glory.

> Our God, our help in ages past,
> Our hope for years to come,
> Our shelter from the stormy blast,
> And our eternal home.
>
> Under the shadow of Thy throne
> Thy saints have dwelt secure;
> Sufficient is Thine arm alone,
> And our defense is sure.
>
> Before the hills in order stood,
> Or earth received her frame,
> From everlasting Thou art God,
> To endless years the same.
>
> *Isaac Watts, 1719*

What's the problem?

Why is it that our modern sermons aren't focusing on Christ? I think there are several reasons, and they are due to the changing theological currents in our modern times. *First*, remember that *preachers* deliver sermons, and they (for the most part) spent several years in college and/or seminary learning how to do it. They took both theology and homiletics classes, and they were called "Masters of Divinity" when they graduated. The problem is that they received what's commonly called a "fire-hose" education – lots of material thrown at them in a short time and regurgitated for exams. Most of that material is still in their notes but not in their heads anymore; they actually aren't masters of anything. And when they move on to their first church, they find that the typical pastorate doesn't allow them the leisure to go back over those notes, let alone do any more studying. So their educational plateau happened at school; they're not in study mode anymore. Maybe you weren't aware of this fact, but most sermons are born out of commentaries, not from studying the text of the Bible itself.

For the *second* reason for sermons without Christ, we have to go back to the seminary itself. There are two problems here. One was terribly misleading, and the other is simple ignorance.

Future pastors are, for the most part, told that the only good information that we have about Jesus is in the New Testament. We are, so the theory goes, New Testament Christians – heirs of the New Covenant in Christ. The Old Testament is relegated to the background as a confusing Jewish document that has only minimal use for Christians. There are all sorts of ways to discredit the Old Testament; and by the time the poor student graduates, he has learned that nobody seems to be agreed on how to interpret the Old Testament – so it's probably safer to stay away from it.

As we shall see in this study, however, that approach to the Old Testament is fatal to the story of Jesus. The New Testament depends on the Old. Though that claim has been made many times as well, it seems that professors are at a loss to show us that principle in action. Which leads us to the second problem in modern schools: they really don't know what the Old Testament has to say about Jesus. They don't seem to know *how* the New Testament depends on the Old. When put to the test, their claim that "all of Scripture is about Christ" is hard for them to prove, given the paltry data at hand. Scholars have come up with the Progressive Revelation theory – that the story of redemption progresses from seed form through the Old Testament history until it blooms fully into the Gospel in the New Testament. But that approach leaves all sorts of hermeneutical questions unanswered: for example, what about the saints of the Old Testament and their brand of "faith"? How could the Jews be held accountable if they didn't have the data? How did the spiritual giants of Israel like Moses and David relate to God, without the Christian realities that we now have? And how exactly do we use Old Testament concepts if the only "useable" doctrine for the Church is exclusive to the New Testament? [1]

So, because pastors got such a bad start in school on how to handle the message of the Bible, they feel pretty much on their own when they get up in the pulpit and start talking about Jesus and our Christian lives. It comes much easier to fall back on more familiar territory – in other words, morality lessons.

How not to do it

It's too bad that people are so easily impressed with the superficial. Many a churchgoer has come out of a service declaring of the pastor that "he really preached Christ today!" when all that happened is that the preacher dropped the name of Christ everywhere in the sermon without telling anything about him.

Let me explain. If you've taken English grammar, you will be familiar with the following diagram:

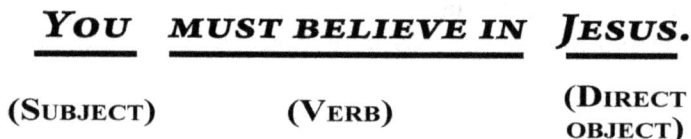

YOU *MUST BELIEVE IN* *JESUS.*

(SUBJECT) **(VERB)** **(DIRECT OBJECT)**

In a typical English sentence, the Subject does the action upon the Direct Object. In this sentence, "You" are doing something to "Jesus." At times this kind of thing needs to be said. But when you listen to the typical modern sermon, it's full of this kind of sentence. "You have to trust in Jesus." "We have to be holy." "You have to follow Jesus." "Stop your sinning and come to God!" "Repent and believe." The subject is almost always *you* – you are doing all the action.

The problem with that is that there's no salvation in it. It's not what *we* do that saves us, it's what Jesus does. He should be the

---

[1] I discuss this subject more at length in my book *A New Model for Biblical Studies*.

primary subject in preaching. That's what the saints need to hear more of.

Dropping Jesus' name all through the sermon like this is not preaching Christ! That's what is confusing people nowadays. They hear the name of Jesus all through the sermon and think that's "preaching Christ." Actually the very opposite is happening. The man is preaching a man-centered sermon; he's telling the congregation that their only hope, their Christian duty, is for *them* to do something for God.

We are told very little about who Jesus is. We could actually change the sentence to read like this –

You must believe in Bob Smith.

– and there wouldn't be any semantic difference between the two sentences.

Focusing on our moral duties appeals to the average conscience because we naturally want to be doing something to secure God's good-will. So, we think, let's just cut to the chase and find out what God wants us to do in order to be in good standing with him.

Some of us, however, would like to know *what* we need to believe about Jesus. Answering that simple question changes the entire makeup of the sermon.

I once sat through a series of sermons on the book of Ephesians in which the preacher was focusing strictly on our duties and responsibilities. "We need to do this" and "we need to do that." As he was moralizing, I started looking in the text for what it said about God and Christ. I found 100 different facts about God in this short letter – all of which are jewels of revelation on what God is like and what he offers us in the Gospel. The whole book is about Jesus, and this preacher was turning it into a book about what *we* should be doing – a string of moralisms. [2]

Moralisms are principles of conduct. It's easy to settle back into moralisms while preaching, because religion so easily ends up in the area of ethics and beliefs. In fact, that's the point of religion, right? To

---

[2] See the *Appendix* for the list from Ephesians.

change our conduct to conform to a standard of what is right versus what is wrong. In other words, changing our morals.

But the difference between Christianity and all other religions is that we believe we can't change our moral makeup or behavior. It requires the hand of God, doing a spiritual miracle and changing our hearts to conform to God's standards. The message of the Gospel is that Jesus came to do it for us; we can't do it ourselves. So the message of every sermon should focus on what God does, not on what we do. Moralisms are for psychologists and Buddhists and Muslims and Jews who demand that you get on the ball and change your behavior. Christianity is for the helpless who need the hand of God.

The standard approach to the Old Testament

I'm going to make a point right here: the Old Testament is critical for our understanding of Jesus. I hope I can demonstrate that principle as we proceed. And every pastor and Bible teacher needs to be skilled at handling the Old Testament. But as I've said before, both seminaries and pastors are really confused about how to use the Old Testament. Most conservatives will agree that the Old Testament is "about Christ," but they haven't much of a clue on what that looks like in practice.

There has always been some kind of attempt at tying the two Testaments together, but the current state of affairs in modern schools is not like it used to be. The approach that modern scholarship uses to analyze how the Old Testament becomes the foundation for the New is made up of several principles:

Prophecy: By far the most popular approach to the Old Testament. There's a standard set of prophecies that Christians use to prove that the message of Christ is indeed in the Old, that people knew back then that there would be a Messiah who would do amazing things. At Christmas and Easter we hear many of them in sermons: the child born to a virgin (Isaiah 7:14); riding into Jerusalem on a donkey (Zechariah 9:9); the Suffering Servant (Isaiah 53); crying out to God on the cross (Psalm 22). These and many other prophecies very obviously point to the One to come who would be our Savior and Redeemer.

The prophecies serve two purposes: *first*, New Testament passages use them to confirm that Jesus really is the Messiah that the Old Testament predicted. And *second*, the prophecies show us what the Jewish hope was in the Messiah. The prophecies in their historical context reveal the kinds of things Israel has been looking for and why.

But once we've made our list of Messianic prophecies, what do we do with the rest of the Old Testament? Is it useless to us? Worse than that, what if those prophecies are actually integrated in complex Old Testament discussions on the nature of the Messiah and his work? If we just pull out the prophecies and say, "Look at these – they predict the coming of Jesus!" and ignore their settings, perhaps we too become as clueless as the Jews were in Jesus' day about what Jesus was doing when he finally arrived. Thus we need the context of the prophecy as well as the prophecy itself.

Typology: A "type" is a pattern or an idea in the Old Testament story that corresponds to the same idea in Jesus. For example, the temple in the Old Testament is a type (as we are told in Hebrews 9:8-9) of Christ. The way into God's presence in the old Temple was closed because of the curtain; that symbolized our separation from the presence of God. But when Jesus died on the cross, the curtain in the Temple was torn in two, foreshadowing the fact that Jesus would open the way to God.

The jury is still out over whether the story of Joseph (the son of Jacob) should be considered a type of Christ, in that he was rejected by his brothers and later rose to second in command in Egypt and saved his family from the famine – corresponding to the same pattern found in Christ's experiences. Without Apostolic confirmation, we're not sure. [3]

Types are a pretty safe way of connecting Old Testament concepts with New Testament realities. In fact, when you follow down through a list of the points of the Old Testament

---

[3] Besides, there's actually a better way to approach this story in the model we will discuss – Distributed Revelation.

character with one finger, and at the same time run down through another list of Jesus doing the same things with the other finger, you feel that you're really on to something.

Types are single events, single individuals that the New Testament uses to explain some feature of Jesus' work. A type is a small-scale version of what we're going to look at later (Distributed Revelation) and not designed to formulate a complete picture of the work of Christ by itself.

Contrast: A favorite way of dealing with Old Testament concepts when the teacher doesn't know what else to say about it! I was reading a commentator on Ecclesiastes lately who said this very thing. To him, the book's main purpose was as a contrast between the way things *ought not* to be (what Ecclesiastes describes) and how they *ought* to be (what we have now in Christ). That's pretty much all he could do with it. My problem with that approach is this: it puts Ecclesiastes on the level of the Bhagavad-Gita or the Egyptian Book of the Dead, or some other non-Christian religious literature that we don't believe in. Why in particular should we study Ecclesiastes if this is what we *don't* want? Again, it convinces the preacher to avoid the Old Testament and just stick with the New, if the Old is simply what we don't have in Christ.

Covenant: There were a number of major covenants, or agreements, recorded in the Old Testament between God and man. We will get into a deeper discussion on the covenants later. For now, however, let's draw our attention to the favorite passage of modern Gospel preachers – the one about the New Covenant.

> By calling this Covenant "new," he has made the first one obsolete. And what is obsolete and aging will soon disappear. (Hebrews 8:13)

Obviously this passage is contrasting the New Covenant with the Old. But before we go charging off in a crusade against the Law, let's ask a question first: which covenant does the writer refer to when talking about the "old" covenant? Most people would answer "the Law," because that's what they've heard since they were children in church. But a closer examination of this passage would show us that this is not exactly true.

> But God *found fault with the people* and said, "The time is coming, declares the Lord, when I will make a new Covenant." (Hebrews 8:8)

The contrast isn't between "the Law" and "the Covenant in Christ." The contrast is between *how* the Law is going to be fulfilled. God had a problem with "the people", not with the Law! If you know the story of the Jews, they had the Law but proved completely unfaithful in keeping that Law. The Covenant at Mt. Sinai, however, was all about that – they were obligated to keep the Law of God upon pain of punishment.

> And if we are careful to obey all of this Law before the LORD our God, as he has commanded us, that will be our righteousness. (Deuteronomy 6:25)

So the "old" Covenant was not the Law, but the agreement on how the Law would be kept – the Jews had to do it themselves, faultlessly. The "new" Covenant is, again, on how the Law would be kept – this time Jesus is going to do it for us. A fine distinction that makes all the difference in the world!

May I point out that my problem with modern sermons revolves precisely around this point: preachers are still prodding their hearers to do something, the very thrust of the "old" Covenant. They themselves have not yet taken the step into the "new" Covenant in which Christ is doing all the work.

Themes: This is probably what most commentators and professors will use to impress their hearers that, yes, they do believe that the Old Testament is the foundation for the New. Most of the themes in the Old (doctrinal and theological) are also found in the New Testament.

For example, the Old Testament idea of the sacrifice that covers over our guilty souls and gives us a substitute is also a foundation of Christ's ministry. The theme of deliverance is found in both Old and New. The Kingdom theme from David is discussed at length in the New. The Old Testament talks

15

about the Creation, and the New talks about the New Creation. Not only do these ideas occur in both Testaments, but the Apostles were careful to point out that fact. Obviously the significance is not to be missed.

But that's pretty much where scholars leave it – significant in some way, but they're afraid to say in what way. The reason they fear to explore this idea is because of the concept of *allegory*.

An allegory is a story full of symbolism. The method is to find a New Testament reality that is symbolized by some aspect in the Old Testament story. For example, Paul says there's an allegory in the story of Hagar and Sarah: Hagar represents the present Jews in their unbelief and rejection, Sarah represents the Christians and their favored status with God.

Allegories can be fun, but turning Old Testament stories everywhere into allegories can also be completely irresponsible. Here's a more dependable rule to follow: let the Apostles tell us where the allegories are. We're not privy to the mind of the Bible's author as Paul was. There may be other allegories in the text, but it would require a good deal of confirmation before the Church can say without hesitation that this was its primary intention. Allegorizing the text goes all way back to the Church Father Origen who first gave this method a bad name because of his inclination to turn the entire Old Testament into allegories. The primary meaning of a text is, first, its plain meaning. After that we need a strong corroboration from the Apostles to proceed further.

A new approach

While all the above are useful in a way, they aren't enough. Without going into a full discussion on the Apostolic use of Old Testament concepts at this point, I'd like to show you a verse from Paul that says it all.

> … the Holy Scriptures, which are able to make you wise for salvation through faith in Christ Jesus. (2 Timothy 3:15)

What he's saying here is fundamental to understanding the Bible, so much so that we don't need any other justification for opening the door to this vast topic. According to Paul, it's the Old Testament that explains Christ. Putting aside for now what the New Testament itself is for, what is the significance of this amazing claim?

- All the doctrinal outlines describing Christ and his work are in the Old Testament.

- The Old Testament saints saw the Christ and understood the truth about him; they had this information about him in *their* Scriptures.

- The New Testament simply borrows the data from the Old when talking about Christ.

- Without the Old Testament (a good understanding of it, not a superficial view!) we can't understand who Christ is or what he does.

Now perhaps you can understand my emphasis on the Old Testament. It's not just a hobbyhorse of mine. It's literally the key to understanding Christ and the Gospel. Without it, you can't understand the truth about Christ, nor can you preach or teach anything resembling what Paul would call the Gospel. Preachers who try are like a doctor attempting to practice medicine without going to medical school first.

I realize that I'm going to have to prove this claim strenuously to convince modern students of the Bible who have seen little of such things themselves. But the authority for my claim is this statement from Paul (along with other passages). If we can't understand why Paul said such a thing, it doesn't therefore mean that Paul was wrong; it means that we have our work cut out for us. It means that we are going to have to dig deeper in the text; we're going to have to find a new approach to uncover what Paul sees.

And in fact this method does exactly that. Like an archaeologist following clues from a manuscript (the New Testament references), we're going to see the bones of the Gospel lying deep in the Old Testament stories. And what's more encouraging, the New Testament writers are going to confirm our discoveries.

Before we start digging, however, let me calm the fears of those who worry about the *differences* between the Testaments. It may seem to them that I'm claiming too much for the Old Testament, as if we don't need the New. Nothing of the sort! The Old Testament has its purposes, and the New has its purposes. To put it succinctly, the Old outlines the doctrines of the Christ, and the New introduces us to him. After learning everything we need to know about our God and his Kingdom in the Old, the New Testament writers reveal the Son of God to us, the one from Heaven, who plans to take us back there to live with God in a new Creation. We learned what had to happen in the Old, but now know that it's going to work because of the One who came to make it happen. The revelation of the Son in the New Testament puts the old story in a new light. We will discuss this at length later.

The Goal

The current state of affairs in the modern church is that people are being treated like they're in kindergarten. Many people in church have college (if not graduate) degrees and are thoroughly familiar with the concept of studying hard to get a good career. But when it comes to the Bible, they're being spoon-fed a baby formula that just doesn't satisfy the soul. From Sunday to Sunday they're told to "believe in Jesus" and "be good." On the other hand, Paul prays for his disciples that they grow in the wisdom of God.

> We continually ask God to fill you with the knowledge of his will through all the wisdom and understanding that the Spirit gives, so that you may live a life worthy of the Lord and please him in every way: bearing fruit in every good work, growing in the knowledge of God, being strengthened with all power according to his glorious might so that you may have great endurance and patience, and giving joyful thanks to the Father, who has qualified you to share in the inheritance of his holy people in the Kingdom of light. (Colossians 1:9-12)

What I'd like to do here is get the modern Christian started in the same way. Let's begin a graduate program on the Christ, who is "the fullness of the Godhead" and the wisdom of God.

GENERAL PRINCIPLES

It should be an easy matter to preach Christ, with all the encouragement that we get from the New Testament writers to do so. Certainly our modern church culture encourages it and advertises to the world around us that we do, in fact, preach Christ. But while the spirit is willing, the intellect is weak. People seem to be lacking the data. They also lack the method as they probe around in passages that look for all the world like encouragements to good conduct!

Like any skilled laborer, we need tools of the trade, and established methods, for taking on this task. Please be aware, however, that simply looking at these tools and methods does not a preacher make! Like any skill, preaching Christ takes time and discipline and practice to get good at it. It's not that it's difficult, and it certainly ought to be enjoyable to see and proclaim the One we love and serve as we study all through the Bible. The problem is the discipline of sticking to the point instead of wandering off into other paths. We all have our own opinions on things, and we all have our own interests. And we so often become lazy and take the easy way out – which usually takes us into worn-out moralisms. But in preaching and teaching, we have to put all that aside and teach the message that God gave us for the church. Getting side-tracked from The Point (which is all too easy!) is not being a responsible servant of the Lord.

So let's look at some principles that will help us focus on the task: how does one successfully preach Christ in a sermon?

It's Christ they need

The first thing to consider is the fact that, by God's design, our souls need him. Just as our bodies survive on physical food, our souls survive only by feeding on the manna from Heaven. You may not understand how that works at this point, but the idea is critical to keep in mind. It keeps us to the task. Talk about Jesus, and you will see life in your hearers. Don't worry about how it happens; the Spirit takes care of that.

19

It's what Jesus is, and what he does, that gives us life. You've no doubt read stories of people starving or doing without food for days, and when given food their faces brighten and they come back to life. In the same way, listening to the words of Christ, watching him perform miracles, seeing him in his glory on his throne – all these bring a spiritual light to the face of starving and hopeless souls. "Sir, we want to see Jesus!" was the plea made to the disciples.

I'm not going to leave you in the dark about how to do that; we're going to examine closely much of what the entire Bible has to say about Jesus. But the point here is that you have to accept this fact as a given in your preaching and teaching: if you come to your task without something about Jesus, you are coming empty-handed to the sheep. By rights they ought to get rid of you and find someone else who *will* feed them!

On the other hand, Paul said something that many people have misunderstood.

> For I resolved to know nothing while I was with you except
> Jesus Christ and him crucified. (1 Corinthians 2:2)

He is *not* saying that he will only focus on the little that the crucifixion story tells us of Christ. What he's saying is that, since Christ alone is our spiritual food, he will bring us no other. We could ask, "Paul, what exactly do you have to say about Christ and him crucified?" And he would delightedly take us to the entire Bible! We know that because that's precisely what he does throughout all his letters.

You may not be a master like Paul when it comes to seeing Christ throughout the Bible, but if you follow his lead you will begin to see more and more. Just be aware that Paul and the Apostles were sent and commissioned by Christ to preach about Christ. And Paul warned us that we too must preach the same message that they received from Christ. We have to do this job the same way that they did it.

> So then, brothers, stand firm and hold fast to the teachings
> we passed on to you, whether by word of mouth or by letter.
> (2 Thessalonians 2:15)

The Old Testament foundation

At the risk of belaboring the point, it's time you learned the basics of the Old Testament if you haven't already done so.

It's not enough to know the stories. If you remember, Jesus embarrassed the Jews repeatedly in this way. They knew the stories of the Old Testament Scriptures; they were experts in it. They could recite them in Hebrew from memory! But they had no idea what those stories were really about. Jesus faulted the Jewish leaders and teachers for not knowing the point of the Bible.

> "You study the Scriptures diligently because you think that in them you have eternal life. These are the very Scriptures that testify about me, yet you refuse to come to me to have life." (Matthew 5:39-40)

> "You are in error because you do not know the Scriptures or the power of God." (Matthew 22:29)

> "You are Israel's teacher," said Jesus, "and do you not understand these things?" (John 3:10)

If you're not familiar with even the stories, the time has come to read the whole Old Testament. Use whatever schedule or method that you wish, but you have to spend some time learning the history and characters. Get a good book that will give you an overview of how the history and events all fit together into one story – the story of God leading his people Israel to the Promised Land and their experiences there. At this point don't worry about the meaning of everything so much as getting the data.

Next you need an overview of the schemes, the themes, the overarching concepts of the Old Testament. You need a good grasp on Creation and its significance in the rest of the Bible. You need to learn about the Covenant with Abraham and why it's important; the Law and Moses, and what all that meant to the future events of Israel; the Kingdom under David and its results on Israel's history. God was doing important things with his people during these centuries, and you need to know what he was doing and why.

Finally, it will be time to graduate to a new level – understanding what significance that all this has for our Christian faith. This is perhaps the hardest thing to find out, because we presently have so little help in this area in our modern literature. I had to find teachers from other centuries for help in this. There are a handful of teachers in our day who understand Paul's principle of "the Old Testament describes Christ", but not many. But until you start seeing this, you won't have much to say about Jesus in your sermons. And don't think that you can rely solely on the New Testament to explain Jesus. Even the New is loaded with assumptions and presuppositions from the Old when it shows us Jesus in action. You will miss huge realities that the Gospel writers could see clearly. [4]

Distributed Revelation

In order to get information about Jesus from Old Testament stories, we need a method. We already looked at what modern scholars use to connect the Old and New Testaments together, but it still lacks a vitality and, more important, the potential for unlocking the data that is within any passage. Try to use the wrong key to open the door and it won't work; use the right key, however, and it will open wide to you.

> He will be the sure foundation for your times, a rich store
> of salvation and wisdom and knowledge; the fear of the LORD
> is the key to this treasure. (Isaiah 33:6)

May I point out here that this passage contains one of the major keys to understanding the Bible? There's a lot behind that idea of fear; it's a concept that scholars in particular need to heed. No scholar will unlock a passage, no matter how brilliant or widely-read he is, without the requisite fear of God – which involves a child-like faith in the spiritual nature of God and his Word.

While you can pursue on your own the other methods that we've mentioned above, the method that we're going to use here is, in my estimation, the most powerful one. I call it "Distributed Revelation." What that means is that in a particular Old Testament story, you will find a complete description of the essentials of some aspect of the person and work of Christ.

---

[4] See my works *Ten Keys to the Bible*, *The Throne of David*, *Mystery Revealed*, and *Where the Paths Meet* for getting started on mastering the Old Testament.

Here's what I mean by "complete." If a scientist were studying, for example, the physics of a billiard ball rolling across the pool table, he would include all aspects of the problem that relate directly to the study – no more, no less. There might be lots of things going on around him, but only those aspects that relate to the study would be important to him. What he would come up with is a model that includes all the essential ingredients that explain the behavior, and together they would describe a perfect system that anybody could duplicate. It's a model that will hold under all circumstances.

ROLLING BILLIARD BALL

- *Mass*
- *Friction*
- *Gravity*
- *Slope of table*
- *Inertia*
- *Force*
- *Formulas*

Now here's an example from Scripture. In Genesis 4 we have the story of the sacrifices of Cain and Abel. Cain offered a sacrifice that God rejected; God accepted Abel's sacrifice, however. What did Abel's sacrifice consist of?

THE RIGHT SACRIFICE

- A sheep from the flock
- A firstborn animal
- The death of the animal – a substitute
- Acceptance based on that substitute's death

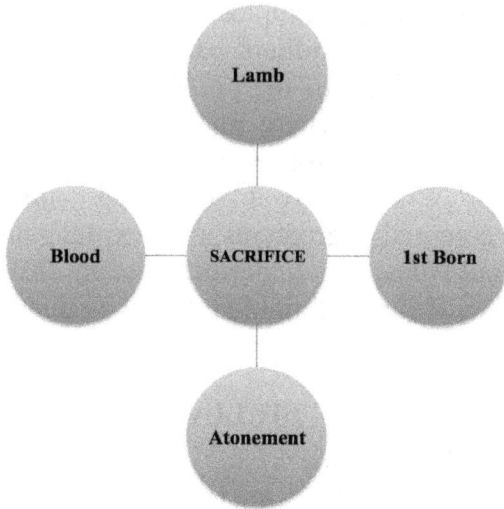

These are all the essentials of a *right sacrifice* – a sacrifice that God will accept. This same list holds true throughout the books of Moses when we read about the sacrifices prescribed for the Temple service, and they also describe the sacrifice of Christ that so effectively takes care of our sin and relationship with God. In other words, here in Genesis is the root idea of an acceptable sacrifice that holds true across the entire Bible. No other passage in the Bible has this description laid out so clearly and concisely as this one; they all start from this list when discussing what God will accept from us as a sacrifice. Abel's story rules; remember what Hebrews tells us – "And by faith he still speaks, even though he is dead." (Hebrews 11:4)

This is not "reverse-engineering." We're not arming ourselves with New Testament data and going to the Old Testament looking for support. The Old Testament actually gives us the data to look for in the New, things that we would have missed on our own without its help. It corrects our thinking with the right data, the right way of looking at things. For example, the story of Creation in Genesis 1 describes three methods that God used to create the universe: God's *Word*, his *command*, and his *miracle*. What we have to do is to meditate on this formula until it becomes ingrained into our thinking. Then when we come to the New Testament and read about Paul describing conversion as a "new *Creation*," the formula will come back to mind and the light will turn on: the Creator makes his "new Creation" in the same ways that he made his first Creation! In other words, people don't become Christians because they want to; God makes them out of nothing. That runs directly contrary to our false notions that dictate how we commonly do evangelism.

In David's story we learn the essentials about the King and his Kingdom. In Moses we see the essentials of the Law and how we become holy. In the Prophets we see the approach that God takes when he encounters us with his Word. In other words, the descriptions of all the important principles of our faith are *distributed* across the Old Testament, and in each story we learn the essentials of that principle. Put all of that together, and you have what Paul described as "the holy Scriptures, which are able to make you wise for salvation through faith in Christ Jesus." [5]

THE OLD TESTAMENT'S CHRISTOLOGICAL SYSTEM

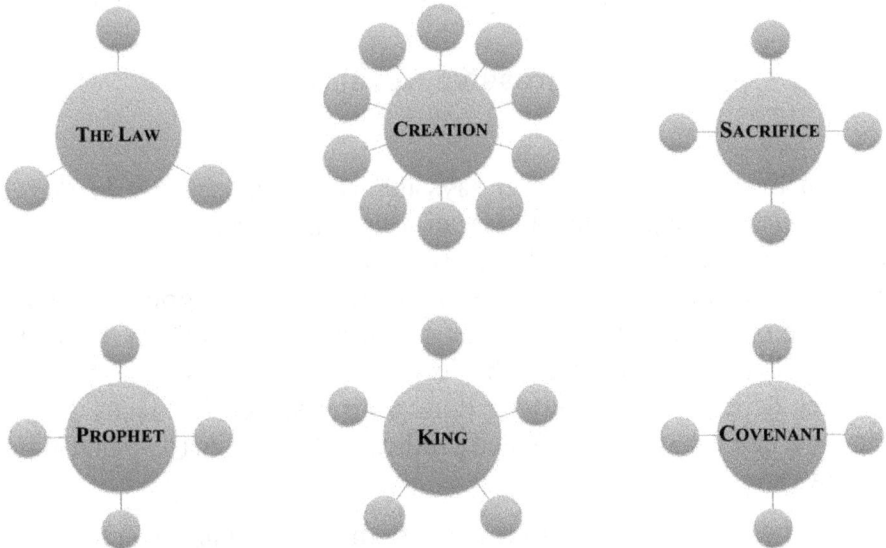

Distributed Revelation – from Genesis to Malachi

---

[5] See *A New Model for Biblical Studies*.

This Distributed model of studying the Bible is different from the traditional "Progressive" model in this way: the "Progressive Revelation" theory states that information about Christ starts out as a "seed" in Genesis 3:15, and gradually and slowly grows throughout the Old Testament, gaining a bit more clarity along the way (but never being fully clear to the Jews!) until we break into the bright light of the New Testament and see the clear picture in Jesus. I hope you see the difference here. According to this theory, nowhere along the way did the Jews know the clear data about Jesus; only we Christians have that. The Progressive model makes the Old Testament pretty much useless to Christians since we have such a clear statement of Christ in the New Testament.

| Abraham | Moses | David | Prophets | Christ |

Progressive Revelation

But the Distributed model says that *nowhere else but in the Old Testament* will we get such a clear description of Jesus. The data is *not* in the New Testament. The New Testament relies on our having studied the basics in the Old Testament first; it's not going to explain that same data again because it has a different task. Which means that we probably won't see those basic lessons repeated in the New; the Apostles depend on you having done your research in "Jesus 101" so that they can go on to advanced studies in "Jesus 201". That's why Hebrews says –

Therefore let us move beyond the elementary teachings about Christ and be taken forward to maturity. (Hebrews 6:1)

We won't belabor this point, but it explains our method in this study. We will use it with great effect as we learn how to preach Christ from the entire Bible. [6]

The Names of Christ

You are probably aware of the fact that Jesus has many names, and they are scattered all through the Bible. This is going to be a rich resource for you as you learn more about him.

A name serves two functions: *first*, it describes something, and *second*, it gets someone's attention. Prayer grasps both functions, but here we will look only at the first.

If it's true that the entire Bible is really about Christ, you can imagine that the depths of who he is must be limitless. There are all kinds of things we can say and know about him. His names actually describe many of those aspects of his nature and work. Turn to the *Appendix* to see a fairly complete list of his many names.

How does one use these names? *First*, notice that each name describes something that Jesus is good at doing, or is unique in that only he can do such a thing. For example, only he knows the way to God, it says in John 14:6. Other ways simply don't bring us into God's presence. *Second*, the name can describe something about his nature – the way we will find him to be when we meet him. For example, when we listen to him teach us, it rings true in our soul – he's showing us the truth as he sees it, and it's obviously true, compared to other points of view which are not true.

These names come from all over the Bible, which is another testimony to the fact that the entire Bible describes Christ. Covering one name every week, you have about three years worth of sermons here!

---

[6] One more note: Distributed Revelation differs from typology in this way: types are individual symbols that correspond to truths in Christ's ministry, and Distributed Revelation describes an entire system laying out the fundamentals of the doctrine of the Christ throughout the Old Testament. Different emphasis, wider scope. It's a system on one hand, and parallel ideas on the other.

Jesus first, then ethics

I'm not sure people really understand the point about ethics and morality. The Bible seems to be so focused on ethics that preachers feel justified in limiting their sermons on what man has to do and what man ought not to do. So they naturally gravitate toward this kind of preaching. They use every passage in the Bible for that purpose.

The worst example of this methodology that I can think of is something I've seen over and over: the story of David and Goliath. Everyone's sermon[7] predictably had one lesson: *we must be like David.* We have to have courage, we have to fight the enemy, we have to trust in God, we have to be a testimony – on and on the moralisms go. But if you look at that story, that's not the point that David himself saw.

> All those gathered here will know that it is not by sword or spear that the LORD saves; for the battle is the LORD's, and he will give all of you into our hands. (1 Samuel 17:47)

The point, as David saw it, was what the God of Israel was about to do to this Philistine. The whole world was about to learn about David's God, not about David. So if you're brave, that doesn't mean that God is going to fight for you. It also doesn't mean that you'll defeat the enemies of God. And it also doesn't mean that you know what you're doing, or that you're doing the right thing. A lot of other things have to be in place before your bravery is considered an asset to God's cause – God has to do his part first before you will get anywhere with your part.

Another classic example is the book of Ephesians. So many preachers spend so much time in Ephesians 4-6 – the section on Christian living – as if it can stand alone from the things that Paul talked about in Ephesians 1-3. It can't. For example, we need the Spirit of wisdom and revelation so that we can know Christ better, so that we can, for instance, love our wives as Christ loves the church.

---

[7] With one exception – I was amazed and encouraged that the man saw the right point!

From Ephesians:

First ...

I keep asking that the God of our Lord Jesus Christ, the glorious Father, may give you the Spirit of wisdom and revelation, so that you may know him better. (Ephesians 1:17)

And next ...

I pray that out of his glorious riches he may strengthen you with power through his Spirit in your inner being, so that Christ may dwell in your hearts through faith. And I pray that you, being rooted and established in love, may have power, together with all the Lord's holy people, to grasp how wide and long and high and deep is the love of Christ, and to know this love that surpasses knowledge — that you may be filled to the measure of all the fullness of God. (Ephesians 3:16-19)

Then, finally ...

Husbands, love your wives, just as Christ loved the church. (Ephesians 5:25)

In other words, God's love is a pattern for a husband's love.

Moral of the story: you ought never to preach a moralistic sermon. Yes, the point about Christianity *is* to change our natures to conform to the image of Christ. But the only reason righteousness happens is that God unites us with his Son, the Perfect man. *He* changes *us*, using a power and wisdom beyond ours.

Encountering Jesus: testimonies

As we keep our task in mind of showing Jesus to people, why not use the examples in Scripture of what happened when real people met the God of the Bible? Show your listeners what happened to others when they saw Jesus. That is, what did they see in him? What happened as a result?

There's no way we can know anything about God until he reveals himself. Information about him doesn't come to us naturally; we can't figure it out on our own. Only when he shows himself will we see and know the truth about him.

But when he reveals himself, what a vision! It shakes us to the very core. We are looking at the One who made us, who keeps us alive, who has standards that are terrifying. It's no wonder that the people in Bible times fell down at his feet in fear and amazement. The experience brought a whole new perspective into their lives; they would never be the same again. If this God really is in our world, that just changes everything.

There is a long list of encounters like this in the Bible. Adam and Eve first experienced guilt in the presence of God. Abraham ended up moving in his old age to a foreign country when God appeared to him, motivated by a hope for something not in this world that God showed him. Joseph never despaired, even through years of rejection and imprisonment, because of his encounter with God. Moses led the Israelites out victoriously from Egypt as he followed God's leading. Joshua took the Promised Land away from the Canaanites only because he let his God fight for him. David did what nobody before him could do, because he was specially trained by God. The prophets spoke the word of God boldly to sinners from kings to commoners, risking persecution, because God was a fire burning in their hearts. The Apostles preached the Gospel around the entire Roman Empire because they believed in the Son of God whom they had seen with their own eyes.

So if you're trying to get your listeners to live a certain way, show them God first. Don't just go to a passage that says "you must be holy" and talk about that. Look at the holy God, how he appeared to people in the past and what he showed them, and what that encounter did to people. Then preach that God who is still the same, bringing the same spiritual realities into our world. You will see (if God is merciful) people responding in the same way that people did in Bible times.

> "Woe to me!" I cried. "I am ruined! For I am a man of unclean lips, and I live among a people of unclean lips, and my eyes have seen the King, the LORD Almighty." (Isaiah 6:5)

Keep to the Mission

There is a great deal of confusion about the last two verses of the Gospel of Matthew. This is traditionally called "the Great Commission" because Jesus gave his disciples the commission of preaching the Gospel to the world. And that's the same commission that we have, we are told.

Well that's true, but that's not the Mission of the church. Let's distinguish between the "commission" and the "mission." The military understands the concept: training comes first, as the soldiers undergo rigorous discipline to learn how to fight and maneuver on the field. Then when their country needs them, they receive a Mission – a clear statement of the objectives to accomplish.

Jesus tells us here to go out and make disciples and teach, but he doesn't tell us in this passage *what* to teach. I'm not splitting hairs; just about every church claims this passage as their mission, but not very many churches are agreed on *what it is that we are supposed to be teaching people.* For example, the Liberals don't teach much at all that resembles what Jesus and the Apostles gave us to work with. And there are many denominations and churches that focus on rabbit trails instead of the primary subjects. So the Mission of the Church is *to accomplish what Jesus wants to see in the Church.*

What is it that Jesus wants to see happen in the church? Not just to teach and make disciples; secular groups teach and make disciples too. The Mission of the Church is twofold and very specific:

Salvation from sin: Sin is the root problem of mankind. In the Garden of Eden, mankind rebelled against God, turned away from him into sin and wickedness, and as a result died to God. It doesn't really matter what our station in life is – rich or poor, sickness or health, king or slave – our hearts are steeped in sin; and unless something is done about it, all is lost. So the primary reason that Jesus came from Heaven was to free us from this sin (and take our punishment for it) and change our hearts so that we will never sin again.

So all the Bible, from the beginning to the end, focuses on this central problem of ours. Though we usually make light of the subject, sin is the first item on God's agenda, and

31

we won't get anywhere with him until we've dealt with it the way he requires.

Getting ready for life with God in Heaven: We mustn't think that Christianity is simply a matter of getting cleaned up morally. It's true, nothing else is going to happen for us until we take care of our sin conclusively. That's the one thing that's keeping us away from light and life. The angels of God bar the doorway to Heaven so that sinners can't approach it. (Genesis 3:24) No pollution there, thank you!

But the second part of the Mission is that, once ready, we can now go into the Temple and see God himself. That's paradise! God is the source of all goodness; he's the spring behind all Creation. To see and touch God directly is going to be an experience beyond our wildest imaginations. Not only that, but Jesus plans to make us sons as he is – with the privilege, with the ability, to go behind the curtain and see and experience his Father as he does.

But there's so much to do. We're not ready yet for that kind of life. We are unfamiliar with the language, with Heaven's spiritual principles, with the house of God. The Old Testament describes life with God, but we are way behind in our homework! There's much to learn, much to change, much to become familiar with before we can step into this new world.

Now the church's job is to work on this two-fold Mission. In fact, the Church has the tools to 1) deliver us from our sin, and 2) get us ready for life with God. When we come together, we show that we understand the whole point of church when we say that we *are* sinners and that we *need* changing.

It's the only organization on earth that can accomplish this otherwise-impossible task. That's why I don't understand these churches that are doing everything else but the Mission. What a golden opportunity to work on *the one thing needful*, and they're wasting it.

Hint: the "treasures of Heaven" that Jesus talked about in Matthew 6:19-21 are spiritual treasures that Jesus has made available for us, treasures in himself that he gives us when we turn to him for

32

them. It's Jesus who saves us and makes us ready for life with God. The way we get hold of this treasure is through the Spirit that Christ pours out on his Church, through the ministry there.

> How good and pleasant it is when God's people live together in unity! It is like precious oil poured on the head, running down on the beard, running down on Aaron's beard, down on the collar of his robe. It is as if the dew of Hermon were falling on Mount Zion. For there the LORD bestows his blessing, even life forevermore. (Psalm 133:1; 3)

Matters of the heart

I am continually amazed when I see so many "Christians" and so little Christian behavior. Something must have gone wrong. Our society is so full of Bibles and literature on the Bible and media transmitting the Bible's lessons that surely we must be close to the goal of converting the entire world. And yet our culture is getting worse and worse – and that includes our modern churches. I think we've lost the message.

In the eighteenth century the Christians believed they were close to the millennial age – the theory that the Post-Millenialists believe. They thought this because the world was effectively shrinking: travel brought the entire world within easy reach for the first time in history. Surely this was going to be the key to spreading the church's influence around the world!

Now we have what they could only dream of. Communication around the world is instant, through the Internet and satellite. Travel only requires hours to get to any part of the world. We all know what everyone is doing because of pervasive news media. But when you visit the modern church that has been empowered beyond belief with technology, there isn't the hundredth part of wisdom and knowledge that the church in the eighteenth century had. It's as if the more powerful we've become and the more overwhelmed with data, the more ignorant and powerless we've become spiritually.

I'm convinced that a large part of this situation is due to the fact that the Gospel has been watered down from the Bible's version to the point that it doesn't do much good at all for people anymore. And the

33

Gospel, as you well know, is the story of Jesus. That must mean that we've changed the Gospel. In fact, if you compare the modern "gospel" with the Gospel that the Apostles preached (for example, in the book of Acts) you will see almost no similarities between them.[8] They preached about Christ; we preach about ourselves. It's no wonder, then, that as our culture has grown more powerful physically, spiritually we've gotten shallower in our faith to the point that there is not much resemblance between our faith and the faith of our spiritual fathers. We've made a lot of excuses for that fact, but it's still a fact.

One way to bring people back to the table, so to speak, is to aim at the heart. That's where Jesus aimed. You'll remember that he tore up the Pharisees, who were "righteous" on the outside, but inside they were "like graves", "full of dead men's bones and everything unclean." He knew what they were really like. I feel that he'd say the same about our generation. Our political correctness has sensitized us to every crime and atrocity except the important ones.

- People don't care about God.
- People don't even know what his Law is, let alone follow it.
- People don't care that they are lost sinners.
- People glorify themselves instead of God.
- People have no interest in the way of escape from the coming destruction.
- People aren't the least interested in life with God.

For most, this list is a real yawner; they have better things to do with their time than seek God. But in God's eyes, this is reason for eternal punishment. It's a shame that so many are going to learn that the hard way.

If you don't know the depths of the spiritual nature of Christ, your heart will never change. The Pharisees, for example, could only see the outward signs of Jesus, and so missed out on salvation. But with faith, we can see the treasures of Heaven in Christ, not just the man. We see the Son of God who can do the impossible, who has come to sit on his throne and rule an eternal, spiritual Kingdom. And in this light we can

---

[8]   See my book *The Gospel of Christ* for an extended discussion of the Apostles' Gospel and our modern form of the Gospel.

see the need for an inner change of the heart and mind so that we can be part of this spiritual Kingdom.

That's how you can tell Jesus is at work – lives change, the interests change, the emotions change. That's the real target of the message of Christ. Jesus goes to the heart, where only he can go, armed with spiritual power and gifts; man's rules only affect the outward behaviors. Take the message of Christ to the heart and the Mission will be accomplished in your church.

> Above all else, guard your heart, for everything you do flows from it. (Proverbs 4:23)

> For the mouth speaks what the heart is full of. A good man brings good things out of the good stored up in him, and an evil man brings evil things out of the evil stored up in him. But I tell you that everyone will have to give account on the day of judgment for every empty word they have spoken. For by your words you will be acquitted, and by your words you will be condemned. (Matthew 12:34-37)

A proper view of the Bible

One more point that we should consider is the way we handle the Bible. You will not preach the message of Christ correctly if you have the wrong outlook on the Book.

An example of what I mean is the notion that the New Testament is more important than the Old Testament. Most people probably think this; many modern Christians call themselves "New Testament Christians" as a mark of distinction, as if the message of salvation in Christ can only be found in the New Testament, that the Old Testament contains things detrimental to their faith in Christ. That's blind ignorance. We've already seen Paul's opinion of the Old Testament. Jesus concurs.

> "They have Moses and the Prophets; let them listen to them." (Luke 16:29)

In fact, someone did a study once and found 350 direct and indirect references to the Old Testament in the pages of the New. The story of Jesus can't be told without the Old Testament. That means that both of them are necessary; one is not more important than the other. Stay with only the New, and that's like trying to walk on one leg!

Another example of how to handle the Bible is to see that the entire book was given to us by God to instruct us in our faith. We need Genesis to instruct us about Jesus; we need Exodus to instruct us about Jesus; we need Leviticus to instruct us about Jesus. The only difference between the Jews and us is that they got the lesson first, in a physical form. But by faith they saw the spiritual side of it (Hebrews 11 tells us that), and it's that same lesson that *all* of God's people must learn from the story. We inherited their faith; we weren't given a new one. The saints of old saw the same Jesus that we see; otherwise their "faith" would have been empty of content. We can only pray that we will see what they saw.

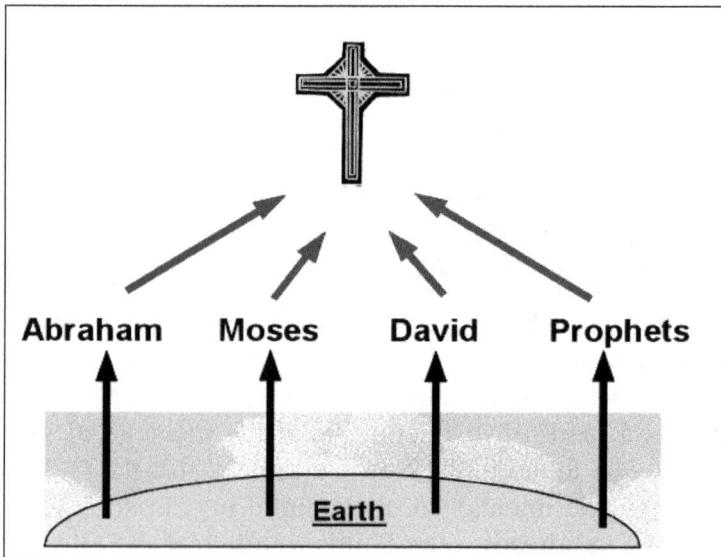

Faith sees Christ in any age!

Section One: Concepts

SECTION ONE: CONCEPTS

Our plan will be this: since the concepts that we need to understand Christ are distributed across the Old Testament, we will visit each one in turn and quickly go over the essentials involved. Then we want to check across the rest of the Old Testament to make sure it's a solid doctrine that holds up in other passages. This is, after all, a description of our God, and we should be able to see the same God from age to age, in every phase of Israelite history. If we have it right, then that same God will show up again in the New Testament in the person and work of Christ.

1. How will we know what to look for? Well, again the Apostles will guide us here. They are the ones who tell us that Jesus is the Creator, the Redeemer, the King, the Lawgiver, the Sacrifice, the Prophet, the Priest that is described in the Old Testament. It's on their authority that we can go back to the Old Testament and investigate what we find there.

2. Really you should take time at that point and practice looking for the points of the doctrine before you leave the Old Testament. It's easier there to spot the different features of God's works. God worked with his people on a physical level, much as an adult would work with a child. If we teach our children with conceptual knowledge, they won't follow us; but show them pictures and tell them stories, and they'll remember it the rest of their lives. And when God taught the Israelites, he did it through their history, through their memorable leaders – and to this day they're still teaching their children the lessons they learned. It works.

3. When we get to the New Testament, we enter the conceptual world, the spiritual world, and it's not going to be so easy to spot these principles. But if you've done your homework, you're at least ready to listen to Jesus and watch

39

him in action. Not that you'll immediately understand what you're looking at; many of the Jews weren't because they were expecting to see a continuation of what they had in the old days. It requires faith to understand the Christ.

But deal with him we must, and so the time comes to apply what we've learned in the Old Testament and interpret passages in the New correctly. In dealing with the Messiah, we need faith – the spiritual light, the spiritual sight, into the world of God. What most see as just a man will be to us the Creator at work, the King, the Judge, the Prophet, the Lawgiver. But if all we see are some precepts to live by, the moralisms that so many see, then we have not yet seen the Christ.

> I do not cease to give thanks for you, remembering you in my prayers, that the God of our Lord Jesus Christ, the Father of glory, may give you the Spirit of wisdom and of revelation in the knowledge of him, having the eyes of your hearts enlightened, that you may know what is the hope to which he has called you, what are the riches of his glorious inheritance in the saints, and what is the immeasurable greatness of his power toward us who believe. (Ephesians 1:16-19)

THE CREATOR

Creation is one of my favorite subjects. The Bible is rich on the theme of Creation; and Jesus worked on all the aspects of Creation from the beginning to the end. In fact, there's no way we can cover all the details of this subject here; we will have to limit ourselves to laying out the important aspects of Creation and how Jesus uses those aspects in his new Creation.[9]

What happened at Creation?

Where is the first place that people go for the story of Creation? Genesis 1. Where is the first place that people go for the story of Jesus? Matthew 1. They don't automatically think of Jesus when they're studying Creation, because there's no mention of him in Genesis 1. After all, he was born long after the event, right?

But we know from other passages in the Bible that Jesus *was* there at the beginning; he had an integral role in the process of Creation. So one of the things we have to tell people in our preaching is that they are coming face to face with the Creator himself. And that has profound implications for our relationship with him. If we truly want to know who Jesus is, we have to learn about him being the Creator.

First we must look at the events of Creation. God created the world using ten principles, and each of these shows us the way that God works. By studying Creation we learn not only who he is but also the methods that he used to create us.

- **Miracle** – In Genesis 1 we read a simple account of the way that God made the universe – by a series of miracles. I know that modern science has talked most people out of the idea of the miracles of Creation; they think that it's a myth; that actually it's a poetic way of describing what evolution and natural law produced over millions of years.

---

[9] For a full-blown treatment of Creation, see the book *The Bible Explains Creation*.

But one of the cardinal rules of Biblical interpretation is to take the plain meaning of a passage first. You have to add all sorts of alien ideas to this chapter to come up with what science is telling us.

A miracle is something that only God can do, because with it he makes something out of nothing. More exactly, when God does a miracle, he skips the steps in between the intent and the result. For example, when we make bread, we know the steps to take – first plant the grain, then harvest it, then grind it up into flour, then mix it up and bake it. We need to perform all the steps to reach the result.

But when God acts, he skips the steps. It's not the kind of thing that we can understand; science is out of its depth here. And the reason he used miracles should be obvious: there was nothing at the beginning! He had to use a miracle to make something out of nothing.

> By faith we understand that the universe was formed at God's command, so that what is seen was not made out of what was visible. (Hebrews 11:3)

- **Command** – The verses in Genesis 1 use a command over and over: "Let there be …" is a form of command in the original Hebrew language. Why a command? Because of who God is!

Let's think this thing through for a minute. Who issues commands? A King does. And if he commands us, what does that make us? His subjects. And obviously what he's putting together here is a Kingdom over which he rules. That means his commands are Law to us – that's where morality and ethics come from; it's all burned into our conscience. But the King won't be satisfied with simply issuing commands; he wants to make sure that we follow through on his orders – and that's why Judgment Day was part of the picture from the very beginning.

We do not belong to ourselves; we are not here to enjoy ourselves and do whatever we please. We are here to serve the King and help with running his Kingdom. If we don't there will be punishment; if we do, rewards.

- **Word** – God was concerned that we understand some critical things about what was going on during Creation. I assume you realize that he could have told us nothing about any of it; he could have simply snapped his fingers, figuratively speaking, and created his universe with no explanations available.

But God prefers to let us in on what's going on. So he spoke during the entire process; his Word is the medium, the foundation, the means of Creation. In fact the entire universe is a medium of information, a revelation of light showing us what's going on around us. Not only is light shining throughout the universe to reveal all of its aspects and levels, our senses are designed to receive that data and process it. This was not an accident; it was by design. We don't see everything, but what we see is enough to live by.

When we can see what's going on, when we can know, then we have *truth* – the way that God the Creator sees everything. He expects a certain behavior and certain works from us, and he faithfully gives us the truth that we will need to accomplish our work. That's the Word at work in God's world. Anything other than God's perspective is not truth; it's a lie, and will most certainly lead us into trouble with him.

- **Wisdom and understanding** – God's wisdom is profound, and so we should expect that his Creation would reflect that. Science can help us here.

The complexity of our universe is staggering. The range reaches from the cosmic end (where relativity rules) to the atomic level (where quantum physics operates). Everything is put together as a whole, a complex system in which all the parts play their roles and nothing is out of its place. In fact, the universe consists of multiple levels which depend on each other. For example, inside our bodies are processes that must work perfectly or we will die. And yet we don't have to know anything about them in order to live; it all works in spite of us, without our knowledge, as we live on a totally different level.

This amazing complexity and unity of the universe speaks of purpose, design and goals. Obviously every part has a role to play, and must do its part, for the system to work. But at no point will we ever have a complete grasp on everything that is going on. Only the Creator knows the beginning from the end, because only the Creator has a goal for the entire system. All that we can do is work with the little that we do understand and make sure we do our part; that's all that we're responsible for.

- **Through Christ** – In the New Testament we read that God made the world "through Christ." This has multiple aspects. For one thing, Jesus was "assigned" the project of Creation because he's going to aim it at certain goals for which he is responsible. The second point is that Christ will need total knowledge and power over every aspect of Creation for the kind of work he will do.

   There's another aspect about "made through Christ" that's vitally important for us, but we will look at that in the next section.

- **The Spirit's power** – At the beginning of Creation the Spirit of God was there. We learn from the rest of the Bible that the Spirit does two things: he reveals, and he empowers. It's through the Spirit that we learn about and understand the spiritual world of God. Because he was there, we now know what happened and how it happened.

   The power of the Spirit is something that this world will never grasp, however. God always works through his Spirit, because he does things that are impossible – and yet they are vitally necessary. This world can't help us when we are in real need; but when God moves, the impossible happens. Mountains move; rivers and seas split apart; millions are fed in the wilderness; the dead are raised. When God brings his own right arm to the problem, nothing stands in his way; the universe is like smoke before the coming of God and offers no resistance to him at all.

- **Witness** – The Spirit played another role at Creation that we shouldn't miss: he witnessed the entire event. The reason for this should be obvious – whoever can provide an eyewitness of an event will be able to prove their claim. Science will never have eyewitnesses of evolution; so they will never be able to prove how the world got its start. But God proves his case with the testimony of the Spirit, who was there and saw the whole thing.

This is important because the kinds of things that went on at Creation were of a spiritual nature; no scientist, no matter how brilliant, would be able to follow what happened and how it happened. There were spiritual forces at work that we will never understand with our scientific instruments. But the Spirit knows and understands the mind of God, and the ways of God. And he faithfully reported to us that God did miracles, he commanded the world into existence, he made the world through Christ – things that we would never have known otherwise if he hadn't told us.

The Spirit then told Moses, the author of the Genesis account, exactly what happened. So again, we aren't forced to depend on a witness who isn't qualified to testify; as Peter tells us, "Above all, you must understand that no prophecy of Scripture came about by the prophet's own interpretation of things. For prophecy never had its origin in the will of man, but men spoke from God as they were carried along by the Holy Spirit." (2 Peter 1:21) Moses, being the greatest of the Old Testament prophets, reported exactly what he heard from the Spirit about the beginning of the world and how it happened.

- **Blessing** – God blessed several elements of his new world, according to the Genesis account. When God blessed something, it involved the ability to *multiply* and fill the earth and *enjoy* the good things of Creation.

  The Creator loves family. The more creatures there are enjoying his world, the better he likes it. He blessed the birds and fish and commanded them multiply – not only would they fill the earth with their progeny (blessing of resources) but the acts of procreation and surviving became a pleasure to them. It's interesting that God attaches pleasure to his commands – he probably did this because it wouldn't happen without the pleasure attached.

  Man also was blessed, and his filling the earth would lead to all sorts of pleasures: the pleasure of procreation, the pleasure of social relationships, the pleasure of ruling over the earth and maintaining God's Kingdom. Not only is God attaining his goal of filling the earth and creating a Kingdom, he also has *willing* servants working with him in this project. He didn't have to add the pleasure to life (he could have made us like rocks!); but God blessed us with the enjoyment of life as we carry out his will. With obedience comes joy.

- **Judgment** – As we mentioned above, the King made this universe, and he expects us his subjects to live for his glory and help maintain his Kingdom. Being the responsible King that he is, he's not going to let us get away with rebellion; he expects results. There will be a Judgment Day to examine our progress.

  Remember that we're dealing with God here. He isn't sitting in Heaven wondering how things are turning out. We're not running around loose in his Kingdom, getting away with whatever we want like children with no adults present. God is always judging us – while we live and work, while we eat and sleep, wherever we go and whatever we do. Nothing is hidden from God. He knows exactly what we are, even if we don't. He always keeps his finger on the pulse of his Kingdom, measuring its progress.

In fact, in his wisdom God designed his world in such a way that it easily reveals what we are inside. Our actions show the state of our hearts. It's no secret what we are inside – we all have a long history of successes and failures behind us, and many witnesses who can testify to the kind of people we really are. When something goes wrong, red flags immediately go up and God targets the problem right away. Nothing is hidden before the eyes of him to whom we must give an account.

Judgment Day will be a simple matter: it's when God gathers all this testimony and evidence in our lives of what we did (or didn't do) for his Kingdom and puts it all on the table for everyone to see.

- **Glory** – There are two meanings to the word "glory." One is "to be heavy," like gold is heavy and therefore a glorious or valuable substance. The other meaning is this: *who is going to get the credit?* And that's a fundamental principle that was at work at Creation.

The whole Bible testifies that God ought to get a lot of credit for what he has done, and is doing, and will do in this world of his. The Creation story gives him the credit for the entire thing; only God can do what Genesis says he did. Only God can do miracles; only God's wisdom can put together the complexity of the universe; only God's Spirit has the power to make the world. Paul says that "from him, and through him, and to him are all things. To him be the glory forever!" (Romans 11:36)

And yet that's precisely what God does *not* get in this Creation. He feeds all of his creatures, he provides for their daily needs and comforts, he decides where men and women will live and what their lives will be like; he raises up nations and tears others down – he's involved in everything in our world. The only thing he won't take credit for is our sin – that's our fault. And yet he gets no

47

mention of any of this in the newspaper; nobody cares whether he gets credit or not.

At the end of time, God is going to fix this situation. He intends to get full glory for everything he has done, if he has to force it out of our lips. We are finally going to quit being self-centered and start focusing on him, the author and perfecter of our faith, the source of all good things. And we will finally be forced to admit that, yes, God did create the universe exactly the way that the Bible describes. He will not share his glory with another.

The Creator in the Old Testament

Just so this book doesn't grow beyond reasonable bounds, I will let you trace these ideas throughout the Old Testament. Keep in mind that the Creator made this world; that's why it looks and works the way it does. If we remember that God made the world, we will look there first when we're trying to figure out what this world is all about.

God had a project in mind from the very beginning, and he kept working on that project throughout the Old Testament. So we find him following up on those Creation themes: setting up a Kingdom, issuing laws, judging the hearts of men. We find the power of the Spirit at work building a spiritual Kingdom to fix the spiritual problems of the first Creation. We should be alert to these realities as we read; it's as if, when starting with the Genesis account, God stated clearly the principle "Here are the important aspects of my Creation, and now I'm going to spend my time developing them over Israel's history." That will help us understand the why's and how's of God's story in the Old Testament. Here is the Creator at work.

The Creator in the New Testament

And in the same way, the only way we will ever understand much of what Jesus did in the New Testament is to remember that he is the Creator.

Learn to ask the right questions: where did Jesus get these powers that he had? Why did he follow certain procedures in his work? What is the agenda that he was working on? What were his goals? What did he expect of the people he worked with? You will find the answers to these questions and many others back in the account of Creation in Genesis.

In other words, you must identify *what* Jesus was doing, and *who* was doing it, and *why* he did it that way, if you want to understand it aright. He was the Creator – not only working on his *first* Creation, fixing it and straightening it and disposing of it, but also starting work on the *second* Creation using the same methods that he used in the first Creation. He had an enormous amount of work to accomplish.

So, since we need to read the New Testament in light of the fact that Jesus is the Creator using those same methods from the Old Testament, let's go back through the list and pick up on the details.

- **Miracle** – God's perfect creation is so broken now that it will require a miracle to fix things. That's why we see Jesus using miracles to heal people in the Gospels. Here is the Creator, in compassion reaching out and healing the broken and crushed, doing what only the Creator can do – but it's showing us the heart of the Creator also, since he would be the one most interested in fixing the beautiful world that he had made in the beginning.

  But this world isn't the only thing that the Creator is interested in working on. He has started a new project – a new Creation to replace the old one. What are the requirements of this new world? That man might see God; that we might learn God's ways and walk in them. That our hearts might be changed from stone to flesh, and we obey willingly everything that the King commands. That we might come back from the dead and live in God's spiritual world and taste him and love him and glorify him. In other words, everything that God wanted from his Creation in the first place. At this point, however, all that is going to take a miracle!

  We find, however, that the Creator is up to the task. We see some of these spiritual miracles at work in the Gospels, but they will come out later more clearly in the

49

letters of the Apostles. A conversion – when a person comes out of the darkness and starts living in the light of Heaven – is a miracle of the Creator, nothing less. It isn't simply an act of the will on someone's part; they don't just decide to become a Christian. The Creator changes the heart from death to life; he brings them back from spiritual death and makes them alive – which means they can see and know God now. This is not the work of man, but a genuine act of the Creator doing what no man can do, skipping the steps in between and doing the impossible.

- **Command** – *Jesus is Lord.* Everyone in church knows that formula. And yet that phrase has such profound implications that I think most people don't understand its true meaning. The Creation account teaches us who this Jesus is – he's the King, and he rules over his subjects with an iron will. There must be no deviation or rebellion against the King, because only his wisdom and power can build a perfect Kingdom. If we don't follow his will, if he isn't making the decisions in a church, then it's doubtful that any new Creation happened in people's lives – the Creator obviously isn't building *his* Kingdom there.

That's why it's staggering when we *do* see it happen. A person who is genuinely converted suddenly sees that Jesus is indeed the Master, the King, the Lord whom we must obey. The proud heart is broken over the sin and rebellion that we've committed against the King; we are ashamed over the trouble we've been, the immorality that we've been wallowing in, the hard heart that has resisted the Word of the King. It sweeps over our hearts that our only hope is if this King has mercy on us, and lifts us up in his presence, and forgets our past, and restores our relationship to him. If he does this, that's an even more staggering reality!

And a true conversion leads to a new passion for following the will of the King. We get into the Bible, and start learning who he is and what he does. We learn about his Kingdom so that we can become part of it. We learn his ways so that we can follow him. We learn his Names so that we can start honoring them and utilizing his spiritual resources in our lives. In other words, whatever belongs to the King, whatever the King does, is now our life's agenda; we are no longer our own but his humble servants. Whatever his will is – even though we must carry the cross and share his shame in this world – that is our will.

That's how you can tell that the Creator has added a new subject to his spiritual Kingdom – when you see these things happening.

- **Word** – Jesus does not treat us like children. "I no longer call you servants, because a servant does not know his master's business. Instead, I have called you friends, for everything that I learned from my Father I have made known to you." (John 15:15) He is going to *reveal* to us, step by step, what it is that he's doing and what our role is in this unfolding new Creation.

He wants us to know the Truth. *Truth* is the way that God sees things – at least what he wants us to see. All of our obedience and faith will depend on being able to see what he's doing, and get clear instructions on what he expects of us. This is going to be a spiritual operation, and a lot of important things have to be done to get us from this world to the next. We can't be in the dark about what's going on.

So Jesus sets up the Church on the foundation of *revelation* – the Word of God shining the light so that we can see our way to God. Preachers and teachers uncover the truth so that we can be informed about God's actions and spiritual realities of Heaven. The Spirit of Christ opens up the text of the Bible so that, not only does it make sense to us, but it becomes real and a real part of our lives. We are children of light now, walking in the light. While the rest of the world is still in darkness, we are growing in wisdom and understanding as Jesus reveals his Kingdom to us.

- **Wisdom and understanding** – There's a prophecy in Isaiah that describes what the Messiah will be like when he comes. He will have a new Kingdom, and we are told how powerful and skillful he will be as he rules over this Kingdom. Isaiah tells us some of his names that describe him – one of which is the "Wonderful Counselor." (Isaiah 9:6)

  The Creator's wisdom behind the first Creation is beyond our imagination. But now that sin and death have entered into the world, getting this mess solved will require an even more profound wisdom, an intellect that is infinite. Untangling the disaster that billions of human beings have caused is not something that an ordinary mortal can do – witness the moral and political and social and educational "solutions" that civilizations keep trying and failing with over the centuries.

  Yet we see Jesus patiently unraveling people's complex problems with the wisdom of the Creator, aiming at the real problems and avoiding the trivia that the religious experts tried to tangle him in. He proscribes the exact course of action, the right remedy, for any problem or situation that people brought to him. In fact, most of what has to be done is going to be counter-intuitive to us; we won't understand at all why his solutions are going to work. Hanging on a cross doesn't seem like a victory to us! But the Creator knows what he's doing. All things are going to work out for the good of those who trust him. He's applying spiritual resources to our problems, which accounts for why they are so perplexing at times to us; but these, though strange to us, are going to prove to be exactly what is needed to restore God's Creation to a new level of eternity and perfection.

- **Through Christ** – What is probably the most amazing aspect of Jesus' role in Creation is how personally involved he is in this project. (See John 1:1-5 and Colossians 1:15-20)

The Father made the world through the Son so that the Son would have all power and authority over the world. It appears that they were both agreed on how this project would unfold. God of course knows what will happen in history, so he knew that man would rebel against him and ruin Creation. But, not surprised in the least, God made plans *at the beginning* to renew his Creation and restore his glory over his Kingdom.

> All inhabitants of the earth will worship the beast — all whose names have not been written in the Lamb's book of life, the Lamb who was slain from the creation of the world. (Revelation 13:8)

What God decided to do was tear down his Creation and start over. But here's where the fascinating part comes in – Jesus himself is going to lead the way from the first to the second Creation. He took upon himself the body of a man, and then destroyed it on the Cross – because this flesh that we have must be destroyed; it can't be preserved as it is in the next world. Then God raised him from the dead as a "new man" with a new body, the first of a new race of men who would never sin against God again. In other words, Jesus went through the necessary transformation himself first, to pave the way for the rest of us.

> Now if we died with Christ, we believe that we will also live with him. For we know that since Christ was raised from the dead, he cannot die again; death no longer has mastery over him. The death he died, he died to sin once for all; but the life he lives, he lives to God. (Romans 6:8-10)

He made this promise to do this in the Gospels, but it's in the Apostles letters that we learn all the details, the amazing transformation and results. The thought that the Son of God shares our humanity so that we can share his glory in Heaven is the story of the ages, a love-story that eclipses all others. Our destiny is to enter Heaven as new creatures, one with the Son of God who has become like us, and live with his Father forever. He is himself his own new Creation – for our sake.

> As was the earthly man, so are those who are of the earth; and as is the Heavenly man, so also are those who are of Heaven. And just as we have borne the image of the earthly man, so shall we bear the image of the Heavenly man. (1 Corinthians 15:48-49)

- **<u>The Spirit's power</u>** – There's a prophecy in Isaiah that best describes the kind of ministry that the Messiah would have.

> The Spirit of the LORD will rest on him — the Spirit of wisdom and of understanding, the Spirit of counsel and of might, the Spirit of the knowledge and fear of the LORD — and he will delight in the fear of the LORD. (Isaiah 11:2-3)

When Jesus was baptized by John, the Spirit came down from Heaven and settled on him – in fulfillment of this prophecy.

> As soon as Jesus was baptized, he went up out of the water. At that moment Heaven was opened, and he saw the Spirit of God descending like a dove and alighting on him. And a voice from Heaven said, "This is my Son, whom I love; with him I am well pleased." (Matthew 3:16-17)

There's been a lot of argument over whether Jesus in his own strength, by virtue of himself being the Son of God, could have done the works that he did without the Spirit's anointing. But I believe that this ignores some of the things that we learn from the Old Testament. As we will see, Jesus was the Son of David, and therefore was destined to sit on David's throne and build the Kingdom of God according to David's Plan. Every king was anointed to this task. And Jesus was the Heir of Abraham; he had to have access to the riches of the Covenant so that he could pass them on to the other heirs. So in light of both of these realities, the man Jesus had to be anointed for his task. It was a requirement for the job. Let's not stumble over the metaphysics involved; the functions proscribe procedure.

So in the power and wisdom of the Spirit (its two main functions) Jesus started his work repairing the brokenness of the first Creation and laying the foundations for the New Creation. It's always the Spirit's power behind God's works, because it's a power that provides what nothing else can provide. Nothing can stop God; and we need nothing less than what only God can do. The works of Christ were a clear proof that here was God himself on the scene, doing what no man could do.

And the new life that we have in Christ is Spirit-filled – Christians have received the Spirit of Christ into their hearts, and now they can live in two worlds at the same time. We can see God in his glory; we see the way of life; we see Jesus and we know now who he is; we are being remade into his likeness by his Spirit – filled with the fruit of the Spirit. The work of the Church goes on because of the Spirit's blessing: through the spiritual gifts we are all built up into the Temple in which God will live with his people forever. Jesus is creating a new world that is filled with the power and wisdom that comes by his Spirit.

- **Witness** – People don't believe in God unless they can see him. And science really doesn't believe that God – if he exists – had anything to do with the Creation of the universe. That's why God had an eyewitness on the scene; he knew we wouldn't believe the Genesis account, so the Spirit testifies that he saw and heard the whole thing. That's a shrewd strategic move on God's part. We can't deny that it happened exactly as the Genesis account says without calling the Spirit a liar.

Well, the Creator has done it again. This time he has provided all kinds of witnesses to testify to the reality of the new Creation that he is making. Many in our society don't believe in conversions, or the salvation through Christ, or the work of the Spirit in the Church – but the Church is full of eyewitnesses who have seen and heard God in their lives. It's not just doctrine; it's a real world that many of us have personally experienced. How can the world deny the personal testimony of someone who has come from darkness to light, from death to life, and now they know the living Christ?

In the Gospel stories there were people from all walks of life who met Jesus and walked away changed; they went home and told their neighbors about this unique man who could do things that nobody else could do. The disciples were themselves eyewitnesses of his glory, and their letters are filled with testimonies of what to expect when you come to this Son of God.

But he's not just a historical figure; he himself was raised from the dead, went back to Heaven and now sits at God's right hand on the throne. He continues to pour out his spiritual treasures in the Church to whoever will come to him in humility and faith. There's just no denying the fact that God's people have experienced a foretaste of Heaven because of their relationship with Jesus Christ. To disprove Christianity, one would have to call millions of people liars – and that won't work in court.

- **Blessing** – The Kingdom that the Creator set up at the beginning was exactly that; everyone is God's subject and bound to obedience to the King. But he's a good King. His commands are not only not burdensome, they are a pleasure to obey. Life is good when we keep his commandments.

Here is where we need to trust the Creator's wisdom as he leads us into the second Creation. Jesus promised us that life will be good if we keep his commands – if we do exactly what he tells us to do, and follow him out of this world into the next world. We may wonder, as we are required to pass by this world's pleasures, whether we are trading the good life for a life of suffering and failure and poverty. But Jesus assures us that, for a time, we may have to suffer; but in the end it will be all worth it.

> And everyone who has left houses or brothers or sisters or father or mother or wife or children or fields for my sake will receive a hundred times as much and will inherit eternal life. (Matthew 19:29)

Don't set your eyes on things in this world; look to the things in the next world. That's where true happiness is. Don't accumulate treasures in this world, where thieves and rust destroy our possessions. Store up treasures in the next world. (Matthew 6; Colossians 3)

The Apostles saw that next world, and they wrote long passages trying to describe it to us. They were amazed at what they saw in Heaven for the saints. We really don't want to miss out on what God has planned for his people. It is pure bliss to serve the King.

> Then the angel showed me the river of the water of life, as clear as crystal, flowing from the throne of God and of the Lamb down the middle of the great street of the city. On each side of the river stood the tree of life, bearing twelve crops of fruit, yielding its fruit every month. And the leaves of the tree are for the healing of the nations. (Revelation 22:1-2)

- **Judgment** – We sinners like our privacy. We really don't want people prying into our lives and asking personal questions. And we also don't like having to measure up to someone else's standards; we do what *we* want to do, not what someone else tells us to do.

But that doesn't work in the Creator's Kingdom. He made us, we belong to him, and we will be expected to produce a profit for him. Which means that he, not we, will be the Judge of whether we measure up to his expectations. If someone doesn't like the sound of this, he or she isn't going to like Heaven.

Jesus showed his glory as the Judge in the way he so easily uncovered the truth about people's hearts. He blasted the Pharisees, whom everyone thought were holy men of God, for their hypocrisy and superficial religion. He knew the true story of the woman at the well and put it out on the table to discuss. He knew exactly what was wrong with the rich young ruler, even though the man didn't know his own heart. Everywhere Jesus went, everyone he dealt with, he showed his deep knowledge of the true state of affairs in people's hearts and minds.

One reason for that is because he needs accurate knowledge of us in order to prescribe the right solution for us. We will inevitably ignore certain deficiencies in our nature, and consider God's affairs of little importance, and avoid the mandates of Heaven because we think we don't need them. Jesus is the perfect Judge, however, and when he prescribes certain remedies – like repentance and humility – and certain resources – like God's Truth – he knows what he's talking about.

So when you read, for example, the Apostles' letters, put yourself in the defendant's seat in the courtroom. This is the Judge analyzing your heart, bringing the truth to light, forcing the subjects that we don't want to talk about, working through necessary issues that we've been ignoring. The Judge knows you far better than you know yourself. Even from Heaven, through the Bible, he uncovers your heart and "reveals the thoughts and attitudes of your heart" in ways that nobody else can, including yourself. (Hebrews 4:12-13)

He *has* to judge us like this – we *have* to submit to his judgment of us – it *has* to be revealed to all and made plain whether we will fit in with his new Creation, and if so, how.

> For we must all appear before the judgment seat of Christ, so that each of us may receive what is due us for the things done while in the body, whether good or bad. (2 Corinthians 5:10)

- **<u>Glory</u>** – Glory, if you recall, is who gets the credit. God made the world in such a way that nobody else can justifiably claim to have done it that way. Nobody else can do miracles; nobody else is the King who can set up a Kingdom with morals and ethics and judgment. Only God could have done what Genesis tells us what happened.

The reason he wants the credit is because nobody else is God. He is the source of all good things; he alone is our "shield and great reward," as he told Abraham. He wants all of his creatures to depend on him alone for everything.

That's what Jesus was telling us when he kept referring to his Father being the source of Jesus' entire ministry.

> Very truly I tell you, the Son can do nothing by himself; he can do only what he sees his Father doing, because whatever the Father does the Son also does. (John 5:19)

Everything Jesus did was because his Father gave him that task; everything he said was a message from the Father to us. Jesus claimed no credit for anything he did or said, because he wanted us to see that God is the source of everything we need.

> "Why do you ask me about what is good?" Jesus replied. "There is only One who is good." (Matthew 19:17)

Jesus' purpose is to bring all the Creation back to God, under the rule of God, depending on God for everything, so that God might finally get the glory that he deserves. Thus Paul writes:

> Then the end will come, when he hands over the Kingdom to God the Father after he has

destroyed all dominion, authority and power. For he must reign until he has put all his enemies under his feet. The last enemy to be destroyed is death. For he "has put everything under his feet." Now when it says that "everything" has been put under him, it is clear that this does not include God himself, who put everything under Christ. When he has done this, then the Son himself will be made subject to him who put everything under him, so that God may be all in all. (1 Corinthians 15:24-28)

Summary

It is vitally important to understand the concept of the Creator. Wherever you turn in the Bible you will see the Creator at work; but if you don't know his methods, if you don't understand what he's working on and how he does it, you will miss the significance of what he's doing in the text. In the Old Testament, God was working in the context of his Creation and using his unique methodology that we learned from the Creation account. But in the New Testament we also see the Creator at work – doing the same kinds of things in the same ways. If we miss what he's doing, that will be quite a surprise to us on Judgment Day when the Creator tells us that we don't fit into his New Creation.

And throw that worthless servant outside, into the darkness, where there will be weeping and gnashing of teeth. (Matthew 25:30)

THE COVENANT WITH ABRAHAM

The promises of God, which we hold so precious, are based on an agreement between God and man that is inflexible, rock-solid, and eternal. We can and must depend on this agreement and his faithfulness to it for our salvation; it is our only hope.

The very salvation that we New Testament Christians rely on is based firmly on the agreement that God made with Abraham; as Paul says, "He is the father of us all." (Romans 4:16) In fact, God made this agreement of salvation *only* for Abraham and his descendants. Only if we can prove that we are the spiritual children of Abraham will we be allowed into the presence of God.

The Agreement with Abraham

In our day we use contracts and lawyers and courts to make agreements with each other, and we have all sorts of ways to make the other party keep their side of the bargain. But in the days of Abraham they had none of these things; so they had to use a different system for making agreements.

The "covenant" was simply a legally binding agreement between two people. In it they agreed to do certain things for each other. But the Hebrew word for "covenant" is *berith*, and the word is used in the phrase "to **cut** a covenant." There is an amazing reason for this. When two people wanted to make this kind of agreement, they would get some animals and, with a sword, cut them into halves and lay the halves out on the ground, making a path down between them. Then one person would walk down the path between the animal halves and declare what he agreed to do for the other person. The idea was that if he failed to do as he agreed, the offended party would have the legal right to take a sword and do to him what was done to the animals! Then when he was finished making his promise, the other person would do the same. As you can imagine, people didn't enter into an agreement like this unless they were serious about it.

Now turn to Genesis 15 for an example of how a covenant was done. In it the Lord instructs Abraham to cut a heifer, a goat and a ram into halves and lay them out on the ground in two rows. Then when Abraham was put into a deep sleep (so that he could see the Lord come down in a vision), the Lord himself walked down through the animal halves and declared his agreement with Abraham.

> When the sun had set and darkness had fallen, a smoking firepot with a blazing torch appeared and passed between the pieces. On that day the LORD made a Covenant with Abram and said, "To your descendants I give this land, from the river of Egypt to the great river, the Euphrates — the land of the Kenites, Kenizzites, Kadmonites, Hittites, Perizzites, Rephaites, Amorites, Canaanites, Girgashites and Jebusites." (Genesis 15:17)

What is truly amazing is that the Lord was submitting himself to the hands of Abraham in this agreement; he (the Author of life!) was putting his own life on the line. He would keep the terms of this agreement or willingly forfeit his life. This should show you how seriously he took the Covenant with Abraham. There was absolutely no question that the Lord was going to do what he promised.

The second amazing thing about this story is that God did *not* require Abraham to walk down between the animal halves. Normally they would both do it; but in this case the Lord knew that Abraham and his descendants would surely put the Covenant in jeopardy if it depended on them in any way. So God took it upon himself to keep both sides of the bargain. Not that he was allowing Abraham to get away with sin in the future. But he knew that Abraham *would* sin — and since the Covenant was tremendously important to the Lord, he was acting now to protect it from any future threats to its fulfillment.

What was this Covenant that the Lord made with Abraham? There *was* a covenant made before this time with Noah; but Abraham was the first important step in the process of salvation. For a long time the Lord was preparing an answer to the sin and death that man had introduced into his perfect creation. Now, in Abraham, he was ready to start unfolding it into human history. The Covenant with Abraham is the beginning of the answer that we have all been looking for.

The Lord promised to do four things for Abraham and his descendants:

To give him a son: Abraham and Sarah had no children when they moved to Canaan in obedience to the Lord's command. They were advanced in years at the time, and had basically given up hope that they ever would have a natural-born son. But the Lord promised them that they would, in fact, have their own son — clearly an impossible thing.

> But Abram said, "O Sovereign LORD, what can you give me since I remain childless and the one who will inherit my estate is Eliezer of Damascus?" And Abram said, "You have given me no children; so a servant in my household will be my heir." Then the word of the LORD came to him: "This man will not be your heir, but a son coming from your own body will be your heir." (Genesis 15:2-4)

> He was too old to have a son, and his wife was long past the child-bearing age for women. God was promising them the impossible — a miracle, which happens to be the very method he uses to build his Kingdom. At one point they both laughed at the idea of having a son in their old age; when the boy was born, then, they named him "Isaac" which means "he laughs" (perhaps because the Lord had the last laugh in this!).

The promise was fulfilled in Genesis 21:

> Now the LORD was gracious to Sarah as he had said, and the LORD did for Sarah what he had promised. Sarah became pregnant and bore a son to Abraham in his old age, at the very time God had promised him. (Genesis 21:1-2)

To give him the land: When the Lord brought Abraham to Canaan, it wasn't just for a sight-seeing tour! He had Abraham look around at this new place and promised him that one day, both he and his descendants would own this land.

> Lift up your eyes from where you are and look north and south, east and west. All the land that you see I will give to you and your offspring forever. (Genesis 13:14)

The problem was that this would have to be as much of a miracle as the first promise. The Canaanites who already lived there wouldn't take kindly to an alien with strange ways and accents settling down among them, taking their valuable pasture and resources — they especially wouldn't appreciate his notions of owning the whole place someday. So they no doubt kept their eye on him at all times and encouraged him to move on, not settle down. (You can see this very thing happen in the story of Isaac — Genesis 26:12-31.)

The fulfillment of this promise came about in a strange way, certainly not in the way that Abraham would have wanted. Sarah his wife eventually died, and after Abraham mourned over her he looked around for a place to bury her. Since he had no land of his own, he went to the Hittites (a Canaanite tribe living near Hebron) and asked to buy from them a field with a cave in it so that he could bury her. They agreed on a price and the deed was made out in Abraham's name; he became the legal owner of a piece of Canaanite property for the first time.

> So Ephron's field in Machpelah near Mamre — both the field and the cave in it, and all the trees within the borders of the field — was deeded to Abraham as his property in the presence of all the Hittites who had come to the gate of the city . . . So the field and the cave in it were deeded to Abraham by the Hittites as a burial site. (Genesis 23:17-18, 20)

The remarkable thing about this transaction was that it was the beginning of the fulfillment of the second promise that God made with Abraham. He was to become owner of the entire land, in spite of the Canaanites already living there. This was the first step to that ownership. It happened in the midst of trial; certainly Abraham didn't want his wife to die. Nevertheless that trial was the means that the Lord used to bring about what otherwise would have never happened. That deed, by the way, stayed in the family until they returned from Egypt hundreds of years later.

To make a great nation from him: The Lord promised Abraham that not only would he get a son, but his descendants would become so numerous that they would be a great nation that nobody could count.

> I will make you into a great nation. (Genesis 12:2)

> He took him outside and said, "Look up at the heavens and count the stars — if indeed you can count them." Then he said to him, "So shall your offspring be." (Genesis 15:5)

Now Abraham couldn't become a nation all by himself. And his son couldn't become a nation without getting married. So they had a problem on their hands: where to find a wife for Isaac? Abraham absolutely refused to get one of the local Canaanite girls for Isaac's wife; they were pagans, worshipers of idols and would lead his son into wickedness and away from the Lord. So Abraham had his servant go back home to Haran where his extended family still lived and find a wife there.

Most people use this story as an example of how to find a suitable marriage partner. But we miss the main point of the story if we limit ourselves to just that. Genesis 24 is really showing us the beginning of the fulfillment of the third promise — the making of a nation. He provided a wife (Rebekah) to be the mother of Jacob, who was the father of twelve sons, who were the fathers of the twelve tribes of Israel. The promise had begun to unfold!

> And they blessed Rebekah and said to her, "Our sister, may you increase to thousands upon thousands; may your offspring possess the gates of their enemies." (Genesis 24:60)

To bless the nations through him: When man first sinned in the Garden of Eden, he brought upon himself and the entire world a tremendous curse of misery and death. As far as God was concerned, this was the worst thing that could have happened to his beautiful creation. He didn't curse us because he liked to, but because he had to. He had to confront sin with the severity of the Law because justice is important to him.

But the Lord never did like that answer for the entire world. From the very beginning he set about putting together a new answer for the problem of sin and death. He hinted at what it might be in Genesis 3:15, but he didn't really say yet what he had in mind.

Now in Abraham's life he was ready to start putting the plan into action. The first step was to promise Abraham that he would be a blessing to the nations:

> And all peoples on earth will be blessed through you. (Genesis 12:3)

> And through your offspring all nations on earth will be blessed. (Genesis 22:18)

This blessing would overturn the original curse that fell on mankind. But what would it look like? Again, Abraham got a "foretaste," a glimpse of what that would look like, in his own experience. The Lord told him one time to take his only son Isaac and sacrifice him to the Lord "on one of the mountains I will tell you about." (Genesis 22:2) So Abraham took Isaac there

THE COVENANT WITH ABRAHAM

and started to draw the sacrificial knife across his son's throat. Immediately the Lord stopped him and commended him for his faith.

What went through Abraham's mind during this crisis? He was about to lose his only hope! Upon Isaac rested the future of the entire Covenant; it didn't make sense to put him to death, even if it *was* in obedience to the Lord. But the Lord showed Abraham a truth there that strengthened him to go on with the act:

> Abraham reasoned that God could raise the
> dead, and figuratively speaking, he did receive
> Isaac back from death. (Hebrews 11:19)

Abraham learned about resurrection that day; he got the first sample himself when the Lord gave Isaac back to him. This was in fulfillment of the fourth promise — the blessing that God had in mind, eventually, for people all around the world: life from the dead, eternal life.

The testimony of the Old Testament

The Covenant rules the rest of the Old Testament. Most think that the Old Testament is dominated by the Law of Moses, when actually the Covenant is the bigger concept. As Paul tells us, the Covenant came first; it's the older agreement. The Law comes under its purview.

> It was not through the Law that Abraham and his
> offspring received the promise that he would be heir of the
> world, but through the righteousness that comes by faith.
> (Romans 4:13)

The *only* reason that the Israelites received anything from their God was because of this Covenant. We can track the different elements of the Covenant through their history.

- **The Heir:** The concept of the Heir is that there had to be someone who would inherit the Covenant blessings from Abraham and pass on those blessings to the rest of the family. In legal terms we call this person the *executor* of the estate.

In Abraham's immediate situation that heir was Isaac – the "miracle baby." Because Isaac was born to Abraham through Sarah, the other children of Abraham (and he had many) were not the legal executors, though through Isaac they would be taken care of.

But then later in Genesis we start to read of how God chose particular people through whom he blessed his people – the "designated Heir." In the story of Genesis it was **Joseph**.[10] If the children of Abraham wanted resources and protection, they had to come to God's chosen executor of the estate and make their claims. That made these designated Heirs extremely important to the rest of the family.

That principle pops up again and again in Israel's history. When God brought his people out of Egypt and sent them on to the Promised Land, he chose **Moses** to be their designated Heir; Moses was a rich resource for Israel, not only in his day but for thousands of years later. Joshua carried on the responsibilities of the designated Heir as he finished Moses' task.

David was obviously the designated Heir in his day; he was a fountain of blessing and guidance just when Israel need it the most. And Solomon carried on his program.

Elijah was the designated Heir in his day, as he brought the Word of the Lord to the Northern Tribes and laid down the principles of the prophetic office. Elisha continued his program. That raises another interesting aspect of this theme of the Heir – in some of these situations we find those clusters of miracles that happen occasionally in the Bible. It's as if the designated Heir has access to not only power and resources of ordinary men, but also has extraordinary powers when needed to bless God's people.

---

[10] For a discussion on Joseph's role in Abraham's family, see below in the chapter "Genesis."

There were other people who qualified as the designated Heirs in their day, because it was through them that God saved, confronted, blessed, and ruled over his people in extraordinary ways and circumstances: see the cases of **Esther**, **Daniel** and **Nehemiah** for examples.

- **The Land:** When God led the Israelites out of Egypt and back to Canaan under Moses, he was keeping this second promise of the Covenant that he made with their father Abraham.

    Joshua divided out the land according to the Tribes of Israel, who were descended from the twelve sons of Jacob. They gave out the land to families. And the Law required that the land stay in the families forever; no tribe was allowed to sell or give away land to someone from another tribe. If by some reason debts and such things made it necessary to rent land to other Israelites, the Year of Jubilee law required that the land go back to the original family that owned it. This was so that the land would always belong to the family, that the promise made to Abraham would be faithfully kept for all of Abraham's descendants, poor or rich.

    If you look at the map, the land that was promised to Abraham's descendants extended from Beersheba in the south to Dan in the north (up beyond the Sea of Galilee), and from the Mediterranean Sea on the west side to the Jordan Plain on the east, including the area surrounding the Jordan River. In other words, the Covenant land included the area where Lot chose to live back in Abraham's day.

    At least that was the ideal. From the time of Joshua on, the Israelites never did get all of that land, for one reason or another. They always had pagans to contend with; they never succeeded on exterminating all of the Canaanites. And that proved to be a thorn in their side for centuries as they struggled with their enemies for possession. And when the Jews went into Exile, matters got worse: they came back to a small percentage of the original Promised Land.

- **The Nation:** At first the family of Abraham was a small group living in Egypt under Joseph's protection. But over the next 400 years the family grew into literally a nation – according to the census in Numbers, the number of fighting men was over 600,000. That means the entire group numbered in the millions.

  During the time of the Judges they got a chance to act like a nation under God. But unfortunately human nature ruined things over and over; instead of obeying God as their King, they worshiped false gods and fought among themselves. Periodically a Judge would pull a tribe or two together to fight off the enemy, but then things would settle back to normal and chaos ensued.

  Then David finally pulled the tribes together into one nation, a crucial step in fulfilling this third promise of the Covenant. Through his 5-point Plan, he defeated their enemies, brought peace and justice to the realm, and led the people back to their God to live according to his Law. His descendants who sat on his throne were supposed to maintain this Plan so that the Covenant promises would extend throughout the nation to everyone, but some of them failed the Lord and things got pretty chaotic again. When the Israelites had thoroughly rejected the Lord, he sent them into Exile and they lost their nation.

  They never recovered from that setback. They did get Jerusalem back and some of the surrounding area, but they were always under someone else's heavy hand – the Persians, the Greeks, the Romans. Most of their troubles during this time between the Exile and the coming of Christ were due to the fact that they no longer had their own nation; the Promise was left hanging for the time being. Without a king, without their own nation and their own laws, they couldn't keep the whole Law as required.

- **The Blessing:** When Abraham received his son Isaac back from the death sentence upon him, he learned several things about this fourth promise. *First*, he learned about the resurrection of the dead (since, as Hebrews says, he "reasoned that God could even raise the dead." (Hebrews 11:19) Second, he learned about the substitutionary sacrifice. Instead of following through on Isaac's death, God provided a ram as a sacrifice – a substitute – that would serve the purpose. Both of these concepts form the foundation of the worship of Israel as it got worked out in the Temple.

Israel's religion was different from the pagan religions. They worshiped their gods with sacrifices also, but for a different purpose – they reasoned that since they were giving up this precious resource for their god's sake, their god owed them something now. In other words, worship was founded on obligating their god to do something for them.

But Israel's worship was founded on an entirely different concept. In God's eyes, mankind fully deserves to die for all the sins that we've committed against him. In fact, if something isn't done, that's exactly what's going to happen – we're all going to die! What God provided for Abraham and his family, however, was a substitution system – we can offer the life of another (in their case, animals from the flock) in their place. The animal would die; they wouldn't have to. It was a system of mercy, not obligation; God didn't have to do anything for them. Out of his compassion for them, instead of requiring their deaths, he accepted the death of a substitute.

All of the worship at the Temple was founded on this concept. And God followed through on his promise and forgave them of their sins – forgave the sin, forgot about the sin, put it completely out of his mind and treated them as if they were righteous. It seemed so unrealistic in that they were still sinners (the proof was that they went right back into their sins!), but it was the foretaste of what was to come in the death of Christ and the cleansing of the sinful heart with his blood.

But as is true with all good things, Israel abused her privileges. She took the sacrifices for granted, turned them into empty ceremonies, and went back to her sins. There are long passages in the Bible that tell about this tragic turn of events – of Israel abusing her most precious possession and treating it like it was worthless. God does not appreciate people abusing his mercy; there were severe punishments in store for his people for their casual attitude toward this promise of life.

Each of these promises defined the nation of Israel; they were the very foundation of their relationship with God. In fact, nobody was allowed to be a part of any of this unless he or she could demonstrate that they were true descendants of Abraham; nothing was taken for granted. For example there were several instances when people were questioned about their genealogy. When the Exiles came back from Babylon and reorganized to start up the Temple services, the men who claimed to be priests (and therefore qualified to work in the Temple) had to provide proof of their genealogy back to Abraham. Some of them couldn't.

> These searched for their family records, but they could not find them and so were excluded from the priesthood as unclean. (Nehemiah 7:64)

What did Abraham know?

Abraham knew about Jesus. People fret about how much Abraham knew, that he couldn't possibly know enough about Christ to fill out an adequate picture of the Gospel. But actually they are worrying about nothing. The way that Abraham knew about Jesus is the same way we know about him: through *faith*.

> Your father Abraham rejoiced at the thought of seeing my day; he saw it and was glad. (John 8:56)

> By faith he made his home in the promised land like a stranger in a foreign country; he lived in tents, as did Isaac and Jacob, who were heirs with him of the same promise. For he was looking forward to the city with foundations, whose architect and builder is God. (Hebrews 11:9-10)

Faith is the ability to see and live in the spiritual world of God. Anybody who lives by the faith that God gives them is able to see clearly who Jesus is. The Lord showed Abraham everything he needed to know about Jesus 2000 years before the Incarnation, just as he shows us 2000 years after the Incarnation – through the Word and the Spirit. That's why Paul says that the Gospel was first announced to Abraham.

> Understand, then, that those who have faith are children of Abraham. Scripture foresaw that God would justify the Gentiles by faith, and announced the gospel in advance to Abraham: "All nations will be blessed through you." So those who rely on faith are blessed along with Abraham, the man of faith. (Galatians 3:7-9)

For some reason people don't appreciate the fact that the Covenant was made with Abraham, not with us. We get it through our father Abraham as an inheritance. This is a legal matter.

> Therefore, the promise comes by faith, so that it may be by grace and may be guaranteed to all Abraham's offspring — not only to those who are of the Law but also to those who have the faith of Abraham. He is the father of us all. (Romans 4:16)

We don't have to wonder how much Abraham knew; the Bible tells us exactly what he knew. Abraham saw that Jesus was the great Heir (John 8); he saw that the land promised was Heaven, an eternal home (Hebrews 11); he saw that the family promised him extends to Jews and Gentiles, the Church (Matthew 8); and he knew about the resurrection from the dead, and our deliverance through a substitutionary sacrifice (Hebrews 11).

The Covenant in Christ

Paul tells us that God had Jesus in mind all along for the job of chief Executor of Abraham's estate.

> The promises were spoken to Abraham and to his Seed. The Scripture does not say "and to seeds," meaning many people, but "and to your Seed," meaning one person, who is Christ. (Galatians 3:16)

There are several reasons for this. First, Abraham – and all of his descendents except for Christ – had no way of accessing all of the children of God throughout history. Each of them would die in their own time. What are the rest of us going to do, then, without Abraham standing in for us defending our right to the promises? Second, the Covenant promises were of a spiritual, eternal nature – they weren't the kind of thing that an ordinary man could deal with. It was Heaven's currency, not earth's. It takes an extraordinary person to be able to even identify what those treasures are, let alone distribute them to those in need of them.

There's another important aspect to that story of the Covenant between God and Abraham. If you look at it again, you will notice that only God walked down through the slain animals. Abraham did not.

> When the sun had set and darkness had fallen, a smoking firepot with a blazing torch appeared and passed between the pieces. (Genesis 15:17)

This was not the usual practice. Usually both parties walked through, symbolizing their willingness to put their lives on the line to keep their side of the bargain. But God, knowing full well that Abraham and his descendents (being weak and sinful) couldn't be trusted to keep their promises, decided to carry Abraham's responsibility as well. God will make sure that his heirs get his promises.

God did this, of course, by himself becoming a man. That gave Jesus a unique position in the Covenant. He was a descendent of Abraham with full legal rights to the Covenant; and he was God's Son with full access to the spiritual depth of the Covenant promises. No wonder, then, that he could make the following statements.

> All things have been committed to me by my Father. No one knows the Son except the Father, and no one knows the Father except the Son and those to whom the Son chooses to reveal him. Come to me, all you who are weary and burdened, and I will give you rest. (Matthew 11:27-28)

> I have spoken to you of earthly things and you do not believe; how then will you believe if I speak of Heavenly

things? No one has ever gone into Heaven except the one who came from Heaven – the Son of Man. (John 3:12-13)

I am the bread of life. He who comes to me will never go hungry, and he who believes in me will never be thirsty. (John 6:35)

I am the way and the truth and the life. No one comes to the Father except through me. (John 14:6)

And I will do whatever you ask in my name, so that the Son may bring glory to the Father. You may ask me for anything in my name, and I will do it. (John 14:13-14)

So the Heir and Seed of Abraham, the Son of God, has the *authority*, the *access*, and the *ability* to distribute the spiritual blessings of the Covenant to Abraham's children. And that's exactly what we see him doing in the Gospels.

- **The Son**

The first order of business is to find the children of Abraham, because Jesus is obliged by the terms of the Covenant to give the promises only to them – upon pain of death. It's a legal contract, and he's going to faithfully execute his duties as Executor of the estate.

These twelve Jesus sent out with the following instructions: "Do not go among the Gentiles or enter any town of the Samaritans. Go rather to the lost sheep of Israel." (Matthew 10:5-6)

He answered, "I was sent only to the lost sheep of Israel." (Matthew 15:24)

What he's looking for are the "family characteristics" inherited from father Abraham: his faith, and his circumcision. But he's looking for the spiritual reality, not just the superficial – the gift of the Spirit, not the works of the Law. When Jesus finds evidence of these characteristics in any particular individual, he rewards the new heir with the Covenant promises.

75

So we often find Jesus turning a corner and discovering yet another child of Abraham by these signs – it was evidence to him that the Spirit had been there, working in this person's heart, to prepare him for the Gospel promises. Jesus could do nothing less than (in fact, he was delighted to) honor God's agreement and give this person salvation and eternal life.

> When Jesus heard this, he was astonished and said to those following him, "I tell you the truth, I have not found anyone in Israel with such great faith. I say to you that many will come from the east and the west, and will take their places at the feast with Abraham, Isaac and Jacob in the Kingdom of Heaven." (Matthew 8:10-11)

> When Jesus saw their faith, he said to the paralytic, "Take heart, son; your sins are forgiven." (Matthew 9:2)

> He said to her, "Daughter, your faith has healed you. Go in peace and be freed from your suffering." (Mark 5:34)

> "Go," said Jesus, "your faith has healed you." (Mark 10:52)

> Then Jesus answered, "Woman, you have great faith! Your request is granted." (Matthew 15:28)

> Jesus said to the woman, "Your faith has saved you; go in peace." (Luke 7:50)

> Then he said to him, "Rise and go; your faith has made you well." (Luke 17:19)

Circumcision was also a sign of the children of Abraham. But as the Law itself describes, God expected a circumcision of the heart, not just the flesh; done by the Spirit, not by man.

> The LORD your God will circumcise your hearts and the hearts of your descendants, so that you may

love him with all your heart and with all your soul, and live. (Deuteronomy 30:6)

He found evidence of a changed heart in Zacchaeus (Luke 19:9), in the tax collector (Luke 18:14), in the crippled woman in the synagogue (Luke 13:16), in Matthew (Matthew 9:9), and in the Samaritan leper (Luke 17:19). Again, the Spirit of God circumcises the heart; it's not something that we can do to ourselves.

On the other side of the coin, he knew a hypocrite when he saw one. The Jews claimed to be Abraham's descendents, but that doesn't impress the Son of God who can see into men's hearts. Even John the Baptist could see that. It was obvious to both that the Pharisees were trying to impress God with their own works and were content with the superficial, not the spiritual, reality. So they will get nothing from God.

> You brood of vipers! Who warned you to flee from the coming wrath? Produce fruit in keeping with repentance. And do not think you can say to yourselves, 'We have Abraham as our father.' I tell you that out of these stones God can raise up children for Abraham. The ax is already at the root of the trees, and every tree that does not produce good fruit will be cut down and thrown into the fire. (Matthew 3:7-10)

"Abraham is our father," they answered. "If you were Abraham's children," said Jesus, "then you would do the things Abraham did. As it is, you are determined to kill me, a man who has told you the truth that I heard from God. Abraham did not do such things. You are doing the things your own father does." "We are not illegitimate children," they protested. "The only Father we have is God himself." Jesus said to them, "If God were your Father, you would love me, for I came from God and now am here. I have not come on my own; but he sent me. Why is my language not clear to you? Because you are unable to hear what I say. You belong to your father, the devil, and you want to carry out your father's desire." (John 8:39-44)

And he had no time for those who refused to come to him. That obstinate rebellion was a sure sign to him that these were not children of Abraham; so he owed them nothing.

And he did not do many miracles there because of their lack of faith. (Matthew 13:58)

You diligently study the Scriptures because you think that by them you possess eternal life. These are the Scriptures that testify about me, yet you refuse to come to me to have life. (John 5:39-40)

O Jerusalem, Jerusalem, you who kill the prophets and stone those sent to you, how often I have longed to gather your children together, as a hen gathers her chicks under her wings, but you were not willing. Look, your house is left to you desolate. For I tell you, you will not see me again until you say, 'Blessed is he who comes in the name of the Lord.' (Matthew 23:37-39)

The children have the right to come to their Father in Heaven, and therefore Jesus' Mission was to make that access possible.

• The Land

Jesus showed almost no interest in this world. You could tell that his mind and heart were back in Heaven, where he shared his Father's glory. He didn't have a place to lay his head; he took little thought about the taxes he owed the Romans; he left his stepfather's carpenter trade to wander around the countryside preaching and teaching, relying on the resources of others for food and drink.

But he was *very* interested in another world.

> My Kingdom is not of this world. If it were, my servants would fight to prevent my arrest by the Jews. But now my Kingdom is from another place. (John 18:36)

Jesus came from there, he longed to return there, and he wanted his people to join him there. He told his disciples that he was going to that other world, after his resurrection, to prepare for our arrival there.

> In my Father's house are many rooms; if it were not so, I would have told you. I am going there to prepare a place for you. And if I go and prepare a place for you, I will come back and take you to be with me that you also may be where I am. You know the way to the place where I am going. (John 13:2-4)

> If anyone would come after me, he must deny himself and take up his cross and follow me. For whoever wants to save his life will lose it, but whoever loses his life for me will find it. What good will it be for a man if he gains the whole world, yet forfeits his soul? Or what can a man give in exchange for his soul? (Matthew 16:24-26)

What will it be like there? It's precious – like a "pearl" of great value (Matthew 13:46) or like a "treasure" found in a field (Matthew 13:44). Once we see that world, we will willingly trade everything we have here in this world for it. In fact, Jesus assured us that it's worth all our efforts to reach that distant land.

> Do not store up for yourselves treasures on earth, where moth and rust destroy, and where thieves break in and steal. But store up for yourselves treasures in Heaven, where moth and rust do not destroy, and where thieves do not break in and steal. For where your treasure is, there your heart will be also. (Matthew 6:19-21)

Jesus draws many comparisons between this world and the next, and assures us that a vision of the abundance and richness of that spiritual world would astonish us.

> And everyone who has left houses or brothers or sisters or father or mother or children or fields for my sake will receive a hundred times as much and will inherit eternal life. (Matthew 19:29)

> Give, and it will be given to you. A good measure, pressed down, shaken together and running over, will be poured into your lap. For with the measure you use, it will be measured to you. (Luke 6:38)

> I tell you, use worldly wealth to gain friends for yourselves, so that when it is gone, you will be welcomed into eternal dwellings. (Luke 16:9)

> Which of you, if his son asks for bread, will give him a stone? Or if he asks for a fish, will give him a snake? If you, then, though you are evil, know how to give good gifts to your children, how much more will your Father in Heaven give good gifts to those who ask him! (Matthew 7:9-11)

As you can see, Jesus intends to take us out of this world and go live with God in his spiritual Kingdom. Just like the Israelites, who found themselves wandering in a desert wasteland on the way to the Promised Land, we too are burdened right now with this world's emptiness and death and brokenness. It's not this world that we need, but God's spiritual world. And since we can't get there on our own, Jesus intends to take us there.

> I will remain in the world no longer, but they are still in the world, and I am coming to you … Father, I want those you have given me to be with me where I am, and to see my glory, the glory you have given me because you loved me before the creation of the world. (John 17:11,24)

Again, however, we find Jesus sticking to the terms of the agreement with Abraham. This inheritance is not for those outside the family. If they can't show their spiritual lineage from father Abraham, they have no right to the Land.

> Therefore I tell you that the Kingdom of God will be taken away from you and given to a people who will produce its fruit. (Matthew 21:43)

> Then the king told the attendants, 'Tie him hand and foot, and throw him outside, into the darkness, where there will be weeping and gnashing of teeth.' For many are invited, but few are chosen. (Matthew 22:13-14)

The children of God have been given Heaven to live in, and Jesus' Mission is to get them there. So he gives them a taste of that spiritual land (through the Spirit) to whet their appetite and motivate them to keep moving through this desert world to that "Heavenly city, that God has prepared for them." (Hebrews 11:16)

- **The Nation**

The family of Abraham is supposed to be a nation. We saw that the Israelites had a difficult time of it trying to pull themselves together in Canaan; a lack of organization meant chaos on many fronts. They couldn't keep to the standards of the Law when twelve tribes were fighting each other and only looking out for their own interests. So David's Plan was crucial for the success of the nation.

In the same way, Jesus, as he follows David's Plan, is going to pull the Church together into an organized Kingdom that will meet the requirements of the Law. Only he won't be satisfied with an outward, superficial fulfillment of the Law; he's going to change every person's heart to complete righteousness and rule over the Church with wisdom and power.

So he set up his Apostles as the foundation for the Church. This means that their writings, their eyewitness testimony, forms the life and rule of the Church. We are not to follow our own opinions; Jesus gave his instructions to the disciples, and they passed those instructions on to us. Anybody who wants to be part of this Kingdom must conform to the will of the King, as published in the Bible.

That's why we have preachers and teachers; they are telling us the will of the King. But we aren't just submitting out of fear; we're supposed to be doing this because we love the family that we're part of.

> Have confidence in your leaders and submit to their authority, because they keep watch over you as those who must give an account. Do this so that their work will be a joy, not a burden, for that would be of no benefit to you. (Hebrews 13:17)

> Therefore if you have any encouragement from being united with Christ, if any comfort from his love, if any common sharing in the Spirit, if any tenderness and compassion, then make my joy complete by being like-minded, having the same love, being one in spirit and of one mind. Do nothing out of selfish ambition or vain conceit. Rather, in humility value others above yourselves, not looking to your own interests but each of you to the interests of the others. (Philippians 2:1-4)

As we obey the Word that we hear, the nation pulls together and we become strong and filled with the blessings of the Covenant.

> We will grow to become in every respect the mature body of him who is the head, that is, Christ. From him the whole body, joined and held together by every supporting ligament, grows and builds itself up in love, as each part does its work. (Ephesians 4:15-16)

As far as earthly families go, Jesus had a dim view of the subject. In the passages where he talks about them, he

THE COVENANT WITH ABRAHAM

either doesn't show much interest in the family or he has grave misgivings about them.

> Brother will betray brother to death, and a father his child; children will rebel against their parents and have them put to death. (Matthew 10:21)

> Only in his hometown and in his own house is a prophet without honor. (Matthew 13:57)

> He said to another man, "Follow me." But the man replied, "Lord, first let me go and bury my father." Jesus said to him, "Let the dead bury their own dead, but you go and proclaim the Kingdom of God." (Luke 9:59-60)

Jesus knows that earthly families won't often follow you as you follow him. In the Old Testament Jewish system, the Jews were born physically into the nation of Israel. But in the new Kingdom of God, you must be born spiritually into God's family – the Covenant is not something that is passed down through the physical family. In fact, you will discover that you have much more in common with your new brothers and sisters in the Church than with your earthly family.

> "Who is my mother, and who are my brothers?" Pointing to his disciples, he said, "Here are my mother and my brothers. For whoever does the will of my Father in Heaven is my brother and sister and mother." (Matthew 12:48-50)

This new spiritual family is the fulfillment of the promise made to Abraham. Instead of being Jewish, you must be a new Creation – patterned after the New Man that Jesus is. This means of course than even Gentiles can now become children of Abraham. A Christian is neither a Jew nor a Gentile; he's a citizen of a spiritual Kingdom that neither of the others had rights to.

The reason this is necessary is because Christ has to change the heart of man – from nasty to nice. The Jew may have been circumcised physically, but he still had that heart

83

of sin inside driving him to rebel against God and do harm to others. And of course the Gentile has lived in darkness, ignorance, and immorality from his birth. The solution is to fill man's heart with the fruit of the Spirit: love, joy, peace, patience, kindness, goodness, gentleness, faithfulness, and self-control. People who are like this are ready to live in Heaven with each other and with God.

> Be perfect, therefore, as your Heavenly Father is perfect. (Matthew 5:48)

> But love your enemies, do good to them, and lend to them without expecting to get anything back. Then your reward will be great, and you will be sons of the Most High, because he is kind to the ungrateful and wicked. Be merciful, just as your Father is merciful. (Luke 6:35-36)

The requirement for becoming part of God's family is going to show the necessity for this new heart, because as we are now, we are not disposed to love God or man. Here is what Jesus expects of us.

> 'Love the Lord your God with all your heart and with all your soul and with all your mind.' This is the first and greatest commandment.

> And the second is like it: 'Love your neighbor as yourself.'

> All the Law and the Prophets hang on these two commandments. (Matthew 22:37-40)

We've seen already that the Son of God knows the Father in a deeper way than any creature under Heaven knows him. The angels, for as close as they are to God, only know so much about him. Jesus has a unique Father-Son relationship that enables him to know, and draw close to, the very heart of God. He knows the mind of God; he is the Wisdom of God; he is the very image of God. He sits at God's right hand. He loves his Father.

That's the relationship that Jesus wants to draw us into.

And now, Father, glorify me in your presence with the glory I had with you before the world began. (John 17:5)

I have given them the glory that you gave me, that they may be one as we are one: I in them and you in me. (John 17:22-23)

We proclaim to you what we have seen and heard, so that you also may have fellowship with us. And our fellowship is with the Father and with his Son, Jesus Christ. (1 John 1:3)

It's an astonishing "giant leap for mankind" – from the universe's most infamous criminals to the children of God! We are destined to know God as Jesus himself knows him. Jesus is going to accomplish this by making us one with him.

And the Church simply can't work unless we love each other. As God's children come together in the Church, they will discover that they need each other (see Paul's discussion of this in 1 Corinthians 12). No one person can do everything; we each have skills that someone else needs. In God's Kingdom we are going to have special skills, abilities that will help our brothers and sisters see Jesus and draw closer to him in faith and practice. This love is what makes the Church, the Body of Christ, live in the presence of God.

It was he who gave some to be Apostles, some to be Prophets, some to be evangelists, and some to be pastors and teachers, to prepare God's people for works of service, so that the body of Christ may be built up until we all reach unity in the faith and in the knowledge of the Son of God and become mature, attaining to the whole measure of the fullness of Christ. (Ephesians 4:11-13)

For this family to work, we have to get along with each other. That's been the second biggest problem of mankind from the very beginning (the first biggest problem is our relationship with God himself). So Jesus gets to work making us a family of peace.

> Then Peter came to Jesus and asked, "Lord, how many times shall I forgive my brother when he sins against me? Up to seven times?" Jesus answered, "I tell you, not seven times, but seventy-seven times." (Matthew 18:21-22)

> You know that the rulers of the Gentiles lord it over them, and their high officials exercise authority over them. Not so with you. Instead, whoever wants to become great among you must be your servant, and whoever wants to be first must be your slave – just as the Son of Man did not come to be served, but to serve, and to give his life as a ransom for many. (Matthew 20:25-28)

> A new command I give you: Love one another. As I have loved you, so you must love one another. By this all men will know that you are my disciples, if you love one another. (John 13:34-35)

Only in the Church, as God works through us, as we reach out to each other in love, will we finally start solving the problems of sin and death. Our brothers and sisters are the only people in the world who care about this aspect of our lives. It's the one opportunity that we have to work on it; nowhere else in the world are we going to find these valuable spiritual resources, or people who care about helping us with them. So Jesus fills his people with his Spirit of love and compassion for one another so that they can help each other learn and grow in their life with God.

> Now that you have purified yourselves by obeying the truth so that you have sincere love for your brothers, love one another deeply, from the heart. (1 Peter 1:22)

> If anyone says, "I love God," yet hates his brother, he is a liar. For anyone who does not love his brother, whom he has seen, cannot love God, whom he has

not seen. And he has given us this command: Whoever loves God must also love his brother. (1 John 4:20-21)

• The Blessing

Death – and the recurring sin that causes it – is a curse that we can't escape. We need someone who can break this curse for us and let us live.

> On this mountain he will destroy the shroud that enfolds all peoples, the sheet that covers all nations; he will swallow up death forever. The Sovereign LORD will wipe away the tears from all faces; he will remove the disgrace of his people from all the earth. The LORD has spoken. (Isaiah 25:7-8)

This is precisely what Jesus, the Executor of Abraham's Covenant, has come to do.

> Since the children have flesh and blood, he too shared in their humanity so that by his death he might destroy him who holds the power of death – that is, the devil – and free those who all their lives were held in slavery by their fear of death. For surely it is not angels he helps, but Abraham's descendants. (Hebrews 2:14-16)

But physical death isn't the worst part of it. If we can define "life" as "the ability to experience," then we also died spiritually when God cut us off from his presence in Genesis 3.

None of us can fully understand how catastrophic that was. You just have to see God in order to come close to understanding how much you need him. He is literally what holds us all together. "For in him we live and move and have our being." (Acts 17:28) "For from him and through him and to him are all things." (Romans 11:36) God is the source of all good things. If we lose contact with him, we will shrivel up and die, first spiritually and then physically.

That's exactly what happened in Genesis 3. The result has been that nobody knows God now, and nobody can come to him.

So Jesus is going to reverse that Curse and bless us with Life.

> I have come that they may have life, and have it to the full. (John 10:10)

And in keeping with the definition of spiritual life, he brings us to God. We will now live in the presence of God, never to be separated from him again.

> Now this is eternal life: that they may know you, the only true God, and Jesus Christ, whom you have sent. (John 17:3)

Death is no barrier to him. He deals with death conclusively, in his own body, so that as he rises to live forever in the presence of God, he brings us with him.

> I am the resurrection and the life. He who believes in me will live, even though he dies; and whoever lives and believes in me will never die. (John 11:25-26)

> Just as Moses lifted up the snake in the desert, so the Son of Man must be lifted up, that everyone who believes in him may have eternal life. (John 3:14-15)

In his own death, Jesus breaks the power of sin over us and frees us from our deadly enemy. This also makes it possible to eat of the Tree of Life, which was formerly off-limits to sinners – because, now that we will never sin again, there is nothing preventing us from having eternal life.

> We were therefore buried with him through baptism into death in order that, just as Christ was raised from the dead through the glory of the Father, we too may live a new life. If we have been united with him like this in his death, we will certainly also

be united with him in his resurrection. (Romans 6:4-5)

The Apostles focused on this amazing turn of events in their sermons about Christ's ministry. The fact that he was resurrected from the dead promises a new life for the rest of us who are in Christ. And this is what God promised Abraham when he said that the nations would be "blessed through him." Abraham's great Heir will finally overcome our worst enemy.

For since death came through a man, the resurrection of the dead comes also through a man. For as in Adam all die, so in Christ all will be made alive. (1 Corinthians 15:21-22)

When the perishable has been clothed with the imperishable, and the mortal with immortality, then the saying that is written will come true: "Death has been swallowed up in victory." (1 Corinthians 15:54)

Jesus will do this in stages. First, he brings us life through his Word –

The words I have spoken to you are spirit and they are life. (John 6:63)

And then through his Spirit.

"Whoever believes in me, as the Scripture has said, streams of living water will flow from within him." By this he meant the Spirit, whom those who believed in him were later to receive. (John 7:38-39)

Finally, he will raise us from the dead on the last day.

And this is the will of him who sent me, that I shall lose none of all that he has given me, but raise them up at the last day. For my Father's will is that everyone who looks to the Son and believes in him shall have eternal life, and I will raise him up at the last day. (John 6:39)

Therefore, if we believe the truth he teaches us, and if we are filled with his Spirit, we will live – even as he lives now.

That if you confess with your mouth, "Jesus is Lord," and believe in your heart that God raised him from the dead, you will be saved. (Romans 10:9)

Therefore I tell you that no one who is speaking by the Spirit of God says, "Jesus be cursed," and no one can say, "Jesus is Lord," except by the Holy Spirit. (1 Corinthians 12:3)

But we miss the second half of this Covenant promise if we forget about the service in the Temple. We will look later at what the High Priest does for us in the Temple, but we should mention here that the whole purpose of the Priest's work was to bring us before God.

Father, I want those you have given me to be with me where I am, and to see my glory, the glory you have given me because you loved me before the creation of the world. (John 17:24)

Jesus, the Priest like Melchizedek, is going to do what the Levitical priests could never do – he's going to bring all of God's children into the throne room of Heaven to live with God forever. There we will see God in his fullness, as the Son sees him, because we're going to be one with the Son and will share in his glory. That's life! To know God the Father as Jesus knows him, to experience the fullness of the inheritance of the Son.

Summary

An interesting aspect of this Covenant with Abraham that we mustn't forget when reading the story of Jesus in the Gospels is that God cut the Covenant with Abraham; remember the halves of animals sacrificed and laid out on the ground, and God walking down between them. That symbolized the seriousness of the agreement: if God ever went back on the terms of the Covenant, Abraham and his descendants would have the right to kill God. At that point in time, we can't imagine killing God. But it's easy to see why Jesus felt obligated to keep the Covenant during his ministry. His life was on the line! He was legally responsible to keep all the promises for all of Abraham's offspring.

That fact alone helps us interpret so much of what was going on in the Gospels. Much of it is obviously God keeping his promises with the Jews. But occasionally we read a story that absolutely perplexes us – like Jesus dealing with the Canaanite woman about her sick daughter. She wasn't Jewish; she had no legal right to anything in the Covenant. That's why Jesus treated her so harshly. So, can we use what we learned about the Covenant to interpret this mystifying story?

> A Canaanite woman from that vicinity came to him, crying out, "Lord, Son of David, have mercy on me! My daughter is demon- possessed and suffering terribly." Jesus did not answer a word. So his disciples came to him and urged him, "Send her away, for she keeps crying out after us." He answered, "I was sent only to the lost sheep of Israel." The woman came and knelt before him. "Lord, help me!" she said. He replied, "It is not right to take the children's bread and toss it to the dogs." (Matthew 15:22-26)

And the disciples agreed with him – these blessings were only for the children of Abraham. But then she said something that revealed the faith that was in her heart.

> "Yes it is, Lord," she said. "Even the dogs eat the crumbs that fall from their master's table." Then Jesus said to her, "Woman, you have great faith! Your request is granted." And her daughter was healed at that moment. (Matthew 15:27-28)

Suddenly Jesus could see the bright light of the family characteristic of all of Abraham's spiritual offspring. Her faith qualified her as a descendant of Abraham. Now he *had* to give her what she asked for, in order to fulfill the terms of the agreement.

The Jesus we all know and have heard about – the gentle Jesus, the shepherd Jesus, the loving Jesus – calling her a dog and refusing her request! This story makes no sense at all until we see it in light of the legal obligations to Abraham's descendants. Without faith this woman had no right to anything; with faith, Jesus was legally obligated to give her whatever she asked for. So the Covenant sheds a lot of light on the ministry of Christ.

Now extend your studies to the rest of the New Testament in the letters of the Apostles and read them in light of the Covenant. Everything that is described there are the spiritual treasures of the Promises, made to all of Abraham's offspring – both Jew and Gentile – because we are Christians now, part of the family. For example, Paul talks about being united to Christ and therefore inheriting the treasures of Heaven (see Ephesians 1). He talks about our future hope in Heaven. (Colossians 3:1-3) All the Apostles' letters were instructions to local churches, and laid out the family characteristics of Abraham's heirs – they will live by faith, and live in holiness. And Paul in his famous passage in 1 Corinthians 15 clearly describes our future hope in the resurrection of Christ from the dead. Link these promises made to us in the New Testament with the Old Testament counterparts of the Covenant and you will begin to understand the importance of the Covenant to the entire Bible.

THE LAW

Probably the one concept in the Bible that causes the most trouble for Christians is the Law, and yet what Paul gave us in Galatians should have cleared up the issue for us long ago.

There are several reasons that the Law is so confusing to us. *First*, it's there in our Bibles, a huge reality that the Old Testament is filled with from Genesis to Malachi. And there are all sorts of commands and threats to take it seriously.

Second, the Law deals with morality, and naturally we take that subject seriously as Christians. We are, after all, obligated to obey God and do what he commands if we want his favor. The Ten Commandments in particular seem to be a natural obligation that all of humanity is under. Whatever we might do with all those strange laws in Leviticus, surely we are responsible to obey the simple commands of ethical behavior.

Third, we may not understand what Paul was saying about the Law in Galatians. Are we to ignore it? Are we to respect it from a distance? Did Jesus take care of it for us? Or are we now enabled, as Spirit-filled Christians, to follow at least the basics of the Law? Are we under grace now, not the Law? There are many theories in the Church about what to do with the Law as Christians.

So we want to try to clear up the confusion here and lay a groundwork for how to deal with the Law, and what Jesus expects of us in regards to the Law.

What is the Law?

There are different things that are meant when we use the word "Law." For one, it refers to the first five books in the Bible, the Books of Moses – Genesis, Exodus, Leviticus, Numbers, and Deuteronomy. The Jews still refer to these books as the Law (or the Torah) when they talk about it, mainly because the Law that God gave Moses is contained in these five books.

Another use of the word Law is, more specifically, the system of Law that God gave the Israelites at Mt. Sinai. There was a Jewish scholar who counted them up once and found 613 separate commands (positive and negative) in this legal system. This Law is the government of the nation of Israel that God gave them after their deliverance from Egypt. They were now God's people, and they had to act like it. It was like a Constitution, if you will, of the new nation. The Law organized the people politically, religiously, socially, economically, militarily.

The Ten Commandments are the summary of these 613 commands; they are found in two places in the Bible (Exodus 20 and Deuteronomy 5). These Ten make it easier to see what the purpose of the Law really is: it governs our relationships with God and man. So the Ten Commandments (which were given to Moses on two stone tablets) list our duties in this way.

TOWARD GOD

You shall have no other gods but the Lord

You shall not make idols

You shall not misuse the Lord's name

You shall observe the Sabbath

TOWARD MAN

Honor your father and mother

You shall not murder

You shall not commit adultery

You shall not steal

You shall not give false testimony

You shall not covet

The Ten Commandments

But Jesus gave us an even simpler version of the Law. When someone asked him what the greatest of the commands were, he answered with two of them – reflecting this natural division of the Law in two tablets.

> 'Love the Lord your God with all your heart and with all your soul and with all your mind.' This is the first and greatest commandment. And the second is like it: 'Love your neighbor as yourself.' All the Law and the Prophets hang on these two commandments. (Matthew 22:37-40)

These were, in fact, two of the 613 commands of the Law – the first was a quote from Deuteronomy 6:5, and the second he quoted from Leviticus 19:18. But they sum up the whole purpose of the Law very neatly.

There are those students who go further and divide up the Law into three types: moral, ceremonial, and civil. The "moral" law would be like the Ten Commandments, incumbent on all to follow. The "ceremonial" law would entail the laws regarding worship in the Temple. The "civil" law would be how to live in a community – the social and political laws that make justice and peace possible in the nation. But what Christians are really after, when they divide them up like this, is to dispose of the ceremonial and even the civil laws so that all we have left to follow are the moral laws. But even though this looks clever and useful, the Jews themselves wouldn't have divided them up like this. In their eyes, all the laws are bound up together – you can't obey one type of law without touching on all kinds of other laws in the process. For example, one way that you're supposed to "love your neighbor" (a moral law) is to keep your bull on your side of the fence. If you don't, the bull will get out and kill someone (civil law). If that happens, you will end up having to go to the Temple and clear your guilt of your neighbor's death (ceremonial law). So to the Jews (who are experts in the Law!) it's all one Law. You can't separate one from another like that.

Three functions of the Law

There are three things that God is doing by giving us his Law.

- **First**, *the Law defines what is right and wrong.* Our system of ethics and morality come from God, not from some other source. There are many religions and philosophies that attempt to define morality, but since we live in God's Creation it behooves us to find out what our Creator thinks. It is he, after all, who will judge us in the end. Remember the principle of Creation: he's the King, we are his subjects, he burned his laws into our hearts to obey, and he will judge us in the end to see whether we lived up to his standards.

- **Second,** *the Law convicts us as sinners.* This is easy to do. God expects all of us to obey his Law, exactly as it's written. But most of us don't even know what the laws are, let alone spend our time and energy obeying them. Five minutes with the Law and we will all know that we fall way short of God's expectations of us. And if the legalists among us need more proof of that, Jesus showed us the spiritual depth of the Law in the Sermon on the Mount, where he stressed perfection in the heart and mind, not just on the outside.

- **Third,** *the Law describes a Perfect Man.* If anybody would keep all of the Law, in the way that God wants to see it done, then that would be a perfect person. Actually the bad press that the Law gets in today's churches is unfortunate; we are told to stay away from the Law as if it will destroy us, when actually it describes a *nice person.* If we would all live like the Law describes, this world would be a nice place to live in. The trouble is that none of us can do this – only Jesus has accomplished the impossible. But the Law still remains the goal that God has in mind for humanity; it always was and always will be. Heaven, you will discover, will be filled with people who are perfect in the eyes of the Law. (How they get that way is another story!)

We need these functions of the Law. *First,* even though we may be Christians now, the need for an eternal standard of right and wrong is always necessary; otherwise sin would rule. *Second,* we are still sinners, and society has to be able to identify sinners and deal with them appropriately – and the Law is the only way to make that charge stick. And *third*, Jesus is still the only perfectly righteous man that God sees. He alone is our only hope for getting through this complex problem of our relationship with the Law of God.

Why the Law is important

Now let's take these three functions and apply them to the life of the Church.

Preachers often make the mistake of setting up rules and regulations and imposing them on the consciences of church members without first checking to see if all these rules are in God's list. A person is obligated to obey God, not man. God is the Judge to whom we must give an account. What God says is right and wrong is the final word, not what man says. It's unfortunate that church leaders resort to rule-making when they're forming their little kingdoms; setting the rules gives them the power they need over the flock, and they use that power by punishing poor sheep who don't obey their rules – or their interpretation of the rules. Jesus and the Apostles referred to this many times in their letters to the Church.

> Since you died with Christ to the elemental spiritual forces of this world, why, as though you still belonged to the world, do you submit to its rules: "Do not handle! Do not taste! Do not touch!"? These rules, which have to do with things that are all destined to perish with use, are based on merely human commands and teachings. Such regulations indeed have an appearance of wisdom, with their self-imposed worship, their false humility and their harsh treatment of the body, but they lack any value in restraining sensual indulgence. (Colossians 2:21)

Jesus targeted the Pharisees with their superficial religion – keeping rules so that they look good on the outside, but actually caring nothing for God's glory or their neighbor's well-being.

> Woe to you, teachers of the Law and Pharisees, you hypocrites! You shut the door of the Kingdom of Heaven in people's faces. You yourselves do not enter, nor will you let those enter who are trying to. (Matthew 23:13)

Whenever we start making our own rules about how to obey God, we end up going in directions that don't help God's Kingdom in the least. These extra rules give us the power, they give us the glory, and they actually take away from God's position as King.

The only way that we will successfully impress the fear of God on people's hearts is if we use God's definition of right and wrong. That's because the Law deals with the heart; it gets down into our attitudes and our opinions that guide our actions. And this is the second function of the Law – to convince us that we aren't nearly as good as we thought we were. It's a difficult thing to convince someone that he or she is a sinner! We are rebels to the core, and we don't like being told that we aren't acceptable. Oh, most people will listen to a hand-slapping sermon that reminds them of a few bad things they did in life. But that's not the power of the Law: when Paul, for example, gets done with us, he has uncovered a sewer of death and rebellion in all our minds and hearts. It's an ugly sight, what's down inside us.

> What shall we conclude then? Do we have any advantage? Not at all! For we have already made the charge that Jews and Gentiles alike are all under the power of sin. As it is written: "There is no one righteous, not even one; there is no one who understands; there is no one who seeks God. All have turned away, they have together become worthless; there is no one who does good, not even one." "Their throats are open graves; their tongues practice deceit." "The poison of vipers is on their lips." "Their mouths are full of cursing and bitterness." "Their feet are swift to shed blood; ruin and misery mark their ways, and the way of peace they do not know." "There is no fear of God before their eyes." Now we know that whatever the Law says, it says to those who are under the Law, so that every mouth may be silenced and the whole world held accountable to God. Therefore no one will be declared righteous in God's sight by the works of the Law; rather, through the Law we become conscious of our sin. (Romans 3:9-20)

That's what the Law sees in *all* of us. The preacher's job is to convince us of that. Because only when we're convinced that we are that bad in the Law's eyes will we see and appreciate God's solution to our problem. If we don't see it, we're going to die. But if we see that Jesus is the only Righteous Man that the Law accepts, we will start heading toward Jesus for his help. "The prayer of a Righteous Man is powerful and effective." (James 5:16)

It's this step-by-step process of using the Law to educate and illuminate that brings people to Christ. Here is what we are supposed to be; we aren't anywhere near what we're supposed to be; but Jesus is, and he can solve this problem for us and make us righteous too. But get ready to explain a lot about the Law, it's true requirements, and prove to hardened sinners that they really do need to take this step-by-step journey to the Christ.

The Covenant at Mt Sinai

So many people confuse what happened at Mt. Sinai with the first Covenant. But that's simply not true. The first Covenant was the agreement that God made with Abraham in Genesis. Mt. Sinai was another Covenant that God made with the Israelites – a totally different matter.

When God delivered the Israelites from Egypt, he took them to Mt. Sinai to form them into a new nation. This was a necessary step for the Covenant people, because law and order and organization are necessary to provide a context for the blessings. They were heirs of the Abrahamic promises, but if they didn't behave themselves they weren't going to get blessings but curses! The calling and election is sure; but righteousness is the prime responsibility of those who are called. That's the whole point of deliverance.

So at Sinai God made an agreement with the Israelites.

> So be careful to do what the LORD your God has commanded you; do not turn aside to the right or to the left. Walk in obedience to all that the LORD your God has commanded you, so that you may live and prosper and prolong your days in the land that you will possess. (Deuteronomy 5:32-33)

In other words, God gave them a Law to live by; they were now obligated to keep this Law. This Law makes everything work perfectly and insures the continuation of the Covenant blessings. The Israelites understood very clearly that the whole thing depended on their obedience to this Law.

> And if we are careful to obey all this Law before the LORD our God, as he has commanded us, that will be our righteousness. (Deuteronomy 6:25)

The agreement at Sinai, then, is that *they had to keep the Law's requirements* if they wanted this Kingdom to work.

So it's not correct to say that the Old Testament is the old Covenant that Hebrews 8 talks about.

> But in fact the ministry Jesus has received is as superior to theirs as the Covenant of which he is mediator is superior to the old one, since the new Covenant is established on better promises. (Hebrews 8:6)

This "old Covenant" refers to the Sinaitic agreement, not with the Abrahamic Covenant. And the old Covenant was *not* the Law. It was the agreement between God and the Israelites that *they* had to keep the Law to make the Kingdom work. Not seeing this difference here makes people think, naturally, that the Law is the problem! The Law itself was not the problem.

> For if there had been nothing wrong with that first covenant, no place would have been sought for another. *But God found fault with the people* and said: "The days are coming, declares the Lord, when I will make a new Covenant … This is the Covenant I will establish with the people of Israel after that time, declares the Lord. I will put my laws in their minds and write them on their hearts. (Hebrews 8:7-8, 10)

God found fault with the people, not with his Law. The problem was that they couldn't keep his Law, not to the extent that God required. The Law is deep; it defines not just outward actions but inner attitudes and feelings. Nobody is able to keep the Law like that.

So why did God go through this pointless exercise with his people just to end up with inevitable failure? Didn't he know they would never measure up? Of course – that's the point. He knew it, but they also had to learn it. Our only hope is if we see how hopeless it is that we try to keep his Law to be righteous. Our sin runs too deeply. Paul describes the point in this way.

> Before the coming of this faith, we were held in custody under the law, locked up until the faith that was to come would be revealed. So the Law was our guardian until Christ came that we might be justified by faith. Now that this faith has come, we are no longer under a guardian. (Galatians 3:23-25)

What Jesus thought of the Law

We had to work through this complex explanation of the Law because we will find Jesus taking the Law very seriously, even though we may not feel inclined to. Preaching Christ will include dealing with Christ's attitude toward the Law.

It's very clear in Scripture what Jesus thinks of the Law.

> Do not think that I have come to abolish the Law or the Prophets; I have not come to abolish them but to fulfill them. For truly I tell you, until Heaven and earth disappear, not the smallest letter, not the least stroke of a pen, will by any means disappear from the Law until everything is accomplished. Therefore anyone who sets aside one of the least of these commands and teaches others accordingly will be called least in the Kingdom of Heaven, but whoever practices and teaches these commands will be called great in the Kingdom of Heaven. (Matthew 5:17-19)

Keep in mind the three functions of the Law, and that will explain why Jesus takes the law seriously. These are in fact critical principles in the Kingdom of Christ, and necessary elements in our deliverance. He would never do away with these functions in his Church. Anybody who thinks so doesn't appreciate the Mission of the Messiah.

There's an amazing passage which shows Jesus' opinion of the Law and its role in the process of salvation. In the story about the rich man and Lazarus, the rich man was in Hell, suffering for his sins, and worrying that his family would end up there with him. He pleaded with

101

father Abraham to send someone to his family and warn them of this judgment to come. But Abraham (as Jesus tells the story) answers with this comment.

> He answered, 'Then I beg you, father, send Lazarus to my family, for I have five brothers. Let him warn them, so that they will not also come to this place of torment.'

> Abraham replied, 'They have Moses and the Prophets; let them listen to them.'

> 'No, father Abraham,' he said, 'but if someone from the dead goes to them, they will repent.'

> He said to him, 'If they do not listen to Moses and the Prophets, they will not be convinced even if someone rises from the dead.' (Luke 16:27-31)

In other words, the way Jesus sees it, the Law of Moses is sufficient to warn us about avoiding Hell and being delivered from our sins! What preacher today uses the Law to such great effect? Most of them are warning their people to stay away from the Law, and Jesus is telling us to go back to the Law and take its counsel seriously. Even the Prophets understood the purpose of the Law and preached about going back to it. It requires a profound understanding of the Law and its functions to do this, however, an understanding that is not common today.

The Law and Christians

Even though Jesus took the Law seriously, it still remains to answer the question – where does that leave us Christians in respect to the Law?

- We've seen that the Law is good; it's the description of a perfect righteousness that God wants to see of all the subjects of his Kingdom. The Law is not going away.

- We've also seen that, given innumerable chances to get it right, the Israelites failed to keep the Law. It's just beyond the reach of sinful man to attain to this high standard of the Law.

102

- And we've seen that if we don't measure up to the perfection of the Law, we only have hell and misery to look forward to in eternity. God is serious about this.

So where does this leave us? The answer is to look for another option. Jesus took on the flesh of man and lived the perfect life, attaining the righteousness required by the Law – and then *gives us that righteousness of his as a gift.* We don't have to do this thing; he does it for us. That solves all kinds of problems. For one thing, our weakness doesn't mess the process up; no matter how weak and sinful we are, we are still covered with the perfect righteousness of Christ and are welcome before God as a result.

Another problem that it solves is that our righteousness, since it comes from Christ, completely satisfies the Law no matter how deeply the Law looks inside us. Jesus isn't going to fulfill the Law of God superficially; his righteousness will stand the test of eternity – never changing, perfect on all levels, to God's highest standards. With that kind of righteousness covering us, we have no fear of rejection or condemnation. And since the Law will never go away – the Law is a description of God's eternal Kingdom – we are ready now to live in that Kingdom.

And how does Jesus transfer his righteousness to us? Through his Spirit. When we believe in Christ, he gives us his Spirit which then brings us into unity with the Son of God and covers us with the righteousness of Christ. So the Spirit accomplishes what the old Covenant (the agreement that the Jews made to keep the Law) could never do.

Therefore, there is now no condemnation for those who are in Christ Jesus, because through Christ Jesus the law of the Spirit who gives life has set you free from the Law of sin and death. For what the Law was powerless to do because it was weakened by the flesh, God did by sending his own Son in the likeness of sinful flesh to be a sin offering. And so he condemned sin in the flesh, in order that the righteous requirement of the Law might be fully met in us, who do not live according to the flesh but according to the Spirit. (Romans 8:1-4)

That's why Jesus could say to us that if we want to be part of this new Kingdom, we must be perfect; nothing less will do.

> For I tell you that unless your righteousness surpasses that of the Pharisees and the teachers of the Law, you will certainly not enter the Kingdom of Heaven. (Matthew 5:20)

As you can see, this new option completely solves our problems about righteousness. We aren't throwing away the Law – it's God's eternal standard of what it means to be a nice person. But then we aren't approaching it in the way the Israelites had to at Sinai; we know better now than to try that impossible task. But we are taking a new road to that righteousness by receiving it from the Spirit as a gift, and remaining in that way as we follow the Spirit of Christ as he transforms us into the image of the Perfect Man.

So when Paul heard that the Galatians were going back to the old Sinaitic solution, he was astonished and angry.

> I am astonished that you are so quickly deserting the one who called you to live in the grace of Christ and are turning to a different gospel — which is really no gospel at all. Evidently some people are throwing you into confusion and are trying to pervert the gospel of Christ. But even if we or an angel from Heaven should preach a gospel other than the one we preached to you, let them be under God's curse! As we have already said, so now I say again: If anybody is preaching to you a gospel other than what you accepted, let them be under God's curse! (Galatians 1:6-9)

Paul's argument in Galatians is not that we can throw away the Law of God. Paul had always respected the Law, because he knew the importance of the Law to God's Kingdom. Remember he was a Jew who was raised in the context of the Law of God. No, he argued that going back to obey the Law (like the Sinai Covenant) was a mistake for sinners to try. Christ is the answer now for getting that righteousness that the Law requires.

> For through the Law I died to the Law so that I might live for God. I have been crucified with Christ and I no longer live, but Christ lives in me. The life I now live in the body, I live by faith in the Son of God, who loved me and gave

himself for me. I do not set aside the grace of God, for if righteousness could be gained through the Law, Christ died for nothing!" (Galatians 2:19-21)

Can Christians now keep the Ten Commandments? There are many who think so; they believe that, with the Spirit in us, we can now go back to the Law and do what we couldn't do before we were Christians. Paul has an answer for these as well.

> I would like to learn just one thing from you: Did you receive the Spirit by the works of the Law, or by believing what you heard? Are you so foolish? After beginning by means of the Spirit, are you now trying to finish by means of the flesh? (Galatians 3:2-3)

In other words, going back to the Law in any of its forms, including the Ten Commandments, is a bad mistake. Our hope is never in keeping the Law for ourselves. The Spirit doesn't enable us to go back to the Law; he enables us to follow Jesus who keeps the Law for us. As we follow the Spirit, the "righteous requirement of the Law will be fully met in us, who do not live according to the flesh but according to the Spirit." (Romans 8:4) [11]

Finally, there are some in every generation who believe that, since we are believers now and "living by grace," we can do whatever we want. If we sin again, the blood of Christ covers us and we will be forgiven. So it's not critical whether we can measure up to the Law as Christians; Jesus has already taken care of the legal side of it, and the Spirit is taking care of the practical side of it.

> What shall we say, then? Shall we go on sinning so that grace may increase? By no means! We are those who have died to sin; how can we live in it any longer? (Romans 6:1-2)

The whole point about being united with Christ through his Spirit is that we might become like him – righteous, a nice person, who loves God and man. If we stay in sin, something is dreadfully wrong! If we stay in sin, that should motivate us to find out if this thing about becoming a Christian didn't work. Christ gives his righteousness to his people as a gift, but he doesn't change our hearts overnight. That

---

[11] What it means to "follow the Spirit" is an entirely different subject.

righteousness of his is like a robe covering us, so that the Law doesn't see what we really are inside and condemn us at the door of the Temple. But there remains a great deal of work to do inside our hearts to make us ready for Heaven. The legal work is done, but now starts the process of sanctification – making our inside match the outside. We certainly don't want to fall under the same judgment that the Pharisees did!

> Woe to you, teachers of the Law and Pharisees, you hypocrites! You are like whitewashed tombs, which look beautiful on the outside but on the inside are full of the bones of the dead and everything unclean. In the same way, on the outside you appear to people as righteous but on the inside you are full of hypocrisy and wickedness. (Matthew 23:27-28)

Summary

Christians all have the same hope: we are united with Christ now; we have a new life through him. But what is it that Jesus is transforming us into? Never forget the Law of God's Kingdom! We are about to step into a perfect Kingdom that sits squarely on God's Law, the perfect system of righteousness that alone brings peace, prosperity, justice and mercy. Jesus' task is to change us from the inside out so that we will fit into this perfect Kingdom. So if people want to see what they will be like in Heaven, take them to the Law. Jesus is going to make us look like that.

THE PRIEST

The Temple had a central location in Israel's life and history. At the beginning, the Israelites built a Tabernacle, or large tent, that they carried with them from Egypt, through the wilderness, and into the Promised Land. In fact they kept the Tabernacle with them during the entire period of the Judges – over 400 years – until the time of the Monarchy.

A Temple for the Lord

It was David who first thought of building a Temple for the Lord's service. He thought it was a shame that he and the rest of the Israelites lived in their own homes, but the Lord had only this worn-out tent that they kept moving around the countryside, depending on who was high priest that year. But while he was planning on building a Temple, the Lord stopped his project.

> I had it in my heart to build a house as a place of rest for the ark of the Covenant of the LORD, for the footstool of our God, and I made plans to build it. But God said to me, 'You are not to build a house for my Name, because you are a warrior and have shed blood.' (1 Chronicles 28:2-3)

David was "a man of blood," but that wasn't a sin, as many interpret it; remember that one of David's tasks was to rid the land of their enemies through warfare. The problem was that the house of God is to be a house of peace, not war. So the task of building the Temple was given to David's son Solomon (a symbolic act) who would have peace throughout his entire reign of 40 years (thanks to his father David!).

But this didn't mean David was out of the picture. His task was to collect the materials and draw up the plans for the Temple. He even organized the work that would go on there, and wrote much of the liturgy that would be used in the Temple worship. The only thing that Solomon had to do was carry out his father's detailed plans.

> Then David gave his son Solomon the plans for the portico of the temple, its buildings, its storerooms, its upper parts, its inner rooms and the place of atonement. He gave him the plans of all that the Spirit had put in his mind for the courts of the temple of the LORD and all the surrounding rooms, for the treasuries of the temple of God and for the treasuries for the dedicated things. (1 Chronicles 28:11-12)

There were two purposes of the Temple. The first was to cleanse sinners of their guilt before God. This was a critical aspect of the life of Israel. No other nation had this great privilege of having their sin-guilt taken away, because no other nation but Israel knew the true God. They knew what he was like, what he expected of them, and where they fell short. And he provided a way to true righteousness – or acceptance by the Law. Without that first step, there was no further steps to eternal life.

> The Law requires that nearly everything be cleansed with blood, and without the shedding of blood there is no forgiveness. (Hebrews 9:22)

The second purpose of the Temple was to be a house where God lived. Of course the Israelites knew that the eternal and infinite God couldn't live in a house made by human hands.

> But will God really dwell on earth with men? The heavens, even the highest heavens, cannot contain you. How much less this temple I have built! (2 Chronicles 6:18)

But Solomon realized that the Lord was putting his Name in this building. If the Israelites would turn toward the Temple and call on his Name, he would hear them and answer them.

> May your eyes be open toward this temple day and night, this place of which you said you would put your Name there. (2 Chronicles 6:20)

The Priesthood

The priests served in the Temple for both functions. It was their job to take the sacrifices that people brought to the Temple and offer the blood on the altar and before the presence of God. By their ministry the Lord forgave the people of their sins.

And the priests also had the right of access into the presence of God – at least to some degree. They were allowed into the Temple itself; the ordinary Israelite wasn't allowed in. When the priests took the blood of the sacrifice into God's house, they received the Lord's forgiveness and blessings and then took those out to the people waiting outside. In a way, the people came to God by proxy – through the priests. At least they had this benefit – other peoples and nations didn't have even this.

But even though the priests were critical for the spiritual life of the nation, they had two shortcomings. First, in their work of sacrifice and getting forgiveness for the people's sins, they couldn't do the *one thing needful* – and that was to change the sinner's heart so that he wouldn't sin again. In spite of all the efforts of everyone involved, the man went home and sinned again throughout the coming year. His heart hadn't been changed in the least. The priest had no power for such a necessary change.

Their second shortcoming was that they could only bring news about God back to the people. The people themselves weren't allowed into the Temple to see God. Now you have to understand something about God to appreciate this situation. God is the highest good there is – he's the Creator who fills our lives with blessing. To see and know him directly would be Paradise; as Jesus says of it later, "To know God is eternal life." (John 17:3) But the priests had to keep the people out of the Temple lest they be destroyed by this holy God who can't look upon sin.

In fact, the priests themselves weren't allowed to see God! They could only go as far as in front of the massive curtain in the Temple. Behind that curtain was the throne of God which none of them were allowed to see. "You cannot see my face, for no one may see me and live." (Exodus 33:20) The only exception to this rule was on the Day of Atonement, Yom Kippur, when the High Priest went into the Holy of Holies and offered a sacrifice for the sins of the entire nation.

> No one is to be in the tent of meeting from the time
> Aaron goes in to make atonement in the Most Holy Place

until he comes out, having made atonement for himself, his household and the whole community of Israel. (Leviticus 16:17)

So, as much as people would love to see God himself, they weren't allowed to. Nobody was. He was just too holy and majestic and fearful to look upon. Any man who dared try would die in the attempt.

There were several incidents in the Old Testament when people were not careful about these strict regulations. For example, when David was moving the ark of the Lord to Jerusalem, one of his Levites reached out and touched the Ark because the oxen carrying it stumbled.

When they came to the threshing floor of Nakon, Uzzah reached out and took hold of the ark of God, because the oxen stumbled. The LORD's anger burned against Uzzah because of his irreverent act; therefore God struck him down, and he died there beside the ark of God. (2 Samuel 6:6-7)

David, of course, since he had a high reverence for the Law of the Lord (see Psalm 119), backed away until the officials could get this procedure straightened out. We can assume that, even though it was through him and his Plan that the Lord richly blessed Israel, he certainly wasn't going to take on the priestly role. That was strictly for others.

One of the descendants of David made that mistake, though, and he was punished for it as a result.

But after Uzziah became powerful, his pride led to his downfall. He was unfaithful to the LORD his God, and entered the temple of the LORD to burn incense on the altar of incense. Azariah the priest with eighty other courageous priests of the LORD followed him in. They confronted King Uzziah and said, "It is not right for you, Uzziah, to burn incense to the LORD. That is for the priests, the descendants of Aaron, who have been consecrated to burn incense. Leave the sanctuary, for you have been unfaithful; and you will not be honored by the LORD God." (2 Chronicles 26:16-18)

He didn't listen to them, and the Lord struck him with leprosy which he suffered with the rest of his life.

Reading all these stories make us wonder if it will ever be possible for the ordinary person to go into God's house and see him face to face.

Jesus the Priest

The reason we learned all this about the priests and their jobs in the Temple was to get us ready for what Jesus came to do. He certainly didn't do away with all the rules! Remember that he called the Temple "my Father's house," and he threw people out who were detracting from its main purpose. What he wanted to do was purify the Temple – to bring God's people back to enjoy its spiritual blessings. And he accomplished what the Levitical priests couldn't do.

The author of Hebrews talks about this. He reviews the limitations of the old system: he says that if the first Temple was good enough, there wouldn't have been any need to fix things. But the priesthood had these two great limitations that they couldn't overcome. They were sinners themselves; how could they reach into the heart and change a sinner into a saint when they couldn't do that to their own hearts? And how could they take others in to see God when they themselves weren't allowed in to see him?

> The gifts and sacrifices being offered were not able to clear the conscience of the worshiper. They are only a matter of food and drink and various ceremonial washings —external regulations applying until the time of the new order. (Hebrews 9:9-10)

But on both counts Jesus can do what the priests couldn't do. Hebrews makes a point of telling us that Jesus was not born in the Levitical tribe; he didn't get his right to the priesthood through genealogy, as did the rest. The Levitical priests had to prove their descent from Levi in order to enter the Temple. Jesus, however, doesn't get his privilege from genealogical descent but by appointment, as did the priest Melchizedek.

> And it was not without an oath! Others became priests without any oath, but he became a priest with an oath when

111

God said to him: "The Lord has sworn and will not change his mind: 'You are a priest forever.'" Because of this oath, Jesus has become the guarantor of a better Covenant. (Hebrews 7:20-22)

And as Melchizedek was the King of Righteousness and King of Peace (Salem), Jesus was bringing the righteousness of God (as the Perfect Man) and eternal peace between God and man (as the Mediator) to the task.

> This Melchizedek was king of Salem and priest of God Most High. He met Abraham returning from the defeat of the kings and blessed him, and Abraham gave him a tenth of everything. First, the name Melchizedek means "king of righteousness"; then also, "king of Salem" means "king of peace." Without father or mother, without genealogy, without beginning of days or end of life, resembling the Son of God, he remains a priest forever. (Hebrews 7:1-3)

Jesus can reach into the heart and change it from a heart of stone to a heart of flesh. He can judge the thoughts and attitudes of the heart when no other man could, and fix whatever is broken to the perfection required by the Law. Jesus can fill us with his Spirit to enable us to live in righteousness and holiness from now on. The whole situation is lifted up from the hopeless to the completely successful. He's a different kind of priest.

And lest we forget this amazing privilege of seeing God, Jesus the Son tears down the curtain separating us from God and brings us directly into the presence of God to meet his Father. Jesus has the right of entry; he's the Son, the Heir of the fullness of God. Whatever the Father has, belongs to the Son. Jesus sees the truth and the depth of the Father like no creature can. He has access to the heart of God, the plans of God, the wisdom of God, the power of God, the majesty of God. There is nothing about God that Jesus is shut out from. So when Jesus takes us by the hand and leads us to God, we are about to see something that no other created being has ever seen, nor had the right to. We are going to know God as Jesus himself knows him.

> The throne of God and of the Lamb will be in the city, and his servants will serve him. They will see his face, and his Name will be on their foreheads. (Revelation 22:3-4)

Now how do we handle this new situation that we have in Jesus when we're reading through the Old Testament? Certainly we have to recognize the fact that Jesus succeeded where the Old Testament priests failed. But that doesn't mean we close the Old Testament! It means that wherever we read of the priestly functions of 1) forgiving us our sins, and 2) going before God, we learn what it takes to do that. It was attempted by the Levites, but they failed; Jesus however succeeds completely and accomplishes the very things they couldn't do.

The laws about the Temple service (laid out in detail in Exodus and Leviticus) show us the depth of the spiritual needs of the human soul; it took all this to get us forgiveness of our many kinds of sin. It also took all this to get man the right into God's presence. Each part of the Temple and the priestly service was critical to the process; if anything was left out, or changed, God rejected their ministry – it had to be done to his stringent standards. Remember what happened when Aaron's two sons changed the ceremony.

> Aaron's sons Nadab and Abihu took their censers, put fire in them and added incense; and they offered unauthorized fire before the LORD, contrary to his command. So fire came out from the presence of the LORD and consumed them, and they died before the LORD. Moses then said to Aaron, "This is what the LORD spoke of when he said: "'Among those who approach me I will be proved holy; in the sight of all the people I will be honored.'" (Leviticus 10:1-3)

So the great detail shouldn't cause us to turn away in boredom. These passages teach us the *depth* of our sin, the *kinds* of sin, the kinds of *blessings and privileges* that God gives his people through the Temple service. They show us the true extent of the holiness of God, the reasons to fear this God, the extent of his mercy that this God would not only allow us to come before him but encourage us to come and live with him.

There are many, for example, who feel that the book of Leviticus is the most boring book in the Bible because of its endless rules and regulations. But to me it's one of the most exciting. Here is God taking care of our most serious problems – sin and death – in a fundamental and complete way. And here is the house of God where he plans to bring us to live with him. Watch God as he cleans his house for the homecoming; as he cleans us up, inside and out, to be ready for him; as he dresses us in his clothes of righteousness so that we "shine like the sun" and "look like his Son" for the occasion. The ladies love to watch the bride get ready for the wedding; in the same way, Leviticus is a picture of getting the Bride of Christ ready for the great banquet with our God. If so much has to be done to make all of this possible, doesn't that shine a bright light on the amazing darkness in our hearts, and the amazing depth of God's compassion toward us to make it possible, and the amazing work that Christ accomplished for us? This is the story of God clearing the way, whatever it takes, to bring sinners to himself. Leviticus is your future and your God, Christian!

Jesus the New Testament Priest

In order to understand what Jesus was doing in the New Testament we have to take the lessons we learned from the Old and use them to interpret the text. The Sermon on the Mount is in the spirit of Leviticus: to be ready for Christ's new Kingdom, where we will live with his Father in Heaven, we will have to be cleaned up and made ready for the occasion. Otherwise we won't be allowed in to see God.

> For I tell you that unless your righteousness surpasses that of the Pharisees and the teachers of the Law, you will certainly not enter the Kingdom of Heaven. (Matthew 5:20)

Cleansing people of their diseases and ailments was the first step at restoration – physical and then spiritual. They got it in that order; but the rest of us will get it in the reverse – spiritual cleansing, then the bodily resurrection. Either way we will be made perfect and fit children of the Father to live with him in his House. Keep in mind that this is the Priest working on our hearts to forgive and cleanse us completely of our sins, with the blood that he brings to the altar.

The Gospel of John in particular is a replay of the theme of Leviticus. Here Jesus talks about going to see the Father, in behind the Holy of Holies. There is the good life! God is the source of all good things; God is fullness and power and wisdom and majesty and beauty in ways that we can't imagine. Jesus knows full well what is in store for us, because he says "I came from the Father," and he knows the plans of the Father completely. And his desire is that we too may know the Father as he does.

> I am the way and the truth and the life. No one comes to
> the Father except through me. If you really know me, you
> will know my Father as well. From now on, you do know
> him and have seen him. (John 14:6-7)

That's the second function of the Priest – going into the presence of God. But Jesus is going to get that privilege for all of God's children, not just himself. All we who are the children of God will finally be able to go to God in Heaven and see the Father as Jesus himself sees and knows him. It will be an astonishing event, this entry into God's presence, and it will be what people have always used the word Paradise for: eternal bliss, joy, peace, and life.

Now these themes of cleansing, forgiving, changing, redeeming, and making us ready fill the entire Bible from beginning to end. And the idea of seeing God is the hope of all of God's saints, finally fulfilled with the coming of the Son who takes us back to see him. You can hardly turn to any part of the Bible and not see these themes in some way – some receiving this great reward, and many being shut out from it. Wherever you read about them, keep in mind that it is Jesus that makes it happen. The Old Testament tells us what to expect; and Jesus gives it to us.

DAVID'S PLAN

The story and influence of David takes up almost a third of the Old Testament. When you count the genealogy of the king (Ruth), the need for the king (Judges), the rise and reign of the king and his son Solomon (1-2 Samuel, 1 Chronicles), the descendants of the king ruling over his Kingdom (1-2 Kings, 2 Chronicles), the writings and teachings of the king (Psalms, Proverbs, Ecclesiastes, Song of Songs) you can begin to understand how integral David is to the story.

And yet modern students relegate King David to the dustbin of history! They inevitably single out the sins that he committed and their results, as if the story focuses on them. The most they can say about him that's positive is that he pulled the nation together and made her strong against her enemies.

And yet they never fail to mention that Jesus was the Son of David, with nothing more to go on than Jesus is building a Kingdom, like David built a Kingdom. I honestly don't see how they could attribute any meaning to that concept, if that's all they have to go on.

What we propose to do here is show that David's Kingdom was the model for all phases of God's Kingdom, Old Testament as well as New. In fact, the modern Church must also be based on this Davidic model if it's going to survive and prosper. The reason that Jesus is called the Son of David is because he (past and present) faithfully follows the 5-point Plan of his father David as he builds his new spiritual Kingdom.

David's Plan

David inherited a mess from King Saul. Under Saul's leadership, Israel fell to her lowest point since some of the disastrous days of the Judges. For centuries, the Israelites had been used to doing whatever they thought was right, without any one person leading the people back to the Law to see what God wanted from them.

116

> In those days Israel had no king; everyone did as he saw fit. (Judges 21:25)

When Saul was king, Israel had hopes that for once the people would be drawn into a single nation under one head, and they would be able to defeat their enemies and prosper for a change. And at first it seemed that this would happen: Saul won victories over the Philistines. But it wasn't long before Saul showed the true nature of his heart. He began to disobey the Lord's commands and do things his own way. For example, when the prophet Samuel passed on the Lord's command to put every living creature in the Amalekite camp to death, Saul evidently thought that this was an unnecessary waste – so he saved the livestock, and even spared the life of the Amalekite king. When Samuel confronted Saul about not carrying out the Lord's orders, Saul made the excuse that –

> The soldiers brought them from the Amalekites; they spared the best of the sheep and cattle to sacrifice to the LORD your God, but we totally destroyed the rest. (1 Samuel 15:15)

But God isn't interested in our opinions; when he gives us a command to carry out, he expects strict obedience:

> Does the LORD delight in burnt offerings and sacrifices as much as in obeying the voice of the LORD? To obey is better than sacrifice, and to heed is better than the fat of rams. For rebellion is like the sin of divination, and arrogance like the evil of idolatry. (1 Samuel 15:22-23)

Obviously Saul wasn't going to work out as the king over God's people. The Lord needs someone for the job who will be careful about the Law of Moses, someone who is filled with the Spirit and knows the mind of God, someone who is primarily interested in God's glory and not his own.

So the Lord sent Samuel out to find a replacement, which he found in the shepherd boy David, the eighth son of Jesse. At the time not even his own family – not even the prophet Samuel himself! – thought that this young boy would measure up to the exacting requirements of this position. But the Lord saw something important in David.

> The LORD does not look at the things man looks at. Man looks at the outward appearance, but the LORD looks at the heart. (1 Samuel 16:7)

David, the Lord could see, was "a man after his own heart" (1 Samuel 13:14) who would work to build God's Kingdom, not his own, over the Lord's people.

When David took over as King (you can read about the ceremony in 2 Samuel 5:1-5) he immediately set about working on five critical areas:

- **First, he established a capital city.** The Jebusites, one of the Canaanite tribes who had remained unconquered from Joshua's day, held the fortified hilltop called Jerusalem and dared David to conquer them. They underestimated him. He quickly took it from them and made it his official residence. The story is in 2 Samuel 5:6-10.

    The king needed a capital in a central location for his realm. Up until this time, even in Saul's day, the center of government was wherever the judge or king happened to live – and that changed frequently. The Israelites from Dan to Beersheba had no one place to bring their problems or concerns to.

    David, however, made his Kingdom much easier to manage by setting up his throne in Jerusalem. His subjects brought him tribute there, came there for his judgments, and gathered there for the religious festivals. He himself sat on the throne in Jerusalem and sent out his officers from there over the entire nation to carry out his commands. In fact, the city of Jerusalem became identified with the King – it was known as the "holy" city because of it being the seat of the King and the place where God also lived in the Temple.

    Setting up Jerusalem as the capital was probably the single most important factor in bringing stability to the nation. Up until this time Israel was just a collection of confused, warring tribes who couldn't pull themselves together to work on anything. But now in one stroke

David had turned Israel into a nation in her own right with a king to be reckoned with – with the resources of a nation behind him, both for war and for peace.

- **<u>Second, David finally crushed the enemies of Israel.</u>** For too long the Israelites had been persecuted, harassed and defeated by her pagan neighbors. The book of Judges is a graphic example of her history: because she hadn't exterminated all the Canaanites living in the land, Israel repeatedly suffered at their hands. The Lord would raise up judges to save them from their oppressors, but in a short time the Israelites would go back to worshiping the false gods of their neighbors, and God would punish them with wars and persecution.

At first it seemed that King Saul was going to break the cycle of war and oppression – he did win a few victories over their enemies in the beginning – but when he fell into sin and rebellion himself the Lord again allowed the Israelites to suffer defeat, especially at the hands of the Philistines.

When David ascended the throne, the time had come to put this issue to rest – permanently. As you can see in 2 Samuel 5, he promptly went to battle against the Philistines and the Moabites and defeated them. What he did to the Moabites shows us how determined he was to settle the issue for good: he put to death two thirds of the men of the nation, in a harsh way! That act alone no doubt impressed the Israelites that they finally had a leader who could deal summarily with the enemy – their foreign policy problems were over.

- **<u>Third, he led the people back to God.</u>** Another problem in Israel was that the pure worship that Moses laid down to them in the Law was almost a thing of the past. Several stories in Judges show us that the people of God had seemingly forgotten how to worship the Lord – false priests, altars to foreign gods, immorality, no justice. The ark traveled around the countryside – it was at Bethel, or at Shiloh, or carried into battle with the army. The religion of the Lord God of Israel seemed to be of little importance to the people. Even the priests – for example, Eli's sons – treated the service of the Lord as an opportunity for personal gain.

It was time to bring the Israelites back to their God. In 2 Samuel 6 we read of David bringing the ark from the house of Abinadab into the city of Jerusalem. After the little problem about Uzzah touching it without authority (and getting put to death for his trouble!) David and the people entered Jerusalem and set up the ark in the tent on Mt. Zion. It was a magnificent ceremony – dancing, singing, worship, food and drink – and it was purposely designed to impress the people with how central the Lord and his worship were to the nation. Whatever the other nations might do, Israel must come together around her God in praise and worship, obeying his Law, offering the stated sacrifices for sin and atonement. David made the principle of centering around God a requirement in his new Kingdom.

The important thing to grasp is that David had to step in and restore the worship of the Lord, because being the head of state he had the authority as well as the responsibility to set an example of what the Israelites must do to please God. The nation will do as the King does; so if David goes back to the Lord, so will his people. And he went on to lead the people again and again to the Lord in worship, as we can see from his many psalms.

- **Fourth, he established a government.** David was only one man. Though he set up Jerusalem as his capital and sat on the throne of Israel, he couldn't go himself and execute the laws of his Kingdom from Dan to Beersheba. He needed a system of government, administrators and officials to carry out his orders.

He made his sons government officials, because he could exert the necessary influence over them to carry out his will. He also had many trusted friends and army comrades whom he made government officials – see the list of some of them in 2 Samuel 8:15-18. These were men who came out to help David when he was an outlaw in the wilderness, hiding from Saul's unjust wrath. Men like these needed to be rewarded for their loyalty.

Of course he wouldn't have picked fools for important government posts. He knew the skills of each man and put them in the places where they would do the most good for the nation. David's goal, remember, was to build up Israel in the fear and knowledge of the Lord. So he's going to make sure that whoever he has in authority over the various aspects of Israel's life will help build that kind of Kingdom.

And the rule of his government was the Law of God. The man who wrote the following lines –

> The Law of the LORD is perfect, reviving the soul. The statutes of the LORD are trustworthy, making wise the simple.
>
> The precepts of the LORD are right, giving joy to the heart. The commands of the LORD are radiant, giving light to the eyes.
>
> The fear of the LORD is pure, enduring forever. The ordinances of the LORD are sure and altogether righteous.
>
> They are more precious than gold, than much pure gold; they are sweeter than honey, than honey from the comb.
>
> By them is your servant warned; in keeping them there is great reward.
>
> Who can discern his errors? Forgive my hidden faults.
>
> Keep your servant also from willful sins; may they not rule over me. Then will I be blameless, innocent of great transgression.

> May the words of my mouth and the
> meditation of my heart be pleasing in your
> sight, O LORD, my Rock and my Redeemer.
> (Psalm 19:7-14)

... knew how important it would be to live by God's
Law as a nation, not just as an individual. To David it
would never be a problem of deciding what was the right
or just thing to do, or what justice would consist of – it's
all written in God's Word.

- **Fifth, he prepared the plans and materials for the
  Temple.** Many people think that Solomon, since he built
  the Temple, must have drawn up the plans for the Temple.
  They are mistaken. It was David who drew up those
  plans. Not only that, he also gathered the materials for the
  Temple. When he was about to die, he handed over the
  entire project to his son Solomon – so that all that
  Solomon had to do was follow the instructions that his
  father had left him!

David at one point had wanted to build a Temple for
the Lord; he felt embarrassed that he had a fine palace to
live in while the ark of the Lord was still sitting in the old,
original tent that Moses had made hundreds of years ago.
But the Lord had someone else in mind as the builder of
the Temple. David, the Lord told him, was a man of
blood:

> You have shed much blood and have
> fought many wars. You are not to build a
> house for my Name, because you have shed
> much blood on the earth in my sight. (1
> Chronicles 22:8)

Not that what David had done was wrong (it was God
who gave him victory over his enemies), but that the
hands which would built this special House must be those
of a man of peace.

> But you will have a son who will be a man
> of peace and rest, and I will give him rest from

122

all his enemies on every side. His name will be
Solomon, and I will grant Israel peace and
quiet during his reign. He is the one who will
build a house for my Name. He will be my son,
and I will be his father. And I will establish the
throne of his Kingdom over Israel forever. (2
Chronicles 22:9-10)

In fact, the name Solomon comes from *shalom* which
means "peace." The Temple is where God will dwell
among his people in peace – peace between God and man,
and between man and man.

But David was going to play an important role in the
Temple. The Lord showed him what the Temple must
look like, what it must be made of, and even what
personnel would work in the Temple and their duties.

"All this," David said, "I have in writing
from the hand of the LORD upon me, and he
gave me understanding in all the details of the
plan." (1 Chronicles 28:19)

This was appropriate for two reasons: *first*, because
David had a special relationship with the Lord and knew
the heart of God. God shared his thoughts and plans with
David so that he could rule over the Israelites in truth,
according to God's Law. So he had an insight into God's
ways and works that would result in the kind of Temple
that would be acceptable to God.

Second, he was the model king for Israel, and what he
did through his realm would be the pattern for all the
kings to follow – especially for the Messiah, the Son of
David who would sit on David's eternal throne. For this
reason the Lord appointed David as the architect of the
Temple – for the sake of the work on God's spiritual
Temple that Jesus would later build, as the Son of David.

David had his share of problems in life, some of them caused by his
own sin and foolishness (for example, his adultery with Bathsheba and
cover-up murder of her husband). And the Lord certainly punished

David for his sins; not even the King of Israel is above the Law. But even when he sinned, he showed that he had the kind of heart that God wants to see in his servants. For example, Psalm 51 shows us a sinner in the agony of guilt and repentance for his sin. The Lord showed himself a merciful God in how he handled the great sins of David.

The point, however, about David is that he successfully accomplished the five tasks that made Israel a great nation under God. Here was a people who lived by God's Law, who treated each other with justice and righteousness, who trusted in God to take care of them, and who regularly came to God's throne for worship and submitting themselves to his will. What more could God want out of a people than this? They were in a perfect position for him to bless them and lead them – and David got them there when generations of leaders and kings before him failed to do so.

The Testimony of the Old Testament

David ruled over Israel for forty years. Being mortal, the time came to turn over the Kingdom to his son Solomon and die. But as it says in Ecclesiastes, we can work hard all of our lives and then turn over all that we've worked for to someone who just may mess everything up!

> I hated all the things I had toiled for under the sun, because I must leave them to the one who comes after me. And who knows whether he will be a wise man or a fool? Yet he will have control over all the work into which I have poured my effort and skill under the sun. This too is meaningless. So my heart began to despair over all my toilsome labor under the sun. For a man may do his work with wisdom, knowledge and skill, and then he must leave all he owns to someone who has not worked for it. This too is meaningless and a great misfortune. (Ecclesiastes 2:18-21)

Fortunately Solomon was the wisest man of his age – so he managed to preserve the Kingdom that his father left him. In fact, he made Israel the richest nation in the Middle East, certainly richer than she had ever been or ever will be, and there was peace along all of her borders during his reign. It was Israel's height of glory. But even Solomon had his faults that laid the seeds for future problems.

> As Solomon grew old, his wives turned his heart after other gods, and his heart was not fully devoted to the LORD his God, as the heart of David his father had been. (1 Kings 11:4)

There are two important things to notice in this passage. *First*, David is used as the pattern, the model king of Israel, to whom all his descendants were compared. In other words, David's works were fundamental to the life of Israel and the glory of God. Any king who succeeded him must do as his father David had done in order to get God's approval.

And that's the *second* thing to notice here – all the descendants of David who sat on the throne of Israel *were* compared to their ancestor David. Here even Solomon strayed from the royal program that God expected his kings to follow: whereas David led the people back to God, Solomon began leading them away from God to worship false gods. The result in the long run was disaster and exile. Do you see? The Scriptures judge a king by whether he followed the five-point plan of David, the model king.

Other kings were judged in the same way:

> He committed all the sins his father had done before him; his heart was not fully devoted to the LORD his God, as the heart of David his forefather had been. (1 Kings 15:3)

> He did what was right in the eyes of the LORD, but not as his father David had done. (2 Kings 14:3)

> He did what was right in the eyes of the LORD, just as his father David had done. (2 Kings 18:3)

The last example was Hezekiah. He was one of the few kings of Judah who got a 100% approval rating from the Lord. And as you can see here, the Lord approved of him because he "did as his father David had done."

Why was it so important for the kings of Israel to maintain David's Plan?

- *First,* it restored the relationship between God and the Israelites that the Law of Moses first set up. For the previous 400 years the Israelites were losing all the benefits that came from being God's people. The sacrifices were intermittent, the priesthood unreliable, so their sins weren't being taken care of. The people worshiped the false gods of their pagan neighbors; even some of the leaders (witness Gideon's ephod) encouraged idolatry. Instead of blessings from Heaven, they were being cursed with internal strife and harassment from their enemies. What was supposed to be a Kingdom of Law providing peace and prosperity had become chaotic.

  So David's plan restored the original Mosaic system that God had set up at Mt. Sinai and put the Israelites back in touch with the promises of the Abrahamic Covenant.

- *Second,* it was up to the leaders to maintain this Plan or it wouldn't get done at all. As the leaders go, so go the people. People are like sheep, and they will follow the leader because he's the one with the power and resources that the nation needs. If he is faithfully following the Lord, the rest will follow; if he rebels against God, then they will too. You can see this in the history of the kings in the books of Kings and Chronicles.

So actually there are three great lights in the Old Testament. **Abraham** receives the Covenant, the promise of the Gospel. **Moses** sets up a Kingdom in which God lives with his people. And **David** brings in a revival of both concepts, being the King who will restore and revive Israel's relationship with her God and maintain it.

Jesus the Son of David

The Scriptures call Jesus the Son of David. For example, these passages use that name when referring to him:

> A record of the genealogy of Jesus Christ the son of David, the son of Abraham. (Matthew 1:1)

As Jesus went on from there, two blind men followed him, calling out, "Have mercy on us, Son of David!" (Matthew 9:27)

All the people were astonished and said, "Could this be the Son of David?" (Matthew 12:23)

The crowds that went ahead of him and those that followed shouted, "Hosanna to the Son of David!" (Matthew 21:9)

While the Pharisees were gathered together, Jesus asked them, "What do you think about the Christ? Whose son is he?" "The son of David," they replied. (Matthew 22:41-42)

It was a popular concept – one which these and other passages emphasize – that the Messiah would not only be a descendant of David but would sit on David's throne, ruling over David's Kingdom. There's a good reason for that. Many people could claim to be descendants of David; even Joseph, Jesus' so-called step-father, was a "son of David." But the Messiah would actually rule over the Kingdom that was given to David – *and do the same things that his father David had done.* This is the key to understanding the ministry of Christ as he sets up his Kingdom.

• The Capital City

The capital of the Kingdom is where all the power and resources come from. That's where the throne is; the government is centered there. The Temple is there, so that's where you will find God. So *where* you put that capital is going to make all the difference in the world.

Jesus is not going to put his capital in this world! He's going to go back to Heaven and set it up there.

My Kingdom is not of this world. If it were, my servants would fight to prevent my arrest by the Jews. But now my Kingdom is from another place. (John 18:36)

This world, with all its attractions, is not what God's people need. Jesus showed almost a disdain for the riches, wealth, comforts and security that so many people long for from this physical world. To him, there is a more important goal in life: to lay hold of the next world and its treasures.

> Do not store up for yourselves treasures on earth, where moth and rust destroy, and where thieves break in and steal. But store up for yourselves treasures in Heaven, where moth and rust do not destroy, and where thieves do not break in and steal. For where your treasure is, there your heart will be also. (Matthew 6:19-21)

Jesus cared little for the comforts and wealth of this world. People should have known that something was up when he, the King, showed up with nothing in his hands!

> Foxes have holes and birds of the air have nests, but the Son of Man has no place to lay his head. (Luke 9:58)

Jesus counseled the rich young ruler to give away all of his wealth to people who could use it, and follow him to a better reward in Heaven. (Matthew 19:21) He shook his head over the fool who dreamed of building bigger barns to hold his increasing wealth, while the angel of death was standing at his door. (Luke 12:16-21) He promised his disciples that they would get back much more in the next world than they gave up here to follow him. (Matthew 19:29) Earthly wealth, he tells us, is better used to help our friends in need – and giving it away has the added advantage of buying real estate for ourselves in the next world. (Luke 16:9)

The Heir of the Covenant has inherited the fullness of the Godhead, and now he is the Executor of the estate, ready to hand out the blessings of that Covenant to all who come and ask. Obviously he could produce physical necessities when the situation required it – he sent Peter off to fish to get the tax that the Romans demanded, for example. But he always seemed to have empty pockets, because such "wealth" meant nothing to him. On the other hand, he was a rich resource of the blessings of the Temple in Heaven, of the Throne in Heaven, of the Priesthood in Heaven, of the Righteousness of Heaven.

Jesus has the Key to Heaven. And though he has returned to Heaven for the time being, he has given that Key to his Apostles so that they too can open Heaven's floodgates and admit all who will come.

> These are the words of him who is holy and true, who holds *the key of David*. What he opens no one can shut, and what he shuts no one can open. (Revelation 3:7)

> I will give you the keys of the Kingdom of Heaven; whatever you bind on earth will be bound in Heaven, and whatever you loose on earth will be loosed in Heaven. (Matthew 16:19)

This is why Jesus promised to send his Holy Spirit when he returned back to the Father.

> When the Counselor comes, whom I will send to you from the Father, the Spirit of truth who goes out from the Father, he will testify about me. (John 15:26)

The Spirit pours out the treasures of Heaven on God's people so that they are changed – cleansed from sin, and prepared to live with God in Heaven. The fruit of the Spirit changes our hearts from nasty to nice – into the image of Christ.

> But the fruit of the Spirit is love, joy, peace, forbearance, kindness, goodness, faithfulness, gentleness and self- control. (Galatians 5:22-23)

And the gifts of the Spirit enable God's people to help with the building of Christ's Kingdom so that others may see and know the glory of the Christ.

> So Christ himself gave the Apostles, the Prophets, the evangelists, the pastors and teachers, to equip his people for works of service, so that the body of Christ may be built up until we all reach unity in the faith and

in the knowledge of the Son of God and become mature, attaining to the whole measure of the fullness of Christ. (Ephesians 4:11-13)

Once a Christian realizes from where all this wealth is coming from – the King's throne in Heaven – he or she will appreciate Paul's injunction.

> Since, then, you have been raised with Christ, set your hearts on things above, where Christ is, seated at the right hand of God. Set your minds on things above, not on earthly things. For you died, and your life is now hidden with Christ in God. (Colossians 3:1-3)

• Defeating the Enemy

War is a fact of life. Some people like to fight, but most of us are peace-loving and will do what we can to avoid a fight. The problem is that we do have enemies, and they won't leave us alone. Jesus, being a realist, knows that in this world there must be war.

> Do not suppose that I have come to bring peace to the earth. I did not come to bring peace, but a sword. (Matthew 10:34)

Our Christian walk will be a struggle against real enemies. There are going to be casualties in this war, pain and hardship, alienation and loneliness. Not only will we have vicious enemies at our front to face, traitors and turncoats will work from behind to bring us down.

> Brother will betray brother to death, and a father his child; children will rebel against their parents and have them put to death. All men will hate you because of me, but he who stands firm to the end will be saved. (Matthew 10:21-22)

But though war is necessary, not everyone knows how to wage war successfully. There's a science and art to war. The first item of business here is to correctly identify the enemy. Contrary to our own opinions, our neighbor is not the enemy!

Jesus can see the battlefield from a higher perspective, and he knows what is driving this world to destruction.

> The reason the Son of God appeared was to destroy the devil's work. (1 John 3:8)

So his first engagement with the enemy is going to be a showdown in the wilderness with the devil. So begins the battle to the finish.

> Jesus, full of the Holy Spirit, returned from the Jordan and was led by the Spirit in the desert, where for forty days he was tempted by the devil. (Luke 4:1-2)

The devil has two allies: this world with its temptations and materialism, and your own fleshly nature that is drawn to those temptations. These too must be destroyed; there can be no compromise with the enemy, in Jesus' opinion.

> If anyone would come after me, he must deny himself and take up his cross and follow me. For whoever wants to save his life will lose it, but whoever loses his life for me and for the gospel will save it. (Mark 8:34-35)

> If the world hates you, keep in mind that it hated me first. If you belonged to the world, it would love you as its own. As it is, you do not belong to the world, but I have chosen you out of the world. That is why the world hates you. (John 15:18-19)

> Do not love the world or anything in the world. If anyone loves the world, the love of the Father is not in him. For everything in the world – the cravings of sinful man, the lust of his eyes and the boasting of what he has and does – comes not from the Father but from the world. The world and its desires pass away, but the man who does the will of God lives forever. (1 John 2:15-17)

The *world* is what man has created on top of, or as a replacement to, God's Creation. We don't like the world that God gave us because it doesn't feed our lusts, our passion for entertainment and power and wealth. So we've created a new world that gives us what we want in abundance, when we want it – pleasures with no responsibilities. But this world is a huge temptation to God's people, and as we try to follow Christ the temptations of this world often create spiritual disasters along the way. So Jesus clears the way for us.

> In this world you will have trouble. But take heart! I have overcome the world. (John 16:33)

The Spirit leads us in God's paths, sometimes lonely paths, but always around the danger. Or if we have to "walk through the valley of the shadow of death," Jesus walks alongside us and protects us from the power of temptation. Just being part of a church helps so many Christians because they live in the safety and like-mindedness of brothers and sisters walking the same path of life.

Our *flesh*, as if we needed any more troubles in life, is another enemy that needs dealing with. It's the part of us that responds positively to the temptations of the world. Pagans, of course, live on that level continuously. But even Christians do battle against their own flesh when they struggle to live the life of faith surrounded by the world's pleasures and other people's examples. There's a saying that if you want to kill a vicious dog, quit feeding it. Our flesh is like a dog that is trying to kill us spiritually, and it's just too strong for us to handle. It's extremely difficult to be a Christian in today's world. But here Jesus provides a strategy that will effectively deaden the enemy's weapons: he leads us to his cross where he will crucify our flesh. And so now we must suffer hardship.

And the *devil* is a constant source of harassment in life. He fights us on two fronts: through lies, and through persecution and suffering. The purpose of his lies is to turn us away from the Truth, the way God sees things. If we don't live by the Truth, we're going to end up in serious trouble spiritually and physically. So Jesus counters with his Word – the Bible, through the Prophets and Apostles and taught to us by pastors and teachers. The ministry of the Word is critical in the life of the Christian. And just so we get the right lesson from the

Word, Jesus sends his Spirit to enlighten us about the depth, the point, the purpose of the Word. In this way Jesus does battle against his and our enemy who is trying to steer us away from God's Truth.

So you see that we have the same problem on our hands that the Israelites had: our enemies are out to destroy us, and they are utterly ruthless. Identifying the right enemy is crucial here: you may or may not have neighbors who don't like you, but the world, the flesh and the devil are going to kill you spiritually if they can. Jesus, however, knows exactly what to do with them.

You can see this spiritual warfare going on all over the New Testament – at least if you've been trained in the art of warfare, as was David. And as the Commander in Chief leads us against our spiritual enemies (see Revelation!) we will learn to "fight the good fight of faith" and win real battles over our enemies.

• Back to God

If there was anything that Jesus cared about, it was that we might "know God." But that does not come naturally; nor does it seem to be a priority for many people who otherwise claim to be God's people. The Jews, particularly in Jesus' day, appeared to be content with going through the motions at the Temple service. Christians as well simply "go to church", go through the motions, and then go home *unchanged spiritually*. That is not knowing God.

Probably the hardest thing for a person to do is get hold of the reality of God. Life in this world doesn't naturally lead us in that direction. So we sin as if God doesn't see us, we value the things that God despises, we ignore the Word that God speaks to us, we walk in places where God told us not to go, and we think we're doing pretty well without him. About the only times we think about getting in touch with him are with rituals at church (which we use like magic charms to bring blessings and protect us from danger), and when we're in deep trouble and need his help.

That is *not* preparation for Heaven. God must become everything to us. If we use God like foreigners often use marriages (simply to get them citizenship), we will find him standing at the door of Heaven very reluctant to let us in.

> Many will say to me on that day, 'Lord, Lord, did we not prophesy in your name, and in your name drive out demons and perform many miracles?' Then I will tell them plainly, 'I never knew you. Away from me, you evildoers!' (Matthew 7:22-23)

Jesus is determined to make God real to us. In fact, that's the whole idea behind God coming in the flesh – so that we can see and know God directly. Now we have no excuse for not knowing him; the whole world can see God, if they will.

> Philip said, "Lord, show us the Father and that will be enough for us." Jesus answered: "Don't you know me, Philip, even after I have been among you such a long time? Anyone who has seen me has seen the Father. How can you say, 'Show us the Father'? Don't you believe that I am in the Father, and that the Father is in me? The words I say to you are not just my own. Rather, it is the Father, living in me, who is doing his work." (John 14:8-10)

Paul told us that Jesus is nothing less than God himself in the body of man.

> For in Christ all the fullness of the Deity lives in bodily form. (Colossians 2:9)

And John calls Jesus the Logos – the very Word of God.

> In the beginning was the Word, and the Word was with God, and the Word was God. (John 1:1)

In effect this puts God right at our fingertips. Now we can hear his voice, we can watch him at work, we can come directly to him with our prayer requests. We don't have to make some extraordinary effort to find God, like people do in other religions.

> Do not say in your heart, 'Who will ascend into Heaven?' (that is, to bring Christ down) or 'Who will descend into the deep?' (that is, to bring Christ up from the dead). But what does it say? 'The word is near you; it is in your mouth and in your heart,' that is, the word of faith we are proclaiming. (Romans 10:6-8)

The point of all this is so that we will become God-centered. The great tragedy of the human race is that we are so independent of God. Man, of all the creatures, was formed to know and glorify God. We were designed to live in two worlds at the same time: in this physical world, carrying out God's mandates over his creation, and in God's spiritual world, in continuous communication with God and enjoying his presence. God is the source of all good; whereas this world, though a blessing from God, was one step removed from that source.

Now Jesus has come to bring us closer to God than even Adam had the right and ability to do. *We were called to live with God, as Jesus lives with him.* This is the idea of the holy.

So to help us live with God, Jesus sends his Spirit into our hearts to make God real to us, and to empower us to use the spiritual realities that we can see in God's world. We pray now in the Spirit – which means we know we are in God's presence, that he's listening to us, that we talk about matters on his heart, that we see things the way he sees them, and we ask for what pleases God. It makes all the difference in the world when we pray like this; it's the difference between a pointless prayer about ourselves, or getting on board with God's Kingdom.

And the Spirit leads us in the way of life. This means we can see why we need to be led (we are full of sin, open to temptations, and we don't know the way to the Father without the Spirit showing us). We now know what Kingdom that we're living in. We know why this world isn't good enough, and why we have to stay away from it. All sorts of spiritual insights pour into our hearts and minds when we come into God's presence and he takes us by the hand to lead us out of this world and into his world.

In the Apostles' letters, Jesus reveals a tremendous amount of information about our new life with God (remember that he gave it to them, and they being eyewitnesses passed it on to us). If we can read the first three chapters of Ephesians without any longing for this God, without any new passion for living with this God, then we aren't living in the Light. The point about these attractive passages about God is to draw us to him, as Jesus shows us the Father, and to motivate us to live with the hope of Heaven with God.

- **A Government**

I recently heard a teacher mention in passing that, when Jesus passes on the throne to his Father (as Paul mentions in 1 Corinthians), there will be no more need of a King or Kingdom because all his enemies will be destroyed. That is totally wrong. Destroying one's enemies is not the sole point of a Kingdom. The idea here is that *only one will* rules the entire Kingdom; as a result, there is peace, prosperity, justice, holiness and righteousness throughout the Kingdom – *forever*. Jesus was assigned the task of setting it up, and then passing on a perfect Kingdom to his Father.

God

Jesus — King

Government | Kingdom—Hierarchy

Standard of rule: | Bible

Apostles—
Pastors &
Teachers

Church
— Gifts

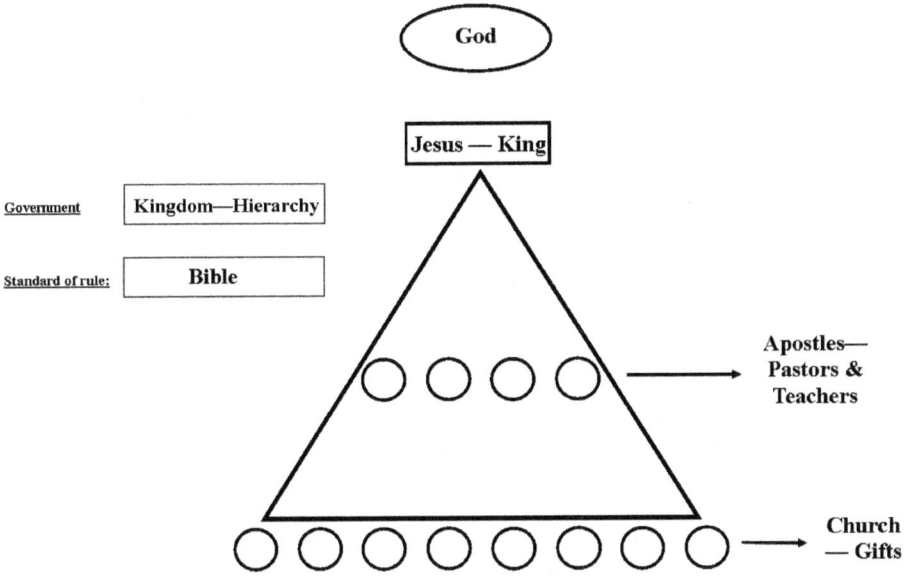

The Kingdom of Christ

The Kingdom of Christ is a *hierarchy*. The point of a hierarchy is that the will of the King might be made known throughout the entire Kingdom, so that everyone will obey that will. A hierarchy is not a democracy (which I'm sure will disappoint most Americans!). Christ is not interested in our opinions. And he particularly doesn't want us to vote on things that he's already issued commands about. Our votes don't change the fact that we are obliged to obey the King upon penalty of death. That's how a kingdom works.

Hopefully everyone realizes that Christ's will is the perfect solution for the daily requirements of the Kingdom. He is, after all, the Creator, so he knows what is best for everyone involved. He knows what works and what doesn't. And he's committed to taking care of all of his creatures. This is not tyranny, he's not doing it for himself; he's dedicated to making a joyous, prosperous Kingdom that everyone will be glad to be a part of. This is the perfect government that human governments have struggled so hard to achieve and failed.

The reason he's harsh with the rebellious is that the rebellious are going to destroy themselves and everyone around them. This is the last thing that the King wants to happen in his perfect Kingdom. Such dangerous traitors must be warned, changed, or disposed of promptly. The King will not tolerate perverse and dangerous behavior when the well-being of the whole is at stake. So Jesus talked about Hell a good bit – the punishment of the wicked.

> This is how it will be at the end of the age. The angels will come and separate the wicked from the righteous and throw them into the blazing furnace, where there will be weeping and gnashing of teeth. (Matthew 13:49-50)

While Jesus was here on earth, he spoke and acted like a King. Of course he only did so much during his ministry because he's not setting up his Kingdom here in this world, not now. His Kingdom is in another world. So he spent his time telling people what things will be like then, when he comes into his Kingdom. That makes people think that they can get away with murder, since he's not yet doing much about the wicked. But that's stupid. The King is most certainly coming, and then he will deal with the wicked as they fully deserve.

> But suppose the servant says to himself, 'My master is taking a long time in coming,' and he then begins to beat the other servants, both men and women, and to eat and drink and get drunk. The master of that servant will come on a day when he does not expect him and at an hour he is not aware of. He will cut him to pieces and assign him a place with the unbelievers. (Luke 12:45-46)

> Above all, you must understand that in the last days scoffers will come, scoffing and following their own evil desires. They will say, "Where is this 'coming' he promised? Ever since our ancestors died, everything goes on as it has since the beginning of creation." ... By the same word the present heavens and earth are

reserved for fire, being kept for the day of judgment and destruction of the ungodly. (2 Peter 3:3-4, 7)

One of the critical concepts to grasp about Christ's Kingdom is the fact that he set a foundation in the Church that extends and maintains the Kingdom of God – the testimony of the Apostles and Prophets. We often look at the Bible as if it's a story about God, and about the Israelites, and about the life of Christ and his disciples. It's much more than that! This book is the will of the King which he gave to his servants who then wrote it down and passed it on to the entire Church.

> Consequently, you are no longer foreigners and strangers, but fellow citizens with God's people and also members of his household, built on the foundation of the Apostles and Prophets, with Christ Jesus himself as the chief cornerstone. In him the whole building is joined together and rises to become a holy temple in the Lord. And in him you too are being built together to become a dwelling in which God lives by his Spirit. (Ephesians 2:19-22)

The Bible is not a human production; it is not the opinions of learned men; it is not on par with the wise sayings of other religions. This is the King's published will – and therefore God requires our knowledge and obedience to what this Book says – period!

• Building the Temple

Jesus, as did his father David, started making plans for the Temple in Heaven. His first order of business was to dig the foundation and lay down stones that the entire structure would rest safely upon.

> As Jesus was walking beside the Sea of Galilee, he saw two brothers, Simon called Peter and his brother Andrew. They were casting a net into the lake, for they were fishermen. "Come, follow me," Jesus said, "and I will make you fishers of men." At once they left their nets and followed him. Going on from there, he saw

two other brothers, James son of Zebedee and his brother John. They were in a boat with their father Zebedee, preparing their nets. Jesus called them, and immediately they left the boat and their father and followed him. (Matthew 4:18-22)

If you didn't catch the significance of what Jesus was doing here, remember that Jesus is building a spiritual Temple for a spiritual Kingdom. His Church needs to be founded on the truth – the Word of God, the Revelation of God. It's his teaching that will keep us afloat in times of storm and confusion (the disciples are the foundation of the new Temple – see Ephesians 2:20).

In order to live with God in his Temple, we ourselves must become priests, because only priests are allowed into God's house.

As you come to him, the living Stone – rejected by men but chosen by God and precious to him – you also, like living stones, are being built into a spiritual house to be a holy priesthood, offering spiritual sacrifices acceptable to God through Jesus Christ. (1 Peter 2:4-5)

By virtue of our union with Christ (we have become "sons of God" now) who is the High Priest, and because we are called to live with God in his house, Jesus commissions us as priests. No wonder, then, that God tore the curtain in the Temple in two when Jesus died – it symbolized Jesus entering into the Holy of Holies and opening the way for us to follow him.

At that moment the curtain of the temple was torn in two from top to bottom. (Matthew 27:51)

Priests are called to service; it's not just an honorary title with a paycheck. For one thing, God must be glorified; he created us all for that purpose, and there's much to do if we're going to make the glory and majesty of God fully known.

You are the light of the world. A city on a hill cannot be hidden. Neither do people light a lamp and put it under a bowl. Instead they put it on its stand, and

140

it gives light to everyone in the house. In the same way, let your light shine before men, that they may see your good deeds and praise your Father in Heaven. (Matthew 5:14-16)

And the other function of priests is to bless our neighbor with the treasures of the Temple. God uses us to reach them; he reveals himself to them in our ministry. This is the new calling that Jesus lays upon all believers: to be priests in God's Temple.

A new command I give you: Love one another. As I have loved you, so you must love one another. By this all men will know that you are my disciples, if you love one another. (John 13:34-35)

Perhaps you haven't yet seen the point of the fruit of the Spirit, mentioned in Galatians. The "works of the flesh" are what we're like naturally, before the Spirit changes our hearts.

The acts of the flesh are obvious: sexual immorality, impurity and debauchery; idolatry and witchcraft; hatred, discord, jealousy, fits of rage, selfish ambition, dissensions, factions and envy; drunkenness, orgies, and the like. (Galatians 5:19-21)

Look at this list carefully, and you will see that it describes what we're like around other people. It's about our relationships with others, including with God. Life is social, we are all in a context with someone, and how we behave affects the others around us. But with hearts like this, we aren't going to be anything but trouble for everyone.

But when the Spirit changes our hearts so that we take on the likeness of the Son, this is what we are like.

But the fruit of the Spirit is love, joy, peace, forbearance, kindness, goodness, faithfulness, gentleness and self- control. (Galatians 5:22-23)

This describes a person who is a blessing to others (conveying the spiritual blessings of Heaven to others) and an obedient servant of the King (growing his Kingdom in his way).

Jesus was so insistent that we take on our new duties as priests in God's house that he added the sharp edge of penalty on slackers. In the story about the talents, he makes it plain that he expects a profit from every one of us.

> You wicked, lazy servant! So you knew that I harvest where I have not sown and gather where I have not scattered seed? Well then, you should have put my money on deposit with the bankers, so that when I returned I would have received it back with interest.

> Take the talent from him and give it to the one who has the ten talents. For everyone who has will be given more, and he will have an abundance. Whoever does not have, even what he has will be taken from him. And throw that worthless servant outside, into the darkness, where there will be weeping and gnashing of teeth. (Matthew 25:24-30)

Jesus will not have his Temple sitting empty while we waste our time on our own pursuits. We are priests now; we're supposed to be aware of our responsibilities, and ready to help – keeping our spiritual antennae up for "works of service." (Ephesians 4:12) We are equipped to minister in the House of God now.

> For we are God's workmanship, created in Christ Jesus to do good works, which God prepared in advance for us to do. (Ephesians 2:10)

Summary

Now that we've seen that Jesus is the Son of David working on David's Plan, we have to start looking for things in the New Testament that correspond to that Plan. Not only was Jesus totally taken up with implementing this Plan, he taught his Apostles to keep working on that Plan as they laid the foundation of the Church. This is, after all, the perfect Kingdom that God has in mind for his people.

First we have to see why David's Plan was so important to the entire Bible, particularly in the way it restored the Abrahamic Covenant and Mosaic Law to the life of Israel and provided a way of maintaining both by means of the Kingdom.

And we must go back to the Old Testament for the details which explain so much about Jesus' implementation of the Plan.

For example, the Lord's Prayer – why is it that Jesus told us to pray for these things? Could it be that they correspond to David's Plan?

Another example: David (in accordance with the Law of Moses) dealt summarily with the Moabites; Jesus also proscribed summary judgment on the sins of the flesh.

> You must destroy all the peoples the LORD your God gives over to you. Do not look on them with pity and do not serve their gods, for that will be a snare to you. (Deuteronomy 7:16)

> David also defeated the Moabites. He made them lie down on the ground and measured them off with a length of cord. Every two lengths of them were put to death, and the third length was allowed to live. So the Moabites became subject to David and brought him tribute. (2 Samuel 8:2)

> If your right eye causes you to stumble, gouge it out and throw it away. It is better for you to lose one part of your body than for your whole body to be thrown into hell. And if your right hand causes you to stumble, cut it off and throw it away. It is better for you to lose one part of your body than for your whole body to go into hell. (Matthew 5:29-30)

The more that we start making these connections between the Covenant, the Law, David's Plan and the ministry of Christ, then the more we will appreciate the concept of Jesus sitting on David's throne. If we don't see all this, our claim that we "make Jesus Lord" is an empty claim.

THE PROPHET

Much of the Old Testament consists of what we Christians call "the Prophets." The Jews would include more than we do, however; they include the historical books under that category as well. Here we will stay with the narrower definition.

A prophet was a man called by God, to speak God's message to God's people. There were several elements involved with being a prophet.

> **First**, his calling came from God, not from himself or another person.

> **Second**, his message came from the Lord word for word. This was not his message; he wasn't a "religious genius" as many Liberals like to style Israel's prophets. He dare not add anything to the message or take anything away from it. He faithfully transmitted the Lord's message to the people; they knew, when they heard the message, that this was God speaking to them, not man.

There's some confusion about the message of the Bible's prophets. Usually people think that it's about the future; our modern day "prophets" that make horoscopes or Wall Street predictions focus mainly on what's going to happen in the future. But Israel's prophets were different. Yes, they did talk about the future, but only in regard to what God had planned for his people according to their behavior. The message about the future was more like "stop doing this or things will get bad for you," or "do this and things will get good." Of course their predictions of the future were accurate, as far as the details. But that's not the main thrust of the prophecy.

The Prophet knows

The prophet only showed up when there was trouble. When times were good, the priests did their work in the Temple, and the king ruled over the land in justice and prosperity. But when particularly the leaders started going bad, the whole nation went bad; and that's when God sent his prophets to confront the people.

The prophet wasn't like your ordinary preacher. Preachers and teachers expound on the words of the Bible and hope they hit the mark; but they really can't tell if you need these things that they're telling you. They rely on the Spirit to apply the Word to whomever it was intended for.

But the prophet knew. God showed him what was in people's hearts and lives. When the prophet spoke, these were words from God targeting specific sins and beliefs in the people's lives. There were no secrets from a prophet; he uncovered a person's heart in public, for everyone to see.

Only God knew the state of his people's hearts. No man, not even Moses, could know what was going on in the hearts and minds of God's people. It's easy to hide your thoughts from others, but it's impossible to deceive God. He knows everything about you; so naturally he would be the only Judge who could accurately and justly pass judgment on you. We would never want to submit to another man's judgment, but there is no appeal from God's court – his judgment on us is more just than what we ourselves would come up with.

That's why nobody liked a prophet. He uncovered their sins, their rebellion, their cold hearts. They cheated their neighbors; they committed adultery; they amassed fortunes at others' expense; they denied justice to the poor. When they went to the Temple to worship, their hearts were far from God; they had no fear of the Lord, no intention of actually examining their hearts to see if they measured up to his standards, no passion about seeking God. The religion that they were supposed to believe in was a tradition, a lie, a superficial covering to fool others into thinking that they were righteous and holy people. Well, they could fool other people, but not God – nor the prophet. He uncovered their hypocrisy easily and thoroughly.

So you can see that the prophet's words weren't his own; this was God speaking to his people. If they ignored the words of the prophet, of course there would be judgment against them. Not heeding the prophet wasn't like ignoring the preacher. God is the last court of appeal; ignore him, and there will be punishment. And that's what the prophet predicted in his prophecies – wrath, the anger of God, punishment. The coming of the prophet was God's last-chance offer for the people to repent or perish.

The greatest Prophets

You may not have known this, but there were two prophets in Israel who were greater than any other prophets. Not just in how much they said, but in *what* they said; not greater in *quantity* but in *quality*.

The first one was Moses. We read this about him in Deuteronomy:

> When there is a prophet among you, I, the LORD, reveal myself to them in visions, I speak to them in dreams. But this is not true of my servant Moses; he is faithful in all my house. With him I speak face to face, clearly and not in riddles; he sees the form of the LORD. Why then were you not afraid to speak against my servant Moses? (Numbers 12:6-8)

> Since then, no prophet has risen in Israel like Moses, whom the LORD knew face to face, who did all those miraculous signs and wonders the LORD sent him to do in Egypt — to Pharaoh and to all his officials and to his whole land. For no one has ever shown the mighty power or performed the awesome deeds that Moses did in the sight of all Israel. (Deuteronomy 34:10-12)

This is a high rating! When Moses' sister and brother tried to cut in on the act and get some glory for themselves, the Lord rebuked them and told them that Moses was special among the prophets. "With him I speak face to face, clearly and not in riddles; he sees the form of the LORD." (Numbers 12:8) There was a reason for this, which we will look at in a minute.

The other great prophet of Israel was Jesus Christ. Moses told us (of course!) that he would be coming: "The LORD your God will raise up for you a prophet like me from among your own brothers. You must listen to him." (Deuteronomy 18:15) Peter confirmed that this was Jesus in Acts 3:22.

Now what did these two men do that made them prophets? Just this: *they revealed the Kingdom of God.* Only they did it in a big way. Let's begin with Moses. When the Israelites left Egypt they headed straight for Mt. Sinai. At this point they were still only a mob, blindly following Moses wherever he led them. When they got to Mt. Sinai they met their God — and there they found out that *he* was their real leader, not Moses.

The next forty years was a crash course on the Kingdom of God. They learned his laws, they learned how to please him, they learned his plans for the future, they were fed and watered by him, they watched the miracles he did for their benefit. The Lord was making a people, a nation, out of these Israelites. He set up his government over them, complete with laws and promises.

How did they learn all this? Remember that they were too afraid to get close enough to God to hear his voice. (Deuteronomy 5:23-27) Moses was the one chosen to take all the words of God to the people; as God built the nation Israel, he did it all through Moses. And the foundation that was laid during these forty years through Moses' ministry lasted for the next 1500 + years until the next prophet could take over — Jesus.

God sent all the Prophets to his people for this reason: the Israelites were getting pretty comfortable in their wickedness, and they thought that God would never come to upset their little world. The prophets, however, brought disturbing news. The Lord *will* come; the wicked had better listen up and change their ways, and the righteous need to hang in there a while longer. They predicted the crashing down of the old world and a new world taking its place. To some it was a dreadful message; to others, their only hope.

When Jesus came, he too announced the Kingdom: "The time has come, the Kingdom of God is near. Repent and believe the good news!" (Mark 1:15) Only this time the Kingdom was to be completely spiritual; nothing on earth would adequately represent the things in the Kingdom of Heaven. He, like Moses, set up a nation of God's people where the Lord would rule over them and they would enjoy his blessings. In this Kingdom, however, people were really saved from their sins. They ate spiritual manna from Heaven; they drank from the spiritual rock in the desert; they felt the Law penetrate their hearts in severe conviction of every thought and act; they received the Spirit who enabled them to obey God; they were protected from spiritual enemies; and so on. It's easy to see, in the work of Christ, a new world in the making; he was forming a new nation out of Jew and Gentile and creating the circumstances necessary for a happy life with God the King.

Moses and Christ were actually working on the same project, the same house, the same Kingdom. After all, this is the Kingdom of God — and he doesn't have two Kingdoms but one. In Hebrews we find this:

> He was faithful to the one who appointed him, just as Moses was faithful in all God's house. Jesus has been found worthy of greater honor than Moses, just as the builder of a house has greater honor than the house itself. For every house is built by someone, but God is the builder of everything. Moses was faithful as a servant in all God's house, testifying to what would be said in the future. But Christ is faithful as a son over God's house. (Hebrews 3:2-6)

This explains in a nutshell why these two prophets were so great — and what they were doing as "prophets." They were responsible for setting up the house, so to speak; through their ministry they revealed to the people the kind of world they were to live in. Through their words, the people saw God in his holiness, in his love, in his anger, in his government, in his redemption, in his promises.

Keep in mind that Moses didn't actually do the work himself; he only revealed the hand of God to the people as the Lord did the work. That's the role of the prophet: to reveal the Kingdom of God. Jesus, however, did what he predicted, or the Father did it through him. He was still a prophet, however, in that he revealed this Kingdom that God was setting up to his followers.

Here then is another connecting point between Jesus and Moses – what Moses did in his ministry, Jesus also does in his ministry.

The Testimony of the Old Testament

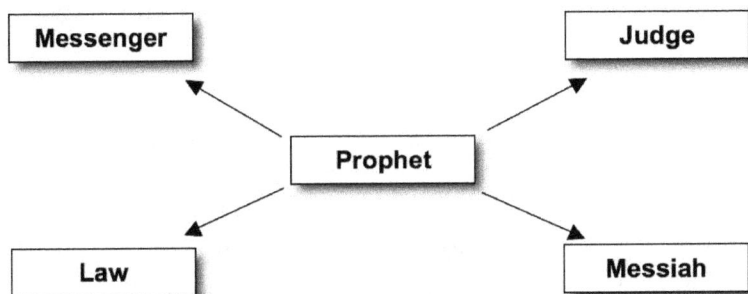

```
┌──────────────┐                          ┌──────────────┐
│  Messenger   │                          │    Judge     │
└──────────────┘ ↖                      ↗ └──────────────┘
                    ┌──────────────┐
                    │   Prophet    │
                    └──────────────┘
┌──────────────┐ ↙                      ↘ ┌──────────────┐
│     Law      │                          │   Messiah    │
└──────────────┘                          └──────────────┘
```

- *Prophecy: A Message Of War*

Perhaps you know how two armies would face each other in the field, in the old days when warriors came against each other to fight. First they would each send a spokesman ahead to parley: the two would deliver messages from their respective kings (usually insults!) and demands for a surrender. Only when that failed would they return to the lines and the battle would begin.

Most people don't know that this is exactly what the prophets of the Bible were doing. The King (God, in this instance) sent his prophets ahead to warn sinners of the coming conquest. Did you ever notice that the prophets almost always confronted the kings of Israel? The heads of state? This was obviously a showdown of kings! The King of kings demanded the surrender of Israel's rebellious leaders who were leading the people into sin and wickedness. He threatened them, through his prophets, with destruction — in fact, his Heavenly hosts were on the way even as the prophet spoke, to deal God's enemies a mortal blow in combat. In other words, the message of the prophets wasn't a game or an idle threat: it was the Lord's challenge to his enemies. War was on its way.

> Listen, a noise on the mountains, like that of a great multitude! Listen, an uproar among the kingdoms, like

149

nations massing together! The LORD Almighty is mustering an army for war. (Isaiah 13:4)

I myself will fight against you with an outstretched hand and a mighty arm in anger and fury and great wrath. (Jeremiah 21:5)

The prophecies are full of warnings like these; we would have to be pretty dense to miss the point. God is declaring war against us rebels, and he is using the prophets to tell us what he intends to do to us if we do not lay down our arms against him. The prophet was given a vision of the Lord and his army – he saw the King assembling his hosts for battle in his spiritual Kingdom, and he saw them start out from Heaven to come to earth here to do battle. The prophet spoke of what he knew.

To God, our problem isn't just a matter of sin and death, destruction and misery, ignorance and materialism (although all that is bad enough!). Rather he sees us in this light: when we sin, *we are attacking him and his Kingdom*. We are a threat to the state, an enemy, someone who wants to replace him with another king more to our liking. We have a deep-seated resentment against the King:

The kings of the earth take their stand and the rulers gather together against the LORD and against his Anointed One. "Let us break their chains," they say, "and throw off their fetters." (Psalm 2:2-3)

We want to rule ourselves, or at least pick a king that we prefer more. So this is a direct insult against the glory of God the King. You may not have realized the true nature of sin — you may have thought that it was just a weakness of the flesh, an occasional lapse in self-discipline — nothing so serious as to warrant God's special attention. But you are wrong if you think this. Sin is *rebellion*: "Everyone who sins breaks the law; in fact, sin is lawlessness." (1 John 3:4)

Sin means to defy the King and his Law. And everyone knows what you have to do with a rebel and traitor: hang him! Governments usually do it with a lot of publicity, as a matter of fact, because of the serious nature of the crime. Rebellion tries to destroy the authority, the laws of the land, the peace of the citizens, and the values that the country holds precious. It is a political threat as well as a moral threat.

God considers sin in this light, and his response is to amass an army and come against us *in war*! Who would have thought that he would take our sin so seriously? But he does, and therefore the message of the prophets ought to scare the wits out of us. I don't know about you, but I would hate to be standing on the wrong side of the battlefield when the Almighty God himself comes to fight his enemies!

There is also a note of hope in this message that the prophet has been sent with. If you surrender *now*, the Lord will accept your surrender and draw you over on his side. He will change you, of course, because he can't let you continue in your rebellion in the middle of his ranks. But to think that he would willingly accept one of his former enemies and then make him part of the army of Christ is an amazing act of grace on the King's part! But you must act on this now. There was always a note of urgency in the prophet's offer. The King is coming soon; you don't want to be caught on the wrong side if he gets to the enemy camp and starts shooting soldiers wearing the enemy's colors! You must change sides now, with all your heart, and give yourself up to God. If you do that, you will find him to be a compassionate and gracious God, ready to make you his servant and (even more amazing!) a part of his family. If you don't surrender, your life is forfeit.

• *Prophecy: Upholding the Law*

If the Israelites would have taken Moses seriously – and the Law that God gave through him – things would have worked out wonderfully for them. Life was good when God took care of them, and when they obeyed God. In his Kingdom they had everything they needed to be happy and prosperous. All they had to do was stay close to him and follow his Law. After all, how could they go wrong when they had the Creator himself for their King?

But sinners are sinners, even when they know they could lose all the good things in life if they turn their backs on God. The Israelites often strayed away from the Law of God, playing around with the sins of their neighbors and being tempted to worship false gods.

What the Prophets did was to confront the Israelites with their commitment to the Lord. They had agreed under Moses to serve the Lord only, to worship him alone, and to obey all of his Law. Now they were rebels against that same Law. It's time to remember our roots and go back to that original agreement.

> Now fear the LORD and serve him with all faithfulness. Throw away the gods your forefathers worshipped beyond the River and in Egypt, and serve the LORD. But if serving the LORD seems undesirable to you, then choose for yourselves this day whom you will serve, whether the gods your forefathers served beyond the River, or the gods of the Amorites, in whose land you are living. But as for me and my household, we will serve the LORD. (Joshua 24:14-15)

> To the Law and to the testimony! If they do not speak according to this word, they have no light of dawn. (Isaiah 8:20)

> Yet they rebelled and grieved his Holy Spirit. So he turned and became their enemy and he himself fought against them. Then his people recalled the days of old, the days of Moses and his people – where is he who brought them through the sea, with the shepherd of his flock? Where is he who set his Holy Spirit among them, who sent his glorious arm of power to be at Moses' right hand. (Isaiah 63:10-12)

> Remember the Law of my servant Moses, the decrees and laws I gave him at Horeb for all Israel. (Malachi 4:4)

Moses had a special relationship with God, as we've already seen. Through him the Lord set up his Kingdom on earth.

God was the King of the Israelites, and naturally a king is going to have a government, a throne, laws to live by, defense against the enemy, and blessings for his people. In order to do this without any confusion, to such a complexity and careful detail, and do it in such a way that it would last for thousands of years – God needed to deal directly with Moses, face to face, not through visions and dreams. So we have this passage that describes how God spoke to Moses:

> Listen to my words: When a prophet of the LORD is among you, I reveal myself to him in visions, I speak to him in dreams. But this is not true of my servant Moses; he is faithful in all my house. With him I speak face to face, clearly and not in riddles; he sees the form of the LORD. (Numbers 12:6-8)

The point is that the system that God laid out through Moses was good enough for the Israelites no matter when or where they lived. The other prophets who followed Moses didn't need to add a thing to his system. All they were supposed to do was bring the people back to the Law of Moses; that was still their righteousness and glory, if they would only follow it. Of course life changes, cultures change, and even the Israelites changed over time. So we find the prophets interpreting the Law of Moses for their own day – applying the individual laws to particular cases. But at no point did they need to preach something new; indeed, they weren't supposed to stray from the same sermon outline, which is righteousness according to the Law.

In a way the Apostles of the New Testament play the same role as the Prophets of the Old. They too preach the Kingdom of Christ to the Church. They aren't supposed to come up with anything new either; they've been called to faithfully pass on the faith of the Gospel to each succeeding generation of Christians. Their role, too, is to bring the Church back to the spiritual Kingdom that Christ set up for us to prepare for and live in.

• **Prophecy: The Judge speaks**

Another reality that the Israelites were faced with in the ministry of the Prophets was that of the Judge. Through their words they heard the voice of God himself, and felt the heat of his white-hot examination of their souls. They couldn't escape the penetrating judgment of God – the Prophet seemed to put his finger right on the problem every time. Even kings squirmed under the scrutiny, their own consciences testifying to the truth of the Prophet's words.

A judge is an important person in a society. His job is to find out what's really going on in a situation. Consider a courtroom: the prosecuting attorney brings a charge against the accused, and the accused tries to defend himself against the charge through his attorney. Both bring in witnesses and evidence to try to prove their point. We need someone to listen to both sides and come to a decision in the matter. That's what a judge does – he weighs the evidence, listens to the testimony, and comes to a final judgment in the case. This, in his opinion, is what really happened. Once he passes his judgment, the court goes with that and either frees the innocent defendant or punishes the convicted felon.

Many people confuse the function of judging with issuing punishments. If being a judge was simply a matter of handing out punishments, then the policeman who first arrested the suspect could have looked up the crime in a book and handed out the punishment right on the spot. But our system doesn't work that way. The suspect has the right to defend himself against the charge in a court of law, and the government's job is to listen to his argument and make its own decision. The judge, therefore, represents the government and has the power of upholding the charge or dismissing it. Once he does his job of finding out what really happened, *then* someone can look up the crime in a book and issue an appropriate punishment. The hard part is making a correct judgment.

An important reason we need a judge is, at bottom, because people don't usually tell the truth about themselves, especially when accused of a crime. If you don't believe this, spend a day in court sometime. Most people plead "innocent" before a judge – you would think by this that the police are arresting a lot of innocent people! Someone who has committed a crime doesn't want to get punished, so he will most likely add to his crimes and lie about what he did. We need a judge who will study the situation and decide whether this person really is innocent. Then, once he has issued his judgment, we don't really care what the person claims about himself; the state has spoken, and that's all we need now.

God is the Judge of all the earth. He has penetrating insight into all people's hearts and minds, and into all situations.

> "Far be it from you to do such a thing – to kill the righteous with the wicked, treating the righteous and the wicked alike. Far be it from you! Will not the Judge of all the earth do right?" The LORD said, "If I find fifty righteous people in the city of Sodom, I will spare the whole place for their sake." (Genesis 18:25-26)

> For the word of God is living and active. Sharper than any double-edged sword, it penetrates even to dividing soul and spirit, joints and marrow; it judges the thoughts and attitudes of the heart. Nothing in all creation is hidden from God's sight Everything is uncovered and laid bare before the eyes of him to whom we must give account. (Hebrews 4:12-13)

> I saw Heaven standing open and there before me was a white horse, whose rider is called Faithful and True. With justice he judges and makes war. His eyes are like blazing fire, and on his head are many crowns. (Revelation 19:12)

When you read the Prophets, you soon learn that nothing escapes God's scrutiny. He knew their hearts so well that he even knew what they were thinking! He knew when they were bringing sacrifices to him out of duty instead from heart-felt devotion. He knew their secret sins – the gods they worshipped, the crimes they committed against each other, the lusts and passions that were unbecoming to the people of God.

God uses a terrifying standard to judge people by: his Law. We've seen already that the Law is very precise about spelling out what is right and wrong. We have no freedom to reinterpret the Law. When it says that a certain activity is righteousness, and another activity is sin, then that's exactly what God thinks about it and we're not going to change his mind – no matter what age or culture we live in! And the Law of God has many levels; we can't just keep the Law on a superficial physical level and satisfy its deep requirements. Jesus and Paul both proved to us, for example, that the Law is also very spiritual. We have an impossible job on our hands if we want to make the Law satisfied with our hearts and lives.

This is the standard that the Judge uses against us. As you can guess, God can make short work with all of us. We know down inside that God is absolutely right about us. Nobody else may know our secret sins, but God knows them and so do we. When he sends the prophet to confront us with our sin, all we can do is wither under his judgment. When David, for example, committed two sins that he probably thought he would get away with, God sent Nathan the prophet to him to expose his sin to public view:

> The LORD sent Nathan to David … Then Nathan said to David, "You are the man! This is what the LORD, the God of Israel, says: 'I anointed you king over Israel, and I delivered you from the hand of Saul …You did it in secret, but I will do this thing in broad daylight before all Israel.'" (2 Samuel 12:1,7,12)

And, perhaps from personal experience, David later said about the searching eyes of the Judge of all the earth –

> O LORD, you have searched me and you know me. You know when I sit and when I rise; you perceive my thoughts from afar. You discern my going out and my lying down; you are familiar with all my ways. Before a word is on my tongue you know it completely, O

LORD. You hem me in − behind and before; you have laid your hand upon me. Such knowledge is too wonderful for me, too lofty for me to attain. Where can I go from your Spirit? Where can I flee from your presence? If I go up to the Heavens, you are there; if I make my bed in the depths, you are there. If I rise on the wings of the dawn, if I settle on the far side of the sea, even there your hand will guide me, your right hand will hold me fast. If I say, "Surely the darkness will hide me and the light become night around me," even the darkness will not be dark to you; the night will shine like the day, for darkness is as light to you. (Psalm 139:1-12)

People lie so much about themselves, even in the face of the Law. How many times have you heard someone say that they think they're basically good (even if they've done a few things wrong in life) and they think that God will let them into Heaven on Judgment Day? Human memory is short; we tend to forget the bad times in life and remember the times that make us look good. God, however, is the perfect Judge. Unlike earthly judges who have to work hard at getting at the truth (at least we hope they will, though sometimes they get it wrong too), God knows the truth about us immediately. He doesn't even need our testimony, or the testimony of others − he's been keeping accurate records of our lives since the day we were born.

His eyes are on the ways of men; he sees their every step. There is no dark place, no deep shadow, where evildoers can hide. *God has no need to examine men further*, that they should come before him for judgment. Without inquiry he shatters the mighty and sets up others in their place. Because he takes note of their deeds, he overthrows them in the night and they are crushed. (Job 34:23)

The Israelites didn't get away with anything while their God had them under such a careful scrutiny. Consider the following passage. The elders thought they were doing their sins in secret, but God sees through walls and brings their sins to light so that others can see.

> Then he brought me to the entrance to the court. I looked, and I saw a hole in the wall. He said to me, "Son of man, now dig into the wall." So I dug into the wall and saw a doorway there. And he said to me, "Go in and see the wicked and detestable things they are doing here." So I went in and looked, and I saw portrayed all over the walls all kinds of crawling things and detestable animals and all the idols of the house of Israel. In front of them stood seventy elders of the house of Israel, and Jaazaniah son of Shaphan was standing among them. Each had a censer in his hand, and a fragrant cloud of incense was rising. He said to me, "Son of man, have you seen what the elders of the house of Israel are doing in the darkness, each at the shrine of his own idol? They say, 'The LORD does not see us; the LORD has forsaken the land.'" (Ezekiel 8:7-12)

God *has* to know everything we do and think; otherwise he couldn't judge the world according to justice. If he were as much in the dark about what's in our hearts as an earthly judge, Judgment Day would be a farce – the wicked would be able to get away with almost everything they've done. But there *will* be justice on that day. Everyone is going to know that the rewards that the righteous get, and the punishment that the wicked get, are fair and just. Everything about us and about our past will come out into the open for all to see, so that nobody will be able to accuse God of being unfair.

> There is nothing concealed that will not be disclosed, or hidden that will not be made known. What you have said in the dark will be heard in the daylight, and what you have whispered in the ear in the inner rooms will be proclaimed from the roofs. (Luke 12:2-3)

Which leads to one more point about the Judge that the Prophets showed us. Though the Israelites first came under the ministry of the Prophets, we need to understand that we too will come under this kind of scrutiny from God. On Judgment Day, he is going to look into our hearts with the same care for detail that we read in the Prophets. He's going to be upset with the same kinds of sins that he found in them, and he's looking for the same kind of righteousness that he called for in them. In other words, this is a preview of what to expect on Judgment Day when we stand before the throne of God to be judged.

• *Prophecy: The need for a spiritual Kingdom*

The Israelites were a special people in history. It was through them that God first worked out the details of his Kingdom on earth, among men. This means that whatever they learned about God is solid doctrine for the rest of us. The Church now has the information that we need to relate to this God, due to the lessons first learned in the Old Testament.

The problem was that the Israelites were sinners as we are. It would have been a nice system if it would have worked; but even though God made demands of them to be righteous, and to be perfect as he is perfect, they just didn't measure up. It's not that God was making the standard too high, it was that the people didn't want to submit to God's rule over them.

There was another problem inherent in the system that made it difficult to meet God's high standard of purity. The following passage says it best:

> The Law is only a shadow of the good things that are coming – not the realities themselves. For this reason it can never, by the same sacrifices repeated endlessly year after year, make perfect those who draw near to worship. If it could, would they not have stopped being offered? For the worshipers would have been cleansed once for all, and would no longer have felt guilty for their sins. But those sacrifices are an annual reminder of sins, because it is impossible for the blood of bulls and goats to take away sins. (Hebrews 10:1-4)

Just about everything in the Old Testament system was on a physical level. Animal blood just can't take away the sin in one's heart. In order to take advantage of the sacrifices, therefore, as well as the many other promises that God gave the Israelites, they needed to approach them *in faith*. They had to be able to see that these physical aspects of their religion – the land, the Temple, the sacrifices, the throne of David – were only shadows of the real treasures that God has in the future for his people. They were dealing with patterns, symbols, clay models, so to speak, which can (if one has the faith to see it) show us the truth of the real items in Heaven.

Without true faith, however, one tends to trust in the shadow and miss the whole point. For example, the Israelites forgot that the Temple sacrifices pointed to the eternal, spiritual sacrifice of Christ. They brought their sacrifices to the Temple, offered them in blood, and then went home and right back to their sins. That sacrifice was designed to *wash away* the sin, not allow them to continue wallowing in it! The sight of the death of the animal, and its shed blood for our sake, should shake us into a fear of this holy God who demanded this payment. So when the Israelites went right back into their sin after worshipping God, the time was ripe for change.

> For when I brought your forefathers out of Egypt and spoke to them, I did not just give them commands about burnt offerings and sacrifices, but I gave them this command: Obey me, and I will be your God and you will be my people. Walk in all the ways I command you, that it may go well with you. But they did not listen or pay attention; instead, they followed the stubborn inclinations of their evil hearts. They went backward and not forward. From the time your forefathers left Egypt until now, day after day, again and again I sent you my servants the prophets. But they did not listen to me or pay attention. They were stiff-necked and did more evil than their forefathers. (Jeremiah 7:22-26)

Again, it's not as if the system itself was to blame – anybody who followed the Lord with his whole heart would have prospered spiritually, even under the Law. But people don't usually follow what they can't see. They think that this spiritual God (wherever he may be) will be satisfied with an outward show of religion, while they go back to living as they please after the service. The result was predictable: if we don't walk in faith, we will walk in rebellion and sin. The Israelites were notoriously wicked by the time that the Lord had to punish them in the Exile.

Something had to give. God would send prophet after prophet to warn the people about their sin, and they would go on ignoring the prophets, live in their sin, worship false gods, yet continue to worship the Lord in the Temple. Things were going from bad to worse. The only way to fix the problem was to fix the heart. So the Prophets promised the coming of the day when God would change sinners hearts and make them follow his decrees:

> I will give you a new heart and put a new spirit in you; I will remove from you your heart of stone and give you a heart of flesh. And I will put my Spirit in you and *move* you to follow my decrees and be careful to keep my laws. (Ezekiel 36:26)

There would be a Messiah for God's people. He will change their hearts with his Spirit; he will cleanse their hearts in a way that animal blood couldn't. He would bring them into an eternal Promised Land where there would be no more sin, crying or pain. He will destroy their enemies (sin, the world, and the devil) once for all; he will sit on David's throne, and set up an eternal Kingdom. He will not only restore the high standards of God's Kingdom according to the Law of Moses, but he will also lift it up to a new spiritual level where nothing can corrupt it. In fact, the promises of the Covenant will reach a new height by bringing the people of God before the very presence of God, to enjoy his treasures from his own hand. This will be a new kind of world where things can't go wrong anymore.

This is a constant theme in the prophets because they were constantly dealing with the shortcomings of the old physical system. Though the Israelites *were* guilty of breaking the Law even in the Old Testament system, one can understand that, in a way, since the system had its shortcomings. So let's put this Kingdom on a level where it can't fail anymore.

This is also the point where the Gentiles come into the picture. During the Old Testament the Covenant was basically a Jewish matter. But the prophets all pointed to the day when God would expand the Covenant to include any who come to God through the Messiah. The Messiah – this Son of David and Son of God – is the solution for turning a physical system into a spiritual one. The Temple is now in Heaven, where all of God's people must worship. And now that Jesus has opened up the veil of the Holy of Holies, anybody who becomes one with Christ through faith in him can also enter into the Temple, into the presence of God, and serve him. Anyone. Now we see that the Jewish race of the Old Testament was, again, just a picture of the entire Church. For a time only the Jews were the receivers of God's grace, the chosen people of God; now anybody who has the faith of Abraham is one of the chosen race. So David's Kingdom will extend around the globe and include all races of men and women in the hands of Christ.

Jesus the Prophet

When we read the story of Jesus in the Gospels, we have to keep in mind his role as a Prophet. He did the same things that the Prophets of the Old Testament did with Israel.

Jesus is not going to be fooled by a superficial observance of the Law that the Pharisees were so good at. The Law has a spiritual depth; it is designed to reform the heart, not just our outward actions. This is where Jesus shows himself the Master even of the Law and its use.

> If you had known what these words mean, 'I desire mercy, not sacrifice,' you would not have condemned the innocent. For the Son of Man is Lord of the Sabbath. (Matthew 12:7-8)

Isaiah was right when he prophesied about you hypocrites; as it is written: 'These people honor me with their lips, but their hearts are far from me. They worship me in vain; their teachings are but rules taught by men.' You have let go of the commands of God and are holding on to the traditions of men. (Matthew 15:7-9)

And he said to them: "You have a fine way of setting aside the commands of God in order to observe your own traditions!" (Mark 7:6-9)

You have heard that it was said, 'Do not commit adultery.' But I tell you that anyone who looks at a woman lustfully has already committed adultery with her in his heart. (Matthew 5:27-28)

This is why nobody could confound him. It's also why he so easily targeted the hearts of his hearers – they knew he could see into their hearts.

They were unable to trap him in what he had said there in public. And astonished by his answer, they became silent. (Luke 20:26)

Woe to you, teachers of the Law and Pharisees, you hypocrites! You are like whitewashed tombs, which look beautiful on the outside but on the inside are full of dead men's bones and everything unclean. In the same way, on the outside you appear to people as righteous but on the inside you are full of hypocrisy and wickedness. (Matthew 23:27-28)

There was urgency in his message, because he knew what was coming next if they didn't accept his message.

You are from below; I am from above. You are of this world; I am not of this world. I told you that you would die in your sins; if you do not believe that I am the one I claim to be, you will indeed die in your sins. (John 8:24)

Jesus knew the real problem of the rich young ruler (Matthew 19:21); he knew what the Samaritan woman really needed (John 4:10); he knew what the Pharisees thought of him (Luke 7:39-40). Jesus could do this so easily that sometimes it makes us laugh to see him scatter his enemies with just a word – something that we could never do. A fascinating example of this was when the Pharisees brought him a woman caught in adultery. They thought they had him: if Jesus let her go, he would be violating the Law of Moses; if he condemned her, so much for his message of salvation! But his answer surprised them.

> They were using this question as a trap, in order to have a basis for accusing him. But Jesus bent down and started to write on the ground with his finger. When they kept on questioning him, he straightened up and said to them, "If any one of you is without sin, let him be the first to throw a stone at her." Again he stooped down and wrote on the ground. (John 8:6-8)

What was Jesus writing on the ground? We Gentiles would have missed the point; but these Pharisees knew their Scriptures. He was writing their names in the dust.

> O LORD, the hope of Israel, all who forsake you will be put to shame. Those who turn away from you will be written in the dust because they have forsaken the LORD, the spring of living water. (Jeremiah 17:13)

He was convicting every man there of being a sinner, of turning away spiritually from God, and hypocritically condemning this woman caught in her sin. They thought they were safe from exposure, hiding behind their outward legalism. They added to their sin by rejecting Jesus, the "spring of living water." And then Jesus looks straight at each man, writes his name in the dust, and forces him to walk away in shame over the state of his own heart.

You don't mess with a Prophet.

As you can imagine, a Prophet makes people very uncomfortable! There's no hiding anything from him. And since he gets his commission from God, he isn't going to tickle the ears of his hearers – he pleases God, not man. He's not going to change his message to make people feel good about themselves; he will faithfully discharge his duty even if it means alienating everyone around him.

Unfortunately that's often what happens. Many of the Prophets of Israel were rejected and persecuted, even put to death, by the Israelites because of their message. They were threatened, beaten, "sawed in two" – anything to shut them up. People don't like to be confronted with their sin and hypocrisy, especially when they know the Prophet is right about them.

Jesus had no misgivings about his own welcome among the Jews. He knew his message would not sit well with them.

> Woe to you, teachers of the Law and Pharisees, you hypocrites! You build tombs for the Prophets and decorate the graves of the righteous. And you say, 'If we had lived in the days of our forefathers, we would not have taken part with them in shedding the blood of the Prophets.' So you testify against yourselves that you are the descendants of those who murdered the Prophets. (Matthew 23:29-31)

> From this time many of his disciples turned back and no longer followed him. (John 6:66)

In other words, they may honor dead Prophets, but they aren't going to like live Prophets any more than their forefathers did. Jesus found resistance wherever he went.

> Then the Pharisees went out and began to plot with the Herodians how they might kill Jesus. (Mark 3:6)

Summary

Now go to the letters of the Apostles. Do we see the same themes of the Prophet there that we saw all through the rest of the Bible? The same careful examination of the heart; the same standard that God used in the Old Testament for righteous living (the Law); the authority of everything that the Apostles tell us (see 1 Thessalonians 2:13 for this). We find the same urgency of the message of salvation.

> With many other words he warned them; and he pleaded with them, "Save yourselves from this corrupt generation." (Acts 2:40)

God knows our hearts, and that becomes plain when we read the words of the Prophets and Jesus Christ and the Apostles – the messengers sent by God to confront us with our sin and bring us back to him.

> We also have the prophetic message as something completely reliable, and you will do well to pay attention to it, as to a light shining in a dark place, until the day dawns and the morning star rises in your hearts. Above all, you must understand that no prophecy of Scripture came about by the prophet's own interpretation of things. For prophecy never had its origin in the will of man, but men spoke from God as they were carried along by the Holy Spirit. (2 Peter 1:19-21)

The spirit of Prophecy is an important plank in the platform of Christ's Kingdom. It would be good if we got more familiar with the works of the Prophet as he lays bare our hearts before the God to whom we must give an account on Judgment Day.

> Worship God! For it is the Spirit of prophecy who bears testimony to Jesus. (Revelation 19:10)

THE MESSIAH [12]

The Old Testament described everything that Jesus came to do for us, but it used ordinary men to describe it. The idea was there, but it fell far short of the reality.

For example, Abraham was the heir of the Covenant; to him God gave the promises of the land, the nation, and the blessing. And he experienced a foretaste of each of these promises in his own lifetime: he acquired a deed to the field of Machpelah in Hebron to bury his wife Sarah (the land – Genesis 23); he found a wife for his son Isaac so that he could start his family (the nation – Genesis 24); and he received Isaac back from the death sentence that God pronounced over him (the blessing – Genesis 22). They were symbolic of the larger fulfillment that the Israelites would later inherit when they came back from Egypt and entered Canaan.

But even the Israelites didn't experience the full extent of these Covenant promises; this physical level was not what God had in mind in the long run. Canaan simply was not Heaven.

> These were all commended for their faith, yet none of them received what had been promised. God had planned something better for us so that only together with us would they be made perfect. (Hebrews 11:39-40)

God always did have the spiritual Kingdom in mind from the very beginning. When he taught these concepts to his people, he gave them the perfect concept first, then gave them the task of working it out the best way they could. The Law is a good example here. God's Law is perfection; it's the description of a Perfect Man, and a perfect nation under God. If everyone would have cooperated and obeyed this Law to the letter (the spirit of the Law – in other words, not just superficially but doing what God really wanted to see in their lives) there would never have been any trouble between God and the Israelites. It would have been a perfect Kingdom.

---

[12] This chapter is taken from the book *The Gospel of Christ*.

And if we are careful to obey all this law before the LORD our God, as he has commanded us, that will be our righteousness. (Deuteronomy 6:25)

But Israel's subsequent history shows that nobody kept this Law perfectly. As Hebrews tells us (Hebrews 8:8), their hearts were flawed: the Law was good, but they were not. At no point do we see any example of someone obeying this Law as God demands – even Moses fell short.

Since the themes of the Old Testament are necessary elements to God's Kingdom, the Israelites' failure to measure up to the spiritual demands of that Kingdom only means one thing: we still need someone to accomplish this great work. The Kingdom can't come to pass without it, and yet we can't do it.

The Spirit of God

The Holy Spirit is the third Person of the Godhead. In Hebrew and in Greek the word "spirit" can also be translated "wind." This refers to the invisible nature of the Spirit, and yet we can feel its influence on our lives as it moves through this world doing its work.

The Spirit of God was there in the beginning of the world.

In the beginning God created the heavens and the earth. Now the earth was formless and empty, darkness was over the surface of the deep, and the Spirit of God was hovering over the waters. (Genesis 1:1-2)

It has always been there, in the background, as God works in our world. It's the power behind all the works of God; and it makes known the presence and nature of God.

The Spirit has two functions.

- **First**, the Spirit *reveals* the world of God to us.

We have not received the spirit of the world but the Spirit who is from God, that we may understand what God has freely given us. This is what we speak, not in words taught us by human wisdom but in words taught

168

by the Spirit, expressing spiritual truths in spiritual words. (1 Corinthians 2:12-13)

Since God is not part of his Creation – he is "completely other" from us and not something that we could even know, let alone understand on our own – the Spirit makes God known to us. We need to know God; our obligations to him depend on accurate knowledge of him. So we find the Spirit revealing the Heavenly Temple to Moses so that he can build the earthly Tabernacle according to the same plan (Exodus 35:30, 34-35; 36:1; Hebrews 8:5). The Spirit told the Prophets what to say (1 Peter 1:21); the Spirit shows us the treasures of Heaven and what to pray for (Romans 8:26). There are many more examples in Scripture of the Spirit revealing the reality of God's world to his people.

▪ **Second**, the Spirit *empowers* us to live in, and take advantage of, that spiritual world of God. It's not enough to see it; we want to taste it, and have it change us into Christ's image.

But you will receive power when the Holy Spirit comes on you; and you will be my witnesses in Jerusalem, and in all Judea and Samaria, and to the ends of the earth. (Acts 1:8)

The Spirit enabled the bones in Ezekiel's vision to come alive (Ezekiel 37:1-14). The Spirit changes our hearts from stone to flesh – in other words, sensitive and alive to God (Ezekiel 36:26-27). The Spirit gives life; he brings us into God's presence so that we can experience his fullness (John 6:63). The Spirit gives joy to his people who enjoy the treasures of the Kingdom (Romans 14:17). Whenever someone needed to do the right thing, or reach out and take something from God's hand, the Spirit was the empowering force making it possible.

The Anointed One

In the Spirit we have the answer to the weakness and ignorance of man. The Old Testament saints tried to follow God, but they fell short of the ideal. Their hearts were still full of sin and rebellion; they focused on this world instead of God's world because that's all they could see; they failed to "bring about the righteous life that God requires" (James 1:20). Just knowing the data, as the Israelites so eloquently proved, is not enough. It has to be real to us. The Spirit, however, can lift man up to a higher level to achieve the impossible. It enables us to be perfectly righteous as the Law requires; it gives us the full spiritual fulfillment of the Covenant and enables us to enjoy them; it creates us into a new man, able to live with God in Heaven.

So the ideal Kingdom described in the Old Testament can now be created by means of the Spirit.

This means, of course, that the Jews should have known that their own efforts apart from the Spirit were not what God had in mind. Most Jews didn't understand this. They were perfectly content with the imperfections of their physical system; they simply ignored the imperfections (and the ignorance and sin that produced those imperfections) and figured that God wouldn't mind.

There were a few Israelites, however, who realized the painful truth that they fell far short of God's expectations. Their view of God wasn't so puerile; they knew he was aiming at a high ideal. And they knew that the Kingdom they lived in was not God's ideal. So from the very beginning they began putting their hopes in a special Person who, being filled with God's Spirit, would achieve what they couldn't achieve. And here is where we learn of the **Messiah**.

In Hebrew the word is מָשִׁיחַ – which means "anointed one." The anointing refers to the Spirit poured down on him from above. Kings and priests were anointed when they assumed their offices, as a symbol of the enlightening and empowering work of the Spirit that would (hopefully) be present in their ministry. Aaron was anointed as Priest; David was anointed as King. But the Spirit wasn't always present in the person who held the office, unfortunately; at best they were sinners whom God helped (anointed) with the power of Heaven to achieve important things in Israel's history. But none of them managed to bring the Kingdom to eternal perfection. Peter, for example, refers to this when he speaks of David. David knew the Lord would raise his "Holy One" from the dead:

Nor will you let your Holy One see decay. (Acts 2:27)

But obviously the prophecy of the Holy One couldn't be David, because he died and was *not* raised.

> Brothers, I can tell you confidently that the patriarch David died and was buried, and his tomb is here to this day. (Acts 2:29)

So we see in the Old Testament that we have crucial issues to solve concerning man's sin and God's Kingdom. But who is equal to the task of bringing it all about?

- *The New Creation* – The first Creation is broken, man has fallen into sin and death, and God is not being glorified in his works. We need a new Creation that will meet and exceed the design specifications of the first Creation – a perfect world, built solidly on a spiritual framework, that will never again fall short of God's purpose for it.

- *The Covenant* – The Promises of the Abrahamic Covenant are of such a nature that we need someone who is completely familiar with them, and is able to hand out the inheritance to all of God's children, whoever they might be, according to their faith.

- *The Kingdom* – David had the right plan, but he couldn't change people's hearts. We need a King who can make saints out of sinners, children of God who love God and follow his will and submit to his rule over them.

- *The Priest* – The Levitical priests oversaw a system of sacrifice and "cleansing" that was only a temporary measure. It forestalled the punishment of the Law; it didn't really take away the root problem of sin in man's heart. We still need a Priest who can answer the depth of the Law's condemnation against us, and cleanse our hearts and minds so thoroughly that we will never rebel against God again.

- *The Prophet* – The Prophets knew the hearts of their hearers but they couldn't get the people to accept their message. We need a Prophet who not only exposes our

171

sin and convicts us of falling short of the Law, but also will convince us of our desperate plight, rescue us from our sin, motivate us to seek God, and reconcile us to God.

- ■ **The Witness** – We have yet to see God in his purity and essence. This ignorance of God is putting us in a terrible position for many reasons. We need someone who can reveal the true God to us, teaching us everything we need to know about him, so that we will *see God* – and then the right things will happen to us. He needs to bring us into that light, and then we can live.

No one man in the Old Testament wore all these hats at the same time. Nobody could perfectly perform even the physical side of the entire program of God's Kingdom, let alone the spiritual side of it.

If someone would come who could do all these things – that is, perform what the concepts teach on a spiritual, permanent, eternal level – he would have to do it by the power of the Spirit. And that's what the saints of the Old Testament looked forward to: the Anointed One, the Messiah, who would bring their hopes to a perfect fulfillment.

The saints of the Old Testament were fully aware of their limitations; they looked forward to another who would accomplish what they couldn't do. Abraham knew about the coming Messiah; David knew about him; the Prophets looked forward to his coming. There is even a Messianic prophecy in the very beginning of the Bible, when the Lord prophesied doom to the kingdom of the devil.

And I will put enmity between you and the woman, and between your offspring and hers; he will crush your head, and you will strike his heel. (Genesis 3:15)

The point to remember here is that the Messiah will accomplish *the entire Old Testament system*. This was the Jews' hope, this is what they were lacking and desperately needed, this is what God promised them. When the Messiah would come, they would know him by his *works* – and the level of their perfection.

By the power of the Spirit

The anointing of the Holy Spirit on the Messiah was so important that every one of the Evangelists record the baptism of Jesus.

> As soon as Jesus was baptized, he went up out of the water. At that moment Heaven was opened, and he saw the Spirit of God descending like a dove and lighting on him. (Matthew 3:16)

> As Jesus was coming up out of the water, he saw Heaven being torn open and the Spirit descending on him like a dove. (Mark 1:10)

> And as he was praying, Heaven was opened and the Holy Spirit descended on him in bodily form like a dove. (Luke 3:21-22)

> Then John gave this testimony: "I saw the Spirit come down from Heaven as a dove and remain on him." (John 1:32)

John baptized Jesus with water, but the Father baptized him with the Holy Spirit – specifically to enable him to build the eternal Kingdom of God. And when Jesus was baptized, the Father's voice could be heard: "This is my Son, whom I love; listen to him!" It was God's confirmation that, finally, someone had arrived with the qualifications to do the job to God's satisfaction – the Christ.[13]

From this point on Jesus did amazing miracles, enlightened God's people, drove away the enemy, set up his government, laid the foundation for a future Temple, brought the people face to face with their God, made holy the children of God, and handed out Covenant treasures to Abraham's true heirs. As it was said of his father David, so it was true of Jesus: "The LORD gave David victory wherever he went." (2 Samuel 8:14)

And while Jesus demonstrated his absolute power and authority and wisdom over the physical realm, he was laying the foundations for the spiritual Kingdom that would begin in earnest in the book of Acts, with

---

[13] "Christ" (Χριστος) is the Greek form of the Hebrew word "Messiah" – they both mean "the anointed one."

the Church. There he poured out his Spirit on his disciples, enabling them to know God as he knows him, and do spiritual work that would build an eternal Temple.

Not Law, but Spirit

Probably the most profound aspect of this Spirit-powered ministry of Christ is the success that he had, compared to the Law-driven Kingdom of the Israelites of the Old Testament.

The Law of Moses laid the burden of obedience on the Israelites. But every law has an inherent shortcoming: it can't touch the heart. It remains on the outside, and can only make threats against lawbreakers. Try as they might, the Israelites weren't able to keep the Law. It's not that the Law was beyond their reach, because actually it's a very reasonable approach to a peaceful and just Kingdom. The problem was that they didn't want to obey it. Their lusts, their ignorance, their apathy, their lack of faith and trust in God, all conspired to make it a failure in the end. Their hearts remained untouched by the Law.

So, the Prophets looked forward to the day when the Messiah would come and do what the Law couldn't do.

> I will sprinkle clean water on you, and you will be clean; I will cleanse you from all your impurities and from all your idols. I will give you a new heart and put a new spirit in you; I will remove from you your heart of stone and give you a heart of flesh. And I will put my Spirit in you and move you to follow my decrees and be careful to keep my laws. (Ezekiel 36:25-27)

The Spirit is the key. It changes the heart first; it doesn't demand righteousness from a sinner as the Law is forced to do. The Spirit creates a person into a child of God, who loves and obeys his Father perfectly.

Paul knew the power of the Spirit over the limitations of the Law; he understood that here is the real solution to the Kingdom of God.

> For what the Law was powerless to do in that it was weakened by the sinful nature, God did by sending his own Son in the likeness of sinful man to be a sin offering. And so

he condemned sin in sinful man, in order that the righteous requirements of the Law might be fully met in us, who do not live according to the sinful nature but according to the Spirit. (Romans 8:3-4)

So the ministry of Christ, through the anointing of the Spirit, brought light and power to what he was doing. Here we see who he is, what he is doing, and where he is going. And the Spirit works on us as well, enlightening and empowering us to enter into his new Kingdom. Jesus was lifting up the Jewish system to a spiritual level.

Section Two: Books

GENESIS: THE BOOK OF THE COVENANT

I once listened to a preacher work through the book of Genesis, and it was a series of moralisms. The church claimed to be God-centered; and the preacher claimed that he didn't preach moralisms, but he did. It was "Judah did a bad thing here, we mustn't be like Judah," and "Joseph did the right thing here, we must be like Joseph." It was dreary. I took the opportunity while he was preaching to explore the book on my own and see what God was really saying.

I already knew that the Covenant with Abraham ruled the entire book. What I still needed was how everyone else in Genesis fit into the Covenant story. What I found was that there are different aspects to the Covenant that are broken out across several characters; we learn about each aspect in a certain person's life, and then put the whole thing together to see how the Covenant works in Christ – who "wears all the hats," so to speak, that the individuals wore in Genesis. What surprised me was the role that Joseph played.

The Covenant with Abraham

These are the four points of the Covenant that God made with Abraham.

- **A Son** – God would give him an heir to inherit not only his property but the Covenant as well. He is the Executor of the estate.

- **The Land** – Someday the Lord would give the land of Canaan to Abraham's descendants.

- **A Nation** – God promised to make Abraham's descendants into a great nation.

179

- **A Blessing** – God told Abraham that he and his descendants would become a blessing to the nations.

There are two things we have to keep in mind about this Covenant:

First, it was made to Abraham and his descendants. Don't miss the significance of the order – God gave these promises to Abraham, and through him to his descendants. It's because of their relationship to Abraham that the rest would receive the promises. Nobody outside of the family gets anything. God doesn't give the treasures of Heaven to anybody apart from that relationship, which means proving the relationship is crucial. Even Christians, as Paul tells us, have to prove their descent from Abraham; we are his children by faith.

Second, we now have a theme at work in the book of Genesis that powers the rest of the book. Each of Abraham's descendants will receive this Covenant. But each one will show a different aspect, like a facet to a diamond, of how the Covenant works. Abraham may be the foundation, but the others will show us other data in the Covenant that we need to know.

There's a practical side to that principle. God chose to teach his truths to the Israelites through history and events and people's lives. When teaching complex ideas to a people who are spiritually immature, it's best to slow it down and use pictures and walk through it step by step. Rather than make this thing too difficult up front, therefore, God split the lesson across several generations so that he could teach each aspect of the Covenant separately. That's the key to interpreting the book of Genesis: it's all about the Covenant, in separate lessons, and we have to look at each in turn and then put the whole thing together for a complete picture. That, in fact, is why God is called "the God of Abraham, Isaac and Jacob." (Exodus 3:6; Matthew 22:32)

So if Abraham is the *source* of the Covenant blessings, we are going to see that at work in Abraham's life. A prime example of this principle at work is the story of Lot. I'm afraid most modern preachers castigate Lot for being a scoundrel for just about everything that he did; what they're deliberately ignoring, however, is Peter's comment about him.

> If he rescued Lot, a *righteous* man, who was distressed by the depraved conduct of the lawless (for that *righteous* man, living among them day after day, was tormented in his *righteous* soul by the lawless deeds he saw and heard) — if this is so, then the Lord knows how to rescue the *godly* from trials and to hold the unrighteous for punishment on the day of judgment. (2 Peter 2:7-9)

Nobody else in Scripture gets such a glowing report as Lot does here! Three times in the same passage he's called a righteous man. Evidently Peter sees something that most of us do not see. It turns out that there are two ways to read the account of Lot; and those who blame Lot for doing everything wrong are reading it the wrong way.

Lot was captured by the local kings in the area of the Dead Sea and carried off as part of the plunder.[14] Abraham was informed of his nephew's predicament and went off to rescue him. They caught up with the marauders, defeated them, and brought Lot and his family safely back home.

Now don't miss the significance of the events: who was it that rescued Lot? Abraham – the *source* of the Covenant blessings. If you're related to Abraham, the Lord is going to take care of you too. The point of the story of Lot is to show us that some of us can get out on the edge of life where we think we have no help, and yet the Lord will still come through if we are part of the family. He is faithful to his Covenant.

The other incident about Lot was when the Lord decided to destroy Sodom for its wickedness. God sent three angels to

---

[14] For those who blame Lot for living in Sodom among sinners – as soon as you move out of the town you're living in then you can blame Lot! It was no sin that he lived among sinners; it's one of the burdens that all believers put up with in this world. Lot gave ample evidence of his opinion of the immorality that surrounded him, which is what prompted Peter to say what he did about him. You miss the point of the story if you focus on the wrong idea; the rescue is the thing.

discuss the matter with Abraham first. Notice what Abraham does right away: he intercedes for the righteous who are living in Sodom. Now who do you think he had in mind? His nephew Lot and his family! Remember Peter's assessment: Lot was a *righteous, righteous, righteous* man. Abraham knew his nephew, and he prays for his nephew's safety. That again is the Covenant at work, protecting the family of Abraham. It turned out that the Lord did rescue Lot by removing him from danger before the destruction of the city. [15]

There are other incidents in Abraham's life that many people wrongly interpret; they are missing the huge reality of the Covenant and focusing on details that we moderns (in our chronological snobbery!) stumble over. For example, twice he found himself in a dangerous situation concerning his wife. Because he was a wanderer and alien wherever he went, his life was an open book to the locals and of course undesirable things often happen to strangers. When the town ruler (or in Egypt, Pharaoh himself) decides he likes the looks of the women in your entourage, and there are a thousand spears pointing at your throat with no escape, then of course you're going to do what you can to protect yourself first.

Keep in mind, however, that Abraham is learning about his God. Modern interpreters roundly blame Abraham for letting the rulers carry off his wife Sarah under the ruse that she was his sister (which *was* true, she was a half-sister). But people should be more charitable toward a man in such dangerous situations and wait for the story to unfold. It turned out both times that the God of the Covenant came through and rescued both Sarah and Abraham from disaster, dealt their enemies a crushing blow as punishment for touching his people, and put Abraham on a more secure footing with the local inhabitants (2 Peter again!). People were learning not to touch God's Covenant people.

What I'm concerned about is that modern interpreters aren't keeping the main point in mind when they read Genesis. They get sidetracked by issues that, to our modern mind, are out of

---

[15] For an extended study of the story of Lot, see "Lot: A Vindication of a Righteous Man" in **Knots Untied**.

sync with our ways of doing things, and they lose sight of what God is doing. That's so typical of moralists.

Isaac – the Heir

Isaac actually doesn't have that big a part in the Genesis story. Aside from his father Abraham getting him a wife, and the story of blessing his two sons, there isn't much to tell.

But his significance is in how he got into the story in the first place. When God promised Abraham and Sarah that they would have a son, she laughed out loud about it – she knew very well that she was too old to have a baby. A woman of ninety years is long past age. But God heard her laugh, and told her that he would have the last laugh – in a year's time she delivered her son Isaac (a Hebrew name meaning "he laughs").

The point here is that this birth was a miracle, an impossible event. Isaac was a "miracle baby." No doubt the story was told over and over whenever he walked through the camp – the son out of nowhere, the son of Promise, the son born by a miracle.

In fact, every part of the Covenant was a miracle; Isaac was the first of four miracles that God did for Abraham. But it was the most startling of the four, and it showed Abraham that he was dealing with Someone who would move Heaven and earth to keep his promises.

Though Isaac was Abraham's immediate heir, the great Heir of the Covenant (Paul tells us) is actually Jesus, which Abraham himself knew.

> The promises were spoken to Abraham and to his seed. Scripture does not say "and to seeds," meaning many people, but "and to your seed," meaning one person, who is Christ. (Galatians 3:16)

> Your father Abraham rejoiced at the thought of seeing my day; he saw it and was glad. (John 8:56)

Everyone knows the circumstances of Jesus' birth – he was another "miracle baby." Only a miracle of God could bring about the birth of the Son of God into human flesh; only a miracle can bring Heaven and earth together into one Man who can solve the problems of sin and death. No ordinary human can do this kind of work. No sinner can be the great Heir that the rest of God's people need to get in touch with the Covenant blessings in Heaven. So the miracle was necessary, just as much so as Isaac's birth to Sarah.

And the principle extends even further – all the heirs of Abraham are going to be "miracle babies" as our hearts are changed from stone to flesh, we are filled with the Spirit of Christ the Son, we are cleansed from our sins permanently, and we take on the likeness of the Son in his resurrection body so that we can live with God in Heaven forever. All this *requires* a miracle on God's part; it can't be done by human means. The principle was laid down at the beginning with Isaac. All the heirs must be "born again" by the Spirit.

Jacob – the richness of the Covenant

Jacob was undoubtedly a rascal. His birth gave pause to his parents – his brother Esau was born first, and Jacob came out next grasping his brother's heel. In Hebrew the name "Jacob" means two things – "he grasps the heel," or "he deceives." An inauspicious beginning.

Jacob was not the outdoorsman that his brother Esau became; he preferred living in camp with the easier life. At one point he took advantage of his brother and made him swear to give him his birthright for a bowl of soup. Later, when it came time to get their blessing from their father Isaac, Jacob took advantage of the fact that his father was nearly blind and put himself in the place of his older brother to get the older brother's blessing. Esau ended up with nothing.

Now the story changes. While trying to escape the wrath of his brother, Jacob runs into the God of his fathers. In a dream he sees a ladder between Heaven and earth and angels going up and down the ladder. God speaks to him there at Bethel in the dream.

184

> I am the LORD, the God of your father Abraham and the God of Isaac. I will give you and your descendants the land on which you are lying. Your descendants will be like the dust of the earth, and you will spread out to the west and to the east, to the north and to the south. All peoples on earth will be blessed through you and your offspring. I am with you and will watch over you wherever you go, and I will bring you back to this land. I will not leave you until I have done what I have promised you. (Genesis 28:13-15)

I don't know why people don't understand the significance of this passage. Jacob woke up a different man. This is where I put the conversion of Jacob. From now on he isn't going to get ahead in life by deceiving others; God himself is going to bless him. He goes to his uncle Laban's camp and ends up with two wives, who give him twelve sons and a daughter (wealth indeed in a time when family was wealth). He gets rich there not by deceiving his uncle, but by a series of miracles that God himself does to thwart Laban. Everywhere Jacob goes, he gets richly blessed in spite of himself! All he does is follow his God.

And when he decides to leave the camp, his wife grabs the family gods (no, this is not a point for modern students to stumble over – it's a political act, not a religious act) and now becomes the family patriarch. He meets his brother Esau who forgets their quarrel, and settles down in Canaan a rich man.

The point to see about Jacob is that God *richly* blesses his people, in spite of what they are or what they've done. We are given treasures "pressed down, shaken together and running over" by God who owns all things – the Covenant is the fullness of God that we inherit in Christ. We do not get the Covenant blessings because we deserve them; far from it. We get them in spite of the fact that we don't deserve them. But there's no holding back – God gives without measure, forgetting the past, as if nothing had happened. Conversion brings a rich new life with God as we follow him.

Joseph – the Designated Heir

What confused me at first about Joseph was that he wasn't one of the three big names in the Covenant. Or at least it didn't appear to me at first that he was. By the time the story gets to Joseph, there are eleven brothers, and they are *all* heirs of the Covenant. So why was Joseph so important in the book of Genesis?

The key is to see the principle that the elements of the Covenant system are spread out over several men in Genesis. We don't see all the elements in any single person. Joseph was only one of the sons of Jacob, but his story of getting singled out is significant to the idea of the Covenant.

The story of Joseph shares a significant place with those of his forefathers Abraham, Isaac and Jacob. Obviously something here is critical for us to understand. God gave Joseph dreams about his future, which he shared with his father and brothers: someday they would all bow down to him. That naturally offended his brothers, because they thought (being near the youngest of the family at the time) that was a pretty arrogant thing to say. They had no intention of bowing down to him. Even his father was offended at the idea. But it turned out that this is exactly what they had to do. As Joseph's life unfolds – being sold as a slave, in prison in Egypt, being freed and becoming Pharaoh's right-hand man, and saving the whole area from a severe famine – it becomes clear how God used this man to deliver his family from disaster. Every one of them was forced to come to Joseph and bow down to him and ask for his help, even his father.

> *You must come to the designated Heir if you want the*
> *Covenant blessings – otherwise you will die!*

Nobody thought that Joseph was the designated Heir of the Covenant; but God chose him to be just that. *Everyone* was required to submit to that idea and come to him; they faced death if they didn't. The story even gets complicated as Joseph forces every one of them to see this absolute necessity; one gets the feeling that it's God himself who is teaching them all a lesson.

All of them had to come to Egypt and get what they needed from Joseph.

The lesson should be plain to all of us.

> I am the way and the truth and the life. No one comes to the Father except through me. (John 14:6)

> Salvation is found in no one else, for there is no other name under Heaven given to mankind by which we must be saved. (Acts 4:12)

So the story of Joseph gives us a necessary element to the Covenant: we must *submit* to the designated Heir and his rule over us if we want to receive anything from God. God has given him the treasures of Heaven, and only he can give them to us. The blessings of the Covenant go to only those who bow down to the Heir of the Covenant. We do not receive anything from God on our own account, nor will we get it from anybody else – only from the designated Heir.

Summary

It's a shame that so many preachers and teachers turn one of the greatest explanations of the work of Christ into a series of moralisms. Of course there were sins committed along the way; we are all sinners – that shouldn't surprise us. They were doing what we would have done. And there were faithful servants of God who did what he told them to do, as we all should. But the book is laying out the Covenant before us, with all of its saving aspects – and that's what all these sinners and saints were dealing with. Genesis is the story of the Covenant God putting together his great system of salvation for Abraham's entire family.

LEVITICUS: LIVING WITH GOD

Leviticus is one of the most problematic books of the Bible. I picked up a commentary once by a scholar who began by apologizing to his readers. It seems that he really didn't know what he could say about the book that would be useful for Christians; but since he was given this task by the general editor of the series, he would do his best and come up with something interesting. I think that's shameful.

Since the book deals with the laws concerning the priesthood, special sacrifices, and purity laws, Christians don't exactly know what to do with it. We know that Jesus took care of these laws for us, so we don't have to now. But does that mean we can ignore Leviticus? Even if we wanted to, we would have a hard time trying to follow some of the laws in Leviticus – especially the "cleanness" laws like dealing with mildew and touching unclean animals. And because there is no Temple now, we certainly can't do anything with the laws specifying particular sacrifices that had to be presented in the Temple, by authorized priests. So do we just dump the entire book?

The way to understand the message of Leviticus is to come at it with faith. Faith will see the bigger picture, something that the Jews usually didn't see. They were satisfied with following the ceremonies and procedures; they simply obeyed the letter of the Law, and they thought that this is all that the Lord was after. We, however, since we can't follow those procedures, are forced to look at it in the light of the entire Bible – and by doing that we will see deeper realities in it. What we will discover is that the Lord was trying to tell the Israelites something by using the physical ceremonies as an object lesson – it shows us how his spiritual world works.

In Exodus the Israelites were taught about the meeting place between themselves and God – the Tabernacle. Here in Leviticus they learned that God expected to be the center of their entire lives. From now on they would be the people of God, and he would be their King and source of all good things in life.

The ceremonies of the Tabernacle were intended to show just how much God was going to be involved in their lives, and they in his. Here they would find forgiveness and cleansing from their sins. Here they would hear the words of God, and receive his blessings through the priests. Here they would spend their free time in festivals and feasts, before the throne of God. Here they would get guidance in all aspects of life – family, nation, business, politics, education, war.

The significance of this lesson is that, up until now, the Israelites had been slaves and not a nation. They pretty much were on their own while living in Egypt. And if God had simply freed them from slavery and sent them on their way to the Promised Land by themselves, we still wouldn't have been able to call them the "people of God." Instead, God sets up his house right in the middle of the people and announces his intention to live there, with them, forever. He is now forever part of their lives. And they, if they don't know it yet, will come to realize the blessing and richness that God is pouring into their laps with this amazing arrangement – he will give them what other nations can only hope for.

But this special relationship with a God living among them has its responsibilities. They learn that God is unutterably holy; one doesn't come before this God with sin in his heart. So the Law shows them how to cleanse themselves in order to prepare for coming before Yahweh. It also teaches them the necessary ceremonies for approaching him. Since he is the Creator, the majestic King over all, and since he expects his subjects to honor him in his presence, the Israelites have a lot to learn. The outcome of this, however, is that they will literally become the one people on earth who know how, and have the right, to deal with the only God. Other nations will have to learn from *them* about what the true God is like, and will have to come to *them* if they want something from God.

We can say this in New Testament terms: the Israelites are learning to have fellowship with God. This is what John meant when he wrote –

> We proclaim to you what we have seen and heard, so that you also may *have fellowship* with us. And our fellowship is with the Father and with his Son, Jesus Christ. (1 John 1:3)

The astonishing thing about this arrangement is the closeness between God and man. It's *family*; he draws us to himself (through a complex system of cleansing and preparation first, to be sure!) and now we're living together. From this point on the Israelites will get everything they need in life from God, and he will direct every detail of their lives.

If we Christians don't have to observe the actual ceremonies now when we come to God – we rely on Jesus to keep them for us – the point is still the same: God intends to live with his people, to richly bless them, to draw them to himself so that they can commune with him and find all that they need in him. And the ceremonies and cleansings must be done, which is why we trust in Jesus. *That's* the lesson of Leviticus for the entire church.

• *Approaching God*

According to the laws in Leviticus, there are very strict rules about how one should approach God. There are several reasons for this:

First, God is holy and expects us to show him honor in this. Isaiah was struck with the holiness of God when he saw him in his Temple in Heaven. If God is this pure, this righteous, this full of glory and majesty, then the only conclusion we can come to is that holiness is the most important thing to God. We may not have been so interested in it up until now, but if we wish to have any dealings at all with this God then it's time to make holiness a priority in our lives.

Second, Heaven is a world in itself with its peculiarities and characteristics. Now that Heaven has come down to earth in the Tabernacle, the Israelites have to learn how to live in this spiritual world. They have to learn the rules of etiquette, so to speak – how to approach the King, how to present their requests to him, what kinds of things to expect from him, what his priorities are, the changes he intends to make to our world, and so on. If someone just blundered into God's presence without knowing the rules or how the game is played, he would look like a fool in front of the angels – who always stand before God's throne to serve him. He also won't get what he wants when he shows such disrespect for the King.

Third, the right of approaching God is a high privilege. Not everyone can claim the right to come close to him. We moderns are so used to seeing even our rulers in a democratic light that we little appreciate how much higher God is than we are, and that we have no right to his throne unless he extends his scepter and honors us with the command to approach him. The priesthood symbolized the high honor and privilege of certain individuals being allowed to serve God.

In other words, God wants to richly bless his people – he wouldn't have given them the opportunity of approaching him if he didn't! But if we want answers to our prayers, we first must learn how to approach God. He won't give anything to a person who won't honor him and respect his glory by first learning the rules of coming to the King.

• *The need for purification*

Leviticus also lays out complex rules for purifying ourselves. It doesn't tell us why in complete detail, but we get that information from other places in the Bible. We are sinners, through and through – God pronounced his judgment over us at the Flood when he looked down on mankind and "saw how great man's wickedness on the earth had become, and that every inclination of the thoughts of his heart was only evil all the time." (Genesis 6:5) And because God is so extremely holy, there is no way we will be allowed into his presence until we clean up our act.

The laws of purification that are spelled out in this book cover both the common Israelite and the priest. Both the one who came close to God, and the one who offered sacrifices to God through the priest, must be made holy and clean before God would accept them. Review the laws, and you will see the depth of the need for cleansing in God's opinion. Things that we wouldn't have thought would make any difference to God were an offense to him. The laws cover personal hygiene, personal relationships, the houses we live in, family practices and marriages, justice in court, business practices – every aspect of our lives. God is telling us two things here:

First, that he expects us to please him in every detail of our lives, not just our religious activities during worship services. Sanctification here means a total dedication of our lives to God.

Second, he sees sin in every aspect of our lives too! If we foolishly declare that we are without sin, he doesn't have to work very hard to prove us liars. It's easy for us to sin, because sin can crop up in any part of our lives.

Not until we purify ourselves will our worship be acceptable to him. He will not relax on that requirement; our worship, when done with sin in our hearts, is an offense to him, even if it's done according to the requirements. He is setting down a principle here that we will see all through the Old and New Testaments – true worship is not only what we do on the physical level, but it's also a complete dedication to God in our hearts and total lifestyle.

My sacrifice, O God, is a broken spirit; a broken and contrite heart, O God, you will not despise. (Psalm 51:17)

• *Sin does not become us*

We don't really know how much the Israelites knew about God when they were living in slavery in Egypt. We do know, however, that they were well-trained in wickedness. See how easily they fell into sin at Mt. Sinai, while Moses was up on the mountain getting the Law. They kept going back to their ways of unbelief and sin all through the journey to the Promised Land. We can assume, therefore, that sin was a deep-seated stain on their souls.

But in the Law we learn what God thinks of sin. It's just not acceptable behavior for God's people. The time has come, he says here, for us to stop sinning. Period.

The Law really threatens disaster for sinners. The message is clear and unmistakable – the Lord expects us to stop our sin and turn to him and be saved. He expects righteousness, not weakness or even excuses. He expects total and complete holiness, not a spotty track record in which we claim we tried but didn't quite make it.

Notice what the penalty for sin is: blood and death. It's a mercy that he didn't require the death of the Israelites; they could offer animal sacrifices for their sins instead of having to suffer execution themselves. But the picture of animals being put to death for their sins was just too graphic to miss. God will not tolerate sin, and the sinner must die – or an acceptable substitute. Sin, to God, is treason against the state and must be answered with severe penalties.

But even if God allows the Israelites to provide a substitute for their own deaths under the penalty of the Law, he still expects them to learn the lesson and stop sinning. Only an ignorant and wicked man would lightly kill a sacrifice for his sin and then go back into his sin, as if it's just an empty ceremony. The lesson is that through the sacrifice we have escaped destruction! Let's not go back to the very thing that got us into this predicament. As Peter says –

> If they have escaped the corruption of the world by knowing our Lord and Savior Jesus Christ and are again entangled in it and overcome, they are worse off at the end than they were at the beginning. It would have been better for them not to have known the way of righteousness, than to have known it and then to turn their backs on the sacred command that was passed on to them. Of them the proverbs are true: "A dog returns to its vomit," and, "A sow that is washed goes back to her wallowing in the mud." (2 Peter 2:20-22)

The Law, therefore, gets right down into the lives of the people and carefully examines every possibility for offending God. It shows no mercy; it misses no detail; it ignores all excuses. If their lives are at stake, the Law can't afford to give an inch – it must carefully describe what a perfect man will look like to God.

- ### *Fellowship with God*

One of the surprising lessons of Leviticus – one that isn't stated in so many words but is there between the lines of the entire book – is that *God wants to live with his people.* He is coming to earth to set his throne among the Israelites. No other nation on earth had been so honored up to this time.

Living with God means living with the **Creator**. He made everything, and he keeps everything alive and moving. He provides for the daily needs of all his creatures (see Psalm 145). So if the Israelites are in need of anything – and who could set a limit on what God can do? – all they have to do is come to the God who lives in their midst and ask him.

Living with God means living with pure **righteousness**. Sin is the terrible and destructive force on earth that makes life so miserable and, in the end, brings death. Wouldn't everyone on earth love to be able to solve this problem of sin and death! Now the Israelites have that opportunity. They can – and are even commanded to – come to the Redeemer who knows how to fix the problem. He can not only cleanse us of sin, but he can undo the damage that sin has done to us in the past and "repay you for the years the locusts have eaten." (Joel 2:25)

Living with God also means that you are living with the **King**. The King rules all; the entire universe is under his hand, and he makes the decisions for mankind that are worked out in history. But the Israelites found themselves called up to the highest place in the universe – they were God's representatives on earth. Even the angels aren't allowed into the secret counsels of God that the Lord will share with his people! They are his children, and therefore heirs of the treasures of Heaven. They are given the wisdom of God, which means they will understand the importance of God's glory, they will know how to target the important problems of life, and how to build up his Kingdom on earth.

David knew the bliss of living with God. In his own writings he longed to be close to God in God's house; here is Psalm 84:

> How lovely is your dwelling place, O LORD Almighty! My soul yearns, even faints, for the courts of the LORD; my heart and my flesh cry out for the living God. Even the sparrow has found a home, and the swallow a nest for herself, where she may have her young – a place near your altar, O LORD Almighty, my King and my God. Blessed are those who dwell in your house; they are ever praising you. Blessed are those whose strength is in you, who have set their hearts on pilgrimage. As they pass through the Valley of Baca, they make it a place of springs; the autumn rains also cover it with pools. They go from strength to strength, till each appears before God in Zion. Hear my prayer, O LORD God Almighty; listen to me, O God of Jacob. Look upon our shield, O God; look with favor on your anointed one. Better is one day in your courts than a thousand elsewhere; I would rather be a doorkeeper in the house of my God than dwell in the tents of the wicked. For the LORD God is a sun and shield; the LORD bestows favor and honor; no good thing does he withhold from those whose walk is blameless. O LORD Almighty, blessed is the man who trusts in you.

You can tell by this that David found tremendous comfort and strength in being close to God. To him, the Temple wasn't a religious chore to carry out but a spiritual bonus.

Working with Leviticus

Leviticus is probably one of the most difficult books in the Bible to work with. Its laws can be bewildering and confusing; what in the world is a Christian supposed to do with all this?

But there is a way to get to the heart of Leviticus – as long as we follow a few simple principles:

First, there are obvious parallels between the legal system in Leviticus and the New Testament realities. We know this because the New Testament itself draws those parallels for us. Those writers who despise drawing parallels between the articles in the Tabernacle and the work of Christ evidently haven't yet mastered, for example, the book of Hebrews! We are told there that –

They serve at a sanctuary *that is a copy and shadow of what is in Heaven*. This is why Moses was warned when he was about to build the tabernacle: "See to it that you make everything according to the *pattern* shown you on the mountain." (Hebrews 8:5)

But we also have to be careful about seeing shadows in things that are fanciful. There are teachers who make up "spiritual realities" that supposedly explain every article in the Tabernacle. Where the Bible explains it to us, we can safely trust in it; but where the Bible leaves it a mystery, the safest thing to do is leave it until we get God's explanation.

Second, Leviticus teaches us some fundamental doctrines of our faith. They aren't hard to see. For example, we learn about the sin of man and the fact that it's so offensive to God. These blood sacrifices are proof that God is very angry over sin – why else would he demand the death of a victim over it? Also, we learn about the holiness of God and his house, the necessity of absolute purity in anybody who approaches God, the kinds of sacrifice needed to atone for sin, the priesthood

196

and how they relate to both God and man, and the high standards for everyday living that God sets for his people. If we learned nothing else from Leviticus, these subjects would keep us busy. They also should give us a healthy fear of God (which is the beginning of wisdom) and the motivation to please God in all things.

Third, the descriptions of the Tabernacle and the sacrificial system here in Leviticus (and in the other books of Moses) are symbols, or shadows, of the real Temple in Heaven. There is a Temple in Heaven – God lives there, and there is where his subjects approach him if they want to relate to him. Heaven is the real destination for all of God's people; it's been the plan that the Church would live with God forever in Heaven since the world was made. But (as we learn here in Leviticus) we must relate to this God in a certain way. We can't just run up to him and do and say as we like! We have to learn the house rules, and show the kind of respect that he deserves in all of our dealings with him. That's what the Temple in Heaven represents – it's the meeting place where we will relate to God. Leviticus is simply a preview of what it will be like there in Heaven.

Fourth, these laws were absolutely rigid – the Israelites were under penalty of law to follow them to the letter. This means that, to God, they are *very* important – even if we don't know exactly why. God wouldn't have laid the penalty of death on breaking these laws of worship if there wasn't something else going on behind the scenes. Obviously the Temple in Heaven, that this Tabernacle represents, is an extremely holy place. If we could get just a glimpse of that Temple, we would understand why such complex and rigid laws are maintained – for example, God's holiness is such that anybody who doesn't approach him in absolute holiness would die immediately. In Leviticus he's getting us used to the idea that the rigidity of the earthly laws are supposed to get us ready to see an even more startling atmosphere in the Heavenly Temple.

Fifth, there will always be a mystery behind the purpose of the ceremonies and requirements. Not everything is explained to us here. Perhaps there are no words to describe the spiritual reality in Heaven that the physical symbols illustrated. It's as if we would ask of God, "why must we do this particular thing – and why must the Tabernacle have this particular article in its making?" God can only respond to us by saying, "You wouldn't understand now. Just do it – it's very important, though you won't know why until you get here in Heaven and see it for what it really is." So we are *commanded* to keep them. Christ honored them all when he fulfilled them *all*. Someday we will know why.

But the reason I like Leviticus is because it parallels a New Testament book – the Gospel of John. They both focus on the two issues that most interest God's people – cleansing us from sin completely, and coming into the presence of God to live with him. In John we see Jesus offering us the solution to the very things that Leviticus promised and yet couldn't produce.

You are already clean because of the word I have spoken to you. Remain in me, as I also remain in you. No branch can bear fruit by itself; it must remain in the vine. Neither can you bear fruit unless you remain in me. (John 15:3-4)

My Father's house has many rooms; if that were not so, would I have told you that I am going there to prepare a place for you? And if I go and prepare a place for you, I will come back and take you to be with me that you also may be where I am. You know the way to the place where I am going. (John 14:2-4)

In fact the entire Gospel is taken up with this subject. Jesus tells us all about what it's like to live with his Father, and his goal is to get his people there, into Heaven's Temple, where they will see the Father as Jesus himself sees him.

Father, I want those you have given me to be with me where I am, and to see my glory. (John 17:24)

If we keep these principles in mind, we ought to gain more respect for Leviticus as we study it. Though we may not understand everything that is going on here, God obviously thinks the whole thing is critical for his Kingdom. Leviticus is showing us our future in Heaven; Jesus, evidently, has done, is doing, and will do far more on our behalf that we realized.

Psalms – Pray for the Kingdom

The book of Psalms is a favorite among Christians. They use it for their worship, both public and private. It is so obviously the cry of the heart towards God, both in times of distress and in times of rejoicing. The Psalmist (whoever he might be, there were several authors involved) strikes universal chords in the human heart: suffering and pain, despair and darkness and loneliness, the need for wisdom and help and strength.

We gravitate so quickly to these heart needs that we miss what perhaps is the greatest feature of the Psalms: they were written by the King of Israel (or under his auspices and/or training). We've already looked at David and his 5-point Plan for the Kingdom of God. He was passionate about this Plan; the Kingdom was always on his heart. He did what nobody before him could do, and he passed this charge down to his descendants to continue – they were supposed to "do as their father David had done." Only in this way would Israel maintain her prosperity, peace and relationship with her God.

What more natural thing to expect, then, than to come into the Temple and hear the King of Israel praying to his God about this 5-point Plan!

David was a man of prayer. Many people claim to be, but David knew how to get in touch with the real God and get answers. If you want this God to listen to you when you pray, you have to approach him a certain way, and you have to talk about the things he wants to hear.

How to approach God

I'm afraid we have much too casual an attitude when it comes to prayer. We forget who we are speaking to. Remember that we first have to get a good view of God, then our part will fall right into place. Without that clear view of him, we end up doing the wrong things.

Our God is a consuming fire. (Hebrews 12:29)

We are so filled with images of the "gentle Jesus" from Sunday school class that we forget our first duty: to fear this God. God is holy, he is righteous to the point of perfection, and he can't stand arrogance and pride and rebellion and lukewarm "Christians" and all the other sins and imperfections that our lives are so filled with. He is merciful to us in spite of what we are, not because of what we are. We may come confidently to the throne of grace, but that's only after seeing that terrifying and sobering vision of Jesus' blood spilled on the altar for our sins. We have a long way to go before we will look like Jesus in our hearts and minds. I would much rather err on the side of caution and come humbly to this God in the way that he prescribes, instead of coming in presumption and pride. Remember Jesus' story of the dinner guests. (Luke 14:7-11)

And our new standing with this holy God depends on some very real and new elements of God's Kingdom in our lives now. Forget these, and you're coming to God unprepared and without the necessities of dealing with God. So if you want God to listen to you, you have to be sure to attend to these things.

- **Pray according to his Word.** God gave us the Bible for a reason – this is a description of God, of his Kingdom, of our true spiritual state, and of the spiritual resources in Christ to solve our problem and bring us back to God. In other words, this is the Agenda for prayer.

- **Call on his Name.** God's many names describe who he is and what he does. Presumably we want *this* God when we pray, and we want what only *this* God can do for us. He can tell when we really want to talk to him – when we call on his name and ask for what he can do, not on some other god for other things. The Name is the door to Heaven.

- **Pray in the Spirit.** The Spirit of God reveals the true God to us. Without the Spirit, the words of Scripture are only words. But in the Spirit we actually leave this world behind and come into the presence of God in Heaven. We taste and see this good God and take hold of spiritual treasures; they are no longer stories but realities.

- **Pray with Faith.** Faith is walking in the light of God's world. It's a gift that the Spirit gives us when he shines the light on the Word and enables us to see. Once we see this real God, we know for certain that whatever he tells us in his Word will come to pass, we can rely on it, and we can now walk in that way as we follow Christ on the road to eternal life. These are the treasures that we fill our lives with.

- **Pray for his Will.** How we fail God here! We bring our "Christmas lists" to God so that he can do what we want. But our God is the King. He wants us to bring willing hearts and an empty list to find out what he wants to do, and *then* what he wants us to do. We come to God in prayer to learn and submit, not to give him orders.

- **Pray for his Glory.** Remember that we were made for no other purpose than to glorify God – that's the fundamental aspect of all Creation. Our one passion should be that, in all things, whether they be good times or bad, our God might get glory. Mature prayer works on that level.

If you study the Psalms carefully, you will see that David kept all six of these principles before him when he prayed. In fact, they had been so ingrained into his thinking (from constant meditation on God) that he didn't have to stop and check his list to see if he was doing it right. He just knew; it came naturally to him. He was a master of prayer, and so he got answers to his prayers.[16]

What God wants to talk about

This is where the Plan of David comes into the picture. The Bible says that David was a "man after God's own heart," so naturally we would expect him to think God's thoughts, share God's vision, hate what God hates and love what God loves.

We already discussed the Plan of David and how it ties in with the entire Old Testament system as well as the work that Christ is doing in his Church. The reason we're looking at Psalms now is because this Plan must form the foundation of our prayers as well. In other words, if we are also "after God's heart" we will pray for the same things. Jesus himself was the Son of David. And if this is the Plan that Jesus is working on in his Church, then we prove that we are "God's co-workers" (2 Corinthians 6:1) if we share his passion and burden.

Rather than go through every Psalm, let's pick out just a few and see what David was really praying about.

• Psalm 1 – the beginning of prayer

This Psalm starts us off on the right foot. The person who prospers in this world is the one who meditates on God's Word. We learn about him there; it describes spiritual treasures that we need from him. The Spirit gives us what we see there, and our lives become enriched as a result. Whoever despises the Word will be left out of the assembly of God's people – because his people want what God promised them in his Word.

How else will we get along with God except to meditate deeply on the things he shows us in the Bible? This is our inheritance! This is what makes us grow

---

[16] You will find an extended discussion on this subject of the essentials of prayer in my book *The Secret to Answered Prayer*.

spiritually. This is what makes us fruitful and useful in the Kingdom. The more you know of the Bible, the deeper your walk with God will become. But despise that knowledge and you will be so shallow and useless to God that you will best be described as chaff.

• *Psalm 2 – the right attitude*

After getting into the Word, the first thing that David sees (the first thing we all must see!) is the glory of the King on his throne. This is the vision of Christ ruling over the nations with an iron scepter (we know this from Acts 13:33). Nothing happens apart from his will; no sin remains unpunished. The only right way to approach this King is in fear and obedience.

> Serve the LORD with fear and celebrate his rule with trembling. Kiss his Son, or he will be angry and your way will lead to your destruction, for his wrath can flare up in a moment. Blessed are all who take refuge in him. (Psalm 2:11-12)

That's quite a sobering picture of the one that we come to in prayer – not at all the Jesus that most have in mind, I'm sure. We are sinners; never forget that. Sin is always at the top of the agenda of prayer – Jesus came to save us from our sins, not leave us in them. And the King is at this moment building a Kingdom – world-wide, eternal, perfect. How do your prayer requests fit in with that? Or perhaps they don't? If we could just see that scene in Heaven – the Throne, angels surrounding the King, servants of the Lord throwing their weight into the Plan, announcements of yet another victory against his enemies and bringing more prisoners over to the cause – maybe we would pause and change our prayers to get in line with the program instead of looking so foolishly self-centered.

• *Psalm 48 – Jerusalem*

Jerusalem was the centerpiece of Israel. Here was where the King's throne was located, here was the site of the Temple, from here the government extended across the nation. The people came from all over the nation to Jerusalem to worship their God and celebrate the feasts. Jerusalem was the source from which flowed the power and wealth of the Kingdom. The city gave cohesion to the nation; it was this that the Israelites were lacking during the time of the Judges.

David knew the importance of the capital for the life of the people. That's why he spent a great deal of time building it up, and strengthening it, and making it prosperous. As Jerusalem prospered, the nation prospered.

This interesting Psalm guides us through Mt. Zion and shows us her wonders. God lives in this city; that's why she prospers. God is the source of all good things for his people. God is the fortress against her enemies. God is the wisdom that guides her rulers and brings justice and peace.

No earthly city now serves that function for God's people. But Jesus and the Apostles encouraged us to look over the Heavenly City in the same way.

> My Father's house has many rooms; if that were not so, would I have told you that I am going there to prepare a place for you? And if I go and prepare a place for you, I will come back and take you to be with me that you also may be where I am. (John 14:2-3)

> Since, then, you have been raised with Christ, set your hearts on things above, where Christ is, seated at the right hand of God. Set your minds on things above, not on earthly things. (Colossians 3:1-2)

For he was looking forward to the city with
foundations, whose architect and builder is God.
(Hebrews 11:10)

What David was seeing was the seat of God's throne,
from which come all good things. A close examination of
this city will inform us, encourage us, give us matter for
prayer. I think this is part of what Jesus meant when he
told us to "store up treasures in Heaven" (Matthew 6:19-
20) – that is, the inheritance waiting for us in Heaven.

- ## *Psalm 18 – The Enemy*

    A major concern on David's heart was the threat of
    Israel's enemies. In many Psalms we find him praying
    about this issue. The problem is that the enemy never
    leaves us alone, and he's so vicious and lethal. The
    common man in the street may turn his attention to other
    matters in life, but the enemy is always on the King's
    mind. Let down your guard for a minute, and you give the
    enemy the opportunity he was waiting for.

    In this Psalm we learn all the essentials of dealing with
    the enemy in God's way.

    - **First**, the fact that our enemy is out to kill us;
      he's not playing games. We're going to die if
      something isn't done. David can see all too
      well the strategy and tactics of the enemy and
      its deadly results.
    - **Second**, the suffering and anguish that
      struggling with the enemy causes in our hearts
      and minds and lives. This is why people all
      around the world struggle in life; here is the
      reason for our pain.
    - **Third**, our only recourse against the enemy –
      God himself. God brings a passion, a power, a
      fearful attack to our enemies that nobody else
      can bring. This is the number one problem in
      God's eyes, and his heart is in this thing.

People ask for all kinds of things from God, but you've never seen the passion of God so supremely revealed as when God goes on the warpath to rescue his children!

- **Fourth**, God rescues us from our enemy by taking us clear away from the danger and putting us on a Rock – a foundation from which we can't be moved by the enemy again. It would be no deliverance if he left us open to another attack.
- **Fifth**, God equips us and trains us so that we can defend ourselves against further advances of the enemy.

Now all these pieces have to be in place for a real rescue; our God does his work thoroughly. David looked for all of them when dealing with the enemy, because he was concerned for the people's present and future well-being. Thus he prayed for all aspects of deliverance.

Do you recognize our New Testament agenda? Remember who our enemies are: the world, the flesh, and the devil. Because of these three, our lives are filled with suffering and pain and isolation and death. We learn the hard way how the enemy destroys us – his strategy to separate us from God and lead us into rebellion and death. Our only hope is if Jesus himself destroys the work of the devil, forgives us of sin and cleanses our hearts, and lifts us up from this world and makes us children of God. It's all his work. And we know his heart concerning all this: out of his great love and compassion he came to rescue his people from the enemy. We even read in Ephesians of how the Lord dresses us in armor and makes us skilled for the next attack.

David was ruthless about dealing with the enemy, which is exactly to the point for all of us. In God's eyes, we can't afford to let this slide; it's always a matter for prayer. And in many of them he prays about the enemy.

- *Psalm 84 – Back to God*

David was not a priest, so we can assume that when he talked about going to God's house that he didn't actually go inside where only the priests were allowed. Neither did his son Solomon. But Korah was a priest, as well as his sons. Both Korah and David went to the house of God for the same reason: to meet God.

> One thing I ask from the LORD, this only do I seek: that I may dwell in the house of the LORD all the days of my life, to gaze on the beauty of the LORD and to seek him in his temple. (Psalm 27:4)

> How lovely is your dwelling place, LORD Almighty! My soul yearns, even faints, for the courts of the LORD; my heart and my flesh cry out for the living God. (Psalm 84:1-2)

I get the feeling that, for some strange reason, modern Christians don't mind getting ready to go in to see God, but they really don't want to go in after they're ready. They're still standing outside on the porch of the Temple, reluctant to go in. Becoming righteous, and being made holy, and getting saved, and following Jesus out of this world – that fills our sermons and Bible lessons, but hardly anybody talks about actually seeing the glory of God. How do I know this? Almost nothing is said about God!

David wanted to see God. He knew that God is life, he is power, he is wisdom. His majesty dazzles and delights the soul. His glory makes us tremble in fear, but that's good because it keeps us submissive and obedient to him. Friends come and go, but God the Father takes us in his arms and protects us and encourages us with his arms of strength and heart of compassion. God is the only source of the riches that our souls need: in him is a limitless supply of the fruit that makes us grow inside.

David knew that separation from God will shrivel up the soul with dryness, with weakness, with despair. It's like taking a coal from the fire – it starts dying down.

But I'm sure that David's vision of God included *data*. He wasn't like so many people who talk about going to God and knowing God but actually they rarely make the connection. When they dial the phone, so to speak, they keep getting the wrong number – or nobody answers. They're not very careful to get in touch with the right God. As a result, they "worshiped" a God they still don't know anything about. David knew what names to call on, he knew where to find God, he knew what moves God's heart. He knew God's home very well and was comfortable there, as if he were part of the family. He considered himself part of the family, and for that reason kept coming back to his Father for all his needs.

Remember that's precisely where Jesus wants us. David is our model here. David didn't let the Levitical laws keep him out of God's house spiritually, and we don't let this world keep us from God's throne in Heaven.

> Therefore, brothers, since we have confidence to enter the Most Holy Place by the blood of Jesus, by a new and living way opened for us through the curtain, that is, his body, and since we have a great priest over the house of God, let us draw near to God with a sincere heart and with the full assurance that faith brings, having our hearts sprinkled to cleanse us from a guilty conscience and having our bodies washed with pure water. (Hebrews 10:19-22)

Not a superficial worship, but a profound insight and faith that takes us directly into God's presence when we pray. Only by making this kind of contact with God will our prayers be heard and answered.

• *Psalm 45 – Government*

David could not rule the entire country himself. History records that he used his faithful army commanders and, later, his sons to organize and run his government over the nation. It was their job to carry the orders of the King to all the people, enforce the King's law, see that justice was done by protecting the innocent and punishing the guilty, promote the well-being and prosperity of all citizens, and keep the peace. It was a big job.

This Psalm talks of an event after David's day, but it describes the same kind of situation. It's the story of the King's wedding. But it focuses on the King's throne, his majesty, the righteousness that he brings to the people. Even the new queen is seen in light of the role she will play in the Kingdom. Their sons will become the future governors – princes – helping to govern the nation.

There are many people interested in power; maybe we all are in some way. But a good king doesn't want power for his own sake. He wants to see the people in his care get the best of life. Jesus expressed the same sentiment.

> Whoever wants to become great among you must be your servant, and whoever wants to be first must be your slave — just as the Son of Man did not come to be served, but to serve, and to give his life as a ransom for many. (Matthew 20:26-28)

So what is on the King's heart?

> So Christ himself gave the Apostles, the Prophets, the evangelists, the pastors and teachers, to equip his people for works of service, so that the body of Christ may be built up until we all reach unity in the faith and in the knowledge of the Son of God and become mature, attaining to the whole measure of the fullness of Christ.
>
> Then we will no longer be infants, tossed back and forth by the waves, and blown here and there

by every wind of teaching and by the cunning and craftiness of people in their deceitful scheming. Instead, speaking the truth in love, we will grow to become in every respect the mature body of him who is the head, that is, Christ. From him the whole body, joined and held together by every supporting ligament, grows and builds itself up in love, as each part does its work. (Ephesians 4:11-16)

In other words, in Christ's Kingdom there is a hierarchy, from the King down to the people in the pews. Christ's will must reign. The Apostles and Prophets recorded that will and passed it on to us in the Bible. Pastors and teachers preach and teach the Lord's will to the people. And the rest of the members of the church are specially gifted to reveal the Lord and his Kingdom to the Church, so that we all come into the presence of this King and are blessed by being in his Kingdom.

Now a mature Christian is going to have this Kingdom on his/her heart at all times. Is the Kingdom growing? Is everyone getting what they need to thrive spiritually? We are all children of the King, and assigned our special duties to extend his Kingdom in the ways that our spiritual skills enable us.

Notice too that the King is really going to rely on his family to help him in this task. They will have his interests at heart more than anybody else will; family sticks together. They care about the family name; they share in the family's successes and failures. Presumably the Christian feels the same way about Christ and his family. The Church comes first.

- ### *Psalm 133 – the Temple*

The Temple is the house of God, and there the priests were assigned the two-fold task of serving both God and man. All priests were descendants of Aaron, Moses'

211

brother. And every priest was anointed with oil to set him apart, or consecrate, him for his work.

There's a lot of imagery in this Psalm. The oil represents the Spirit who gives insight and power to accomplish the work of Heaven. Aaron of course represents the High Priest, who we know now is Jesus himself serving in his Father's house.

But we also know that every Christian has been made a priest to serve in the spiritual Temple in Heaven.

> You also, like living stones, are being built into a spiritual house to be a holy priesthood, offering spiritual sacrifices acceptable to God through Jesus Christ. (1 Peter 2:5)

Through us God gets praise, as each one of us testifies to his power and grace in our lives. Through us the grace of God pours out to our brothers and sisters, as we minister God's fullness to each other through our spiritual gifts. David was concerned that the right things were happening in the Temple, that the Lord would get glory and his people be blessed with the treasures of Heaven.

> Praise the LORD. Praise the name of the LORD; praise him, you servants of the LORD, you who minister in the house of the LORD, in the courts of the house of our God. Praise the LORD, for the LORD is good; sing praise to his name, for that is pleasant. (Psalm 135:1-3)

Since David knew God, and since he himself has tasted the goodness of God, it weighed on his heart when the Temple wasn't working like it was supposed to. The same thing weighs on my heart as I see the modern church doing without God, without Christ. It's too often a shallow religion that isn't connecting people with Heaven. It's a man-centered religion, earth-based. The system that the Son of David has set up for us has been set aside and replaced with the ways of the world. People are drying up and dying as a result.

But when we are all doing our part in the Church, it's a beautiful thing to see. The Spirit fills us with what we need to do our work. David longed for this kind of cooperation between the people of God, instead of the usual fighting and jealousy and self-serving that usually goes on. The Spirit brings the Kingdom of God down to earth when we don't resist him. Grieve him, and all our sins come out and we destroy each other; follow him, and there is life in the Church.

David organized the Temple service (1 Chronicles 22-29). And he knew and appreciated those dedicated servants who worked for God's glory and the benefit of others. He gave credit where credit was due, too: there were always priests assigned to Temple duty, even at night when no one was there to see, and David appreciated their labor for the Lord.

> Praise the LORD, all you servants of the LORD who minister by night in the house of the LORD. Lift up your hands in the sanctuary and praise the LORD. May the LORD bless you from Zion, he who is the Maker of heaven and earth. (Psalm 134)

That must have been a lonely vigil! And it certainly doesn't get the glory that the day-shift received in the public eye. But there are some who are doing their job not for personal glory, but for God's glory. They deserve special mention.

Summary

Psalms is a huge book and we can't analyze all of it here. I'll let you continue on your own. Hopefully you get the idea: follow David's 5-Point Plan and learn from David as he prays over these issues. It's all about the Kingdom of Christ; that's the key to interpreting the book.

And you will find that most Psalms deal with multiple issues – like Psalm 68. There we read about the capital city being the source of blessing for God's people; we read about God defeating the enemy; we also read about the worship in the Temple. It's an interesting study to see how these ideas fit together.

But what if we don't pray like this? Does everyone have to pray on this level? Won't God hear our prayers about food and clothing and health? Well, the question points us to the answer.

> So do not worry, saying, 'What shall we eat?' or 'What shall we drink?' or 'What shall we wear?' For the pagans run after all these things, and your Heavenly Father knows that you need them. But seek first his Kingdom and his righteousness, and all these things will be given to you as well. Therefore do not worry about tomorrow, for tomorrow will worry about itself. Each day has enough trouble of its own. (Matthew 6:31-34)

The immature keep coming to God with prayers about themselves, and their material wants. David prayed for the prosperity of God's Kingdom.

ECCLESIASTES – THE PROBLEM OF TWO WORLDS

When people read the book of Ecclesiastes they get the impression that Solomon was having a bad day. He had tried every pleasure in life that money can buy, and it all ended up empty and a cheat. Vanity, as he says at the beginning of his book – all is vanity. Nothing has any purpose or meaning, so all we can do is enjoy what we're doing at the moment.

And yet there are clues that this is not the writings of a man in despair. Rather this is a man with deep faith who sees this world for what it really is.

> In all this my wisdom stayed with me. (Ecclesiastes 2:9)

> Not only was the Teacher wise, but he also imparted knowledge to the people. He pondered and searched out and set in order many proverbs. The Teacher searched to find just the right words, and what he wrote was upright and true. (Ecclesiastes 12:9-10)

What did Solomon see? For that, we have to go back to the Creation and remember the lessons we learned there.

A two-sided world

The world was made by miracle, by command, by God's Word. There were spiritual forces at work making a universe that is both physical and spiritual. That means that this is a two-sided creation, and man is living in both sides at the same time. When God first made mankind, we of course had the ability to know and take advantage of that spiritual side of God's world; we needed it in order to carry out our duties in his Kingdom.

God provides meaning and purpose and value. His act of creation makes whatever he creates valuable to him, and by extension gives us a sense of value. Man was created "in God's image" and therefore bears a glory and honor and responsibility bestowed upon him from outside (it's not intrinsic), from God's authority and intent. Creation immediately established a relationship between God and man that makes every act that we do historic, and every act that God does with us of great moment. The universe awaits the outcome of this arrangement as we follow the will of the King – supposedly helping to guide and maintain and grow his Kingdom. Nothing that we do is unimportant; everything we do is pregnant with meaning and purpose and power and glory.

In order to accomplish this, however, man had to be in constant and direct communication with God so that he knew what to do, and when, to make it successful. This picture shows our relationship to God and each other.

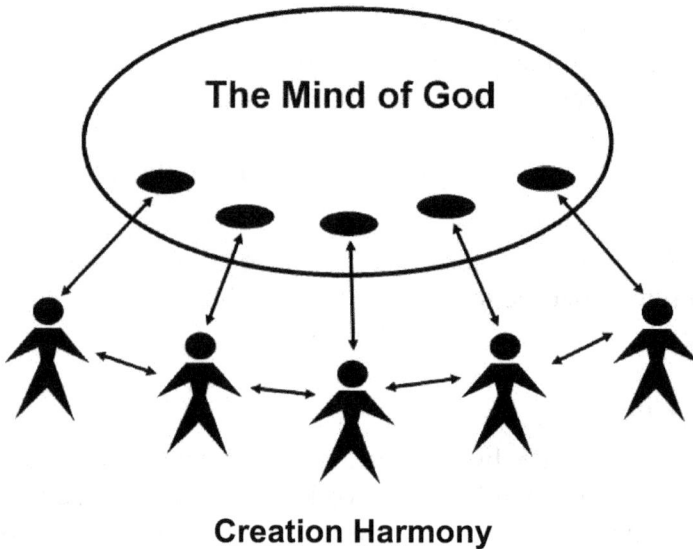

The Mind of God

Creation Harmony

Each human being was in contact with a part of the mind and will of God. No one person knew the fullness of God, but then they didn't have to. All that they had to know was the part that

216

God had them to play. If they would follow God's commands for them exactly, their actions would not only fulfill God's plans for them, but they would also fit in peacefully with their neighbors, without friction. We wouldn't have to know what our neighbor was supposed to do, because our actions (defined by God) would work alongside the actions of others who were also following God's will for them. All the parts of the system would work together perfectly, like the planets revolving around the sun according to law. It would have been a glorious testimony to God's infinite wisdom and understanding, and it would have resulted in a harmonious Kingdom in which each and all would prosper under his rule.

Remember too that Solomon also wrote the book of Proverbs. There he described God's creation from its design aspect: the Lord made things a certain way, and he filled our lives with certain resources, and therefore *these are the principles to live by if you want to succeed and prosper in the world that God created for you.* If we work *with* God and his design, then we will get along fine. But if we work *contrary* to God's will, we will only fail and destroy ourselves. So it will be abundantly clear to everyone whether we have wisdom.

Wisdom is being able to see things the way they really are, and how best to take advantage of them. Solomon had that in abundance.

Blind and dead

But when man fell into sin, we lost the ability to know that spiritual world. We still have an intuition that it's there, but we are dead to God now, and we can't know what's out there unless someone pulls away the veil and shows us.

Here's what happens when we have all lost touch with God.

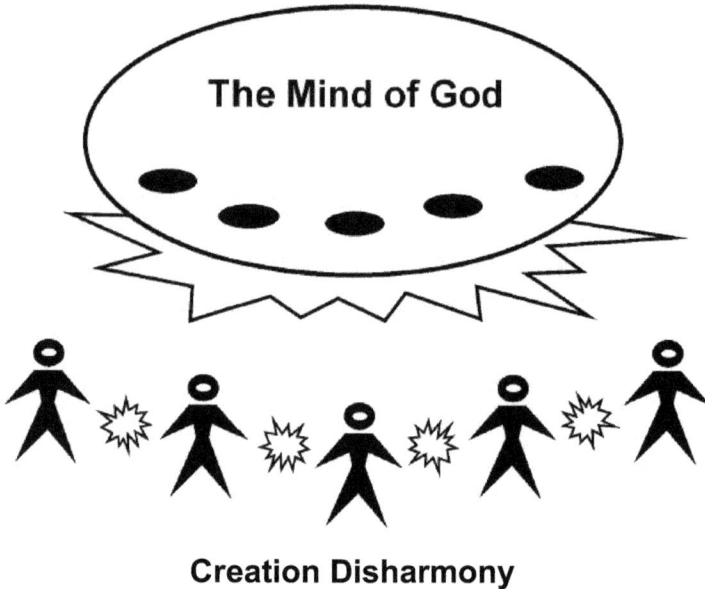

The Mind of God

Creation Disharmony

Now we don't know what God wants us to do. We don't even know what he's like – or if he's even out there. We can't see the design of God's world anymore; the lessons in Proverbs are lost on us. We show by our actions that we just don't get the point about living in God's Kingdom when we focus on ourselves instead of our responsibilities, and our own lusts and desires instead of righteousness. We are on the stage of the world and we have not only forgotten our lines, we are ruining the whole production.

We're on our own now, blind to the spiritual world of God. And blindness produces foolishness: we invent new ethical systems, and hope that things work out. We try to come up with governments in which we can all get along peacefully and get what we need in life, yet the very opposite is happening in our world.

The results of spiritual blindness to God are not what we were hoping for from all our efforts. We invent the wrong ethical systems and end up hurting ourselves and others in our struggle for happiness and wealth. We invent governments that oppress

218

the poor and promote injustice. We go to war with each other because we all have conflicting goals and desires. In other words, without God life turns into suffering and death.

And when someone tries to tell us about the true God and what life is supposed to be like, we turn a deaf ear – we actually reject the truth because it doesn't make sense to us. Stupidly we choose death instead of life. If we could just see God, and hear his voice, that would answer all sorts of questions and solve all sorts of problems that our society is filled with; instead, we go the way of the fool and turn away from God.

A one-sided worldview

So what Solomon is realizing in his wisdom is that we lost something vital when we turned away from God. We are living in darkness now; that's why people do so many foolish things. The world is upside down: he sees crazy things going on in this world like the wicked getting the good things of this world, and the righteous suffering want and oppression. He sees fools ruling over the righteous and wise. He sees people working all their lives for wealth, and then laying down to die in despair over the pointlessness of it all. He sees people gaining wisdom but it doesn't get them any further in life. He sees friendship and laughter and family and wealth in the lives of fools.

This may sound like despair, but actually it's a necessary lesson to learn. It should humble us to know what things used to be like, what things could have been, and what we've done to ourselves in our sin. Our world is ruined because of our foolishness and now we can't do anything to fix it; in fact, we keep making matters worse. So much for our wisdom!

People try to make sense out of life, and they try to fix the problems of the world, but they don't bring the right resources to the problem. This world can't bear the weight of righteousness, and meaning and purpose, and right and wrong; the structure isn't there in the physical world to account for such things. Scientists are right: evolution doesn't produce ethical systems, and physical laws don't create meaning and purpose and value. The physical

219

world is devoid of spiritual content. So governments and schools and parents and everyone else in positions of responsibility aren't fixing anything; the solutions they come up with only make things worse than they are. There will never be justice and righteousness and wisdom in this world, not as long as blinded sinners are running the show. They're leaving the Creator out of the picture, so therefore they are not true and they don't work.

All this is because we've lost the connection to the spiritual world – the other side of the coin that would explain everything if we had it.

Unfortunately you're not going to understand much of what God is doing either, even though you may have become a Christian and have some wisdom now. The kind of wisdom that God gives his people isn't what we need to fix our world. We try, but the Church has been trying and failing to fix the world since the days of Christ. Every generation takes whatever good has been done by its fathers and throws it all away.

> For a person may labor with wisdom, knowledge and skill, and then they must leave all they own to another who has not toiled for it. This too is meaningless and a great misfortune. What do people get for all the toil and anxious striving with which they labor under the sun? (Ecclesiastes 2:21-22)

The lesson to learn here is to let go of your grand hope of fixing this world; you aren't going to do it. And you aren't going to accomplish much that is useful, to either yourself or to others – and particularly toward God. There's a good reason for this: we've lost the ability to understand and follow God's deep purposes for us. We may have had that ability at one point, but now our sin and ignorance and death has crippled our judgment and understanding in dealing with spiritual matters. You may be able to get through life yourself, and you may be of help to others, but nobody knows what is needed, or when to act, or what the outcome will be – only God knows. The wiring that we used to have as perfect men and women is short-circuited now, and we can't be the help that we were supposed to be.

When I applied my mind to know wisdom and to observe the labor that is done on earth — people getting no sleep day or night — then I saw all that God has done. No one can comprehend what goes on under the sun. Despite all their efforts to search it out, no one can discover its meaning. Even if the wise claim they know, they cannot really comprehend it. (Ecclesiastes 8:16-17)

So I reflected on all this and concluded that the righteous and the wise and what they do are in God's hands, but no one knows whether love or hate awaits them. All share a common destiny — the righteous and the wicked, the good and the bad, the clean and the unclean, those who offer sacrifices and those who do not. (Ecclesiastes 9:1-2)

It's humbling to think that we are such children now regarding what used to be matters of state, but there it is. Our lives have been reduced to simple survival because of our sin.

Wisdom's role

This all sounds very dark, but it's necessary to get it all on the table for discussion. Like Solomon says, "Better to go to the house of mourning than the house of feasting." "Death is the destiny of every man; the living should take this to heart."

Is there a bright side to this picture? Well, at least being able to see the problem is half the solution. Solomon knows the futility in trying to force what we want from a physical world. It doesn't work. We can use it for what it was designed for – the good things in life are for our physical pleasures – but it wasn't made to do what we want from them: meaning and purpose, value and accomplishment. The things of this world aren't mean to replace the resources of Heaven.

Actually Ecclesiastes is the necessary first chapter to the book of Hebrews in the New Testament. The two work together. In Ecclesiastes we learn that we lost the Creation ability of living in two worlds at the same time; without that, we can't do what the

Creator made us to do – we can't even survive our problems. But in Hebrews we learn that we've been given a new sense of vision – not to replace what we lost, but to lift us up to a new Creation where God is preparing a new home for us.

It turns out that Jesus is going to create a new world in which we will be not only restored to the original perfect system, but included in a grander scheme. We will once again "know the mind of God" through his Spirit, and we will take our place in the Church, the Temple, and do our part to glorify God and minister to each other. The plan that God had for humanity at the beginning is going to be accomplished. You can be sure that this new world isn't going to have the problems that we have in this one!

At the beginning we were given the necessary senses to live in this physical world – our five senses – and we had the ability to sense God's spiritual world, so that we could do his will in his Kingdom. But in this New Creation we've been given a new spiritual sense – *faith*. As we shall see later on, faith is the ability to live in God's spiritual world. It doesn't straighten out things here, but it certainly gets us ready to move out of this world and into Heaven when the time comes. More on that later.

What Solomon does tell us is that we still have a chance to redeem ourselves in this situation. Wisdom may not reveal to us the spiritual side of *this* world – that insight is beyond us now – but it can help us deal with our present broken situation. Now that we know how we stand as blinded sinners, we can at least turn toward the right direction and stop acting like fools headed in the wrong direction.

> The wise have eyes in their heads, while the fool walks in the darkness. (Ecclesiastes 2:14)

> Guard your steps when you go to the house of God. Go near to listen rather than to offer the sacrifice of fools, who do not know that they do wrong. (Ecclesiastes 5:1)

> This is what I have observed to be good: that it is appropriate for a person to eat, to drink and to find

satisfaction in their toilsome labor under the sun during the few days of life God has given them — for this is their lot. Moreover, when God gives someone wealth and possessions, and the ability to enjoy them, to accept their lot and be happy in their toil—this is a gift of God. (Ecclesiastes 5:18-19)

Death is the destiny of everyone; the living should take this to heart. (Ecclesiastes 7:2)

Summary

Ecclesiastes is actually teaching the same truths that the rest of the Bible teaches. Abraham was told that his "great reward" was not this world but God himself. Hebrews 11 tells us that all the saints in the Old Testament looked not to this world but the next one.

Instead, they were longing for a better country — a Heavenly one. Therefore God is not ashamed to be called their God, for he has prepared a city for them. (Hebrews 11:16)

That's a necessary lesson for us to learn. Instead of insisting on the pleasures of this life, it's time to turn spend less time on physical things and start focusing on what we really need. It's when we try to figure out this world, or try to get ahead in it, that we get into trouble.

But God said to him, 'You fool! This very night your life will be demanded from you. Then who will get what you have prepared for yourself?' This is how it will be with whoever stores up things for themselves but is not rich toward God. (Luke 12:20-21)

Do not store up for yourselves treasures on earth, where moths and vermin destroy, and where thieves break in and steal. But store up for yourselves treasures in Heaven, where moths and vermin do not destroy, and where thieves do not break in and steal.

For where your treasure is, there your heart will be also. (Matthew 6:19-21)

Since, then, you have been raised with Christ, set your hearts on things above, where Christ is, seated at the right hand of God. Set your minds on things above, not on earthly things. (Colossians 3:1-2)

It's as if God had Solomon write Ecclesiastes to put our noses in the dirty fact that we've been focusing on the wrong things in life. Do the best you can in a fallen world, but put your hope in the new world that only faith can show you.

MALACHI – GIVE THEM JESUS!

The book of Malachi would make an interesting study in the annals of the history of preaching. It's been used both to support the Law and to predict its demise. Preachers seem not to notice how completely polarized these two approaches are; they are after something, and no amount of reasoning is going to talk them out of it.

There are two reasons people preach from Malachi: *first*, they want to "lay the law down," so to speak, about tithing. Our modern churches require a great deal of maintenance, and costs have pushed the prices of building and upkeep into the hundreds of thousands, if not millions. Obviously the group needs to honor its commitment that it made at the beginning of the building program and keep paying the bills. And of course there is the pastor's salary, along with whatever other staff the church is paying for.

There is perhaps no other passage in the Bible so sharp about "paying your bills" as Malachi 3. The Lord himself steps in with a rebuke, and it's hard to argue against it.

> Will a mere mortal rob God? Yet you rob me.
>
> But you ask, 'How are we robbing you?'
>
> In tithes and offerings. You are under a curse — your whole nation — because you are robbing me. Bring the whole tithe into the storehouse, that there may be food in my house. (Malachi 3:8-10)

Press that passage on people's hearts, and they feel so guilty about "robbing God" that they will usually submit and start giving more to the church. Malachi 3 is a favorite text that preachers bring out every once in a while to give the finances a boost.

The *second* reason people preach from Malachi, though less often, is found in chapter 4 – the prophecy of the coming of Elijah.

> See, I will send the prophet Elijah to you before
> that great and dreadful day of the LORD comes.
> (Malachi 4:5)

Jesus himself makes a reference to this prophecy when he spoke of John the Baptist.

> Truly I tell you, among those born of women there
> has not risen anyone greater than John the Baptist ...
> And if you are willing to accept it, he is the Elijah
> who was to come. (Matthew 11:11, 14)

The reason I say that this passage is preached from less often is because they are usually preaching through Matthew, and they reach back here in Malachi to pick up this prophecy to explain what Jesus was talking about. Rarely will preachers use the Malachi text itself as the basis of a sermon.

Problems in interpretation

Let's start by examining how preachers abuse the book of Malachi. First the tithing issue.

Tithing is not what most people think it is. Most think it's a matter of giving ten percent of your income to the church so that they can pay the bills – building costs, the pastor's paycheck, maintenance costs, mission projects, and so on. To "tithe" means to commit to paying your fair share of the costs. Seen in this light, it's no wonder the preacher will pin you to the wall and make you feel guilty if you're not doing your fair share.

But that's a terrible misunderstanding of the concept of tithing. If the pastor would take the time to investigate, he would learn all about the tithing law in Deuteronomy.

> You must not eat in your own towns the tithe of
> your grain and new wine and olive oil, or the
> firstborn of your herds and flocks, or whatever you

have vowed to give, or your freewill offerings or special gifts. Instead, you are to eat them in the presence of the LORD your God at the place the LORD your God will choose. (Deuteronomy 12:17-18)

Be sure to set aside a tenth of all that your fields produce each year. Eat the tithe of your grain, new wine and olive oil, and the firstborn of your herds and flocks in the presence of the LORD your God at the place he will choose as a dwelling for his Name, so that you may learn to revere the LORD your God always. (Deuteronomy 14:22-23)

There are other passages which you can look into on your own: Leviticus 27:30-33; Numbers 18:25-29; Deuteronomy 12:17-19; Deuteronomy 14:22-29.

The idea was this: the Israelites were required to come to Jerusalem three times a year for their religious festivals. With millions of people in town, the shopkeepers in Jerusalem would have found it impossible to feed all those people. So the Levites were supposed to roam through the country during harvest time and collect a tenth of the grain and harvest from each household and take it to the storage rooms at the Temple. When everyone came to town for the festivals, there would be plenty for everyone to eat. There was even a law for those who couldn't get their grain to Jerusalem – they *could* change it into money.

But if that place is too distant and you have been blessed by the LORD your God and cannot carry your tithe (because the place where the LORD will choose to put his Name is so far away), then exchange your tithe for silver, and take the silver with you and go to the place the LORD your God will choose. Use the silver to buy whatever you like: cattle, sheep, wine or other fermented drink, or anything you wish. Then you and your household shall eat there in the presence of the LORD your God and rejoice. (Deuteronomy 14:24-26)

So the point of the tithe was not money, but food. And it wasn't used for Temple maintenance and costs (there was a half-shekel tax law to cover that – Exodus 30:11-16) but to feed everyone when millions were in town. And in effect, the tithe that a family would send to Jerusalem was going to be *their* food when they went later to the festival. It was more like a pot-luck supper at the Temple feasts.

In other words, we've changed the meaning of the word "tithe" to suit our own purposes; it no longer reflects the intent of the Law of God.

The reason there was a law to cover this situation is because of human nature – there are going to be some who don't want to give up their income, and they'll devise a scheme on how to eat their neighbor's food and save their own. Remember Paul's comment about the Law being given to expose sin. (Romans 5:20)

But what bothers me more about how preachers handle this text is that they are using no discernment at all about preaching the Law to Christians. This tithing law comes straight out of the Law of Moses. It was not optional, it was mandatory – upon pain of expulsion from the community of faith. The Law's penalty is not "oh well, if you can't do it this year, try again next year." You have to obey it or you're a law-breaker and open to the penalties of the law. But there isn't a preacher in the land (I hope!) who would carry out that penalty and throw people out of the church if they didn't pay their tithe. They know better than to treat Christians like that.

Now if this is the Law, then preach it like the Law. But if it's not appropriate to use this Law to impale a Christian's conscience and force him to obey, then don't dare go there! Either we are obliged to follow the Law, or as Christians we have another route in Christ. If you have any confusion about this issue, please go to Paul as he discusses the Law in his book to the Galatians.

There's something else that is *not* happening that shows me that preachers are handling Malachi with abysmal ignorance: I don't remember hearing any preacher talking about other passages in Malachi. For example, Malachi talks about bringing crippled animals to the sacrifice (Malachi 1:8); about the priests violating the covenant with Levi (Malachi 2:8); and about Judah desecrating the sanctuary (Malachi 2:11). If preachers must preach the passage about tithing, why don't they talk about breaking the other laws that Malachi complains about? The reason is because they know full well that they can't go there! It's the Law, and we can't preach obedience to the Law to the Church.

So that tells me that their constant harping on this passage on tithing in Malachi is a panic solution to their financial situation: they really don't know how else to solve the problem but try to make people guilty with the Law and start obeying it. Again they fall back on morality lessons – "You must do this for God." But the other laws – well, we don't have to worry about that. [17]

The long and the short of it is, preachers are a long ways from preaching Christ when they handle the book of Malachi in this way.

Malachi: Give them Jesus!

So let's start over. Let's assume again that the Lord is after our salvation. Although we are required to measure up to the Law's demands, God knows that we can't do it. We need help. So the point of Malachi, as is the point of the entire Bible, is that we might be saved from our sins. Using the Law to expose our sin is the first step to salvation; we have to admit, first of all, that we are indeed sinners before we will be motivated to find a cure for our spiritual sickness.

One of the grosser sins that we're guilty of is the manner in which we worship God. Malachi's message is all about that: exposing the Jews' hearts and proving that their outward actions don't match their inward spiritual state. Their worship of God is actually alienating them from God.

There are five issues that Malachi brings up to prove his point.

- **Polluted offerings** – the Jews are bringing the lame and blind of their flock for sacrifice instead of bringing the best of their flock.

- **Unfaithful priests** – the priests are not instructing the people to turn away from sin; they craft their messages more for the people's pleasure and spiritual laziness.

---

[17]   For an extended discussion on tithing and church support, see the chapter "Christians and Tithing" in **Knots Untied**.

- **Faithless worship** – the Jews are going through the motions of worship but their hearts aren't in it; it's like being married to a woman but not loving her. A jealous God can't stand that!

- **Withholding the Tithe** – people aren't contributing their fair share to the festivals; they're eating the labors of others but withholding their own.

- **Accusing God of injustice** – they say that, apparently, it doesn't pay to be a follower of the Lord when the wicked get everything they want and the righteous get nothing.

When we think about these charges that Malachi (or God, as he works through Malachi) makes against the Jews, the passage at the beginning of the book stands out all the more plainly. The Jews have inherited a precious treasure from their God.

> "I have loved you," says the LORD.

> "But you ask, 'How have you loved us? '

> "Was not Esau Jacob's brother?" declares the LORD. "Yet I have loved Jacob, but Esau I have hated, and I have turned his hill country into a wasteland and left his inheritance to the desert jackals." (Malachi 1:2-3)

The Lord has chosen the Jews, above all other nations, to be the heirs of the Covenant with Abraham. Esau got nothing; Jacob got everything. It's interesting that God referred to Jacob here, because at first Jacob was the least deserving of the Patriarchs – he was a liar and deceiver. But in spite of his sins, the Lord chose him to be the heir of what Paul later calls the Gospel. (Galatians 3:8) And these Jews in Malachi's day (though sinners) were also Abraham's heirs. But they certainly weren't acting like it! They didn't seem to understand at all the value of the treasures of the Temple or how to use them. They were treating the treasures and privileges of Heaven of little importance, yet they had in their hands the answers to the problems of humanity.

It's true that following the Law is not our hope; but the other side of that coin is that it's the Law that Jesus came to fulfill. The Law defines our relationship with God and man; it's the definition of true righteousness and holiness. But it's what Jesus does to us and for us that fulfills that Law in us. We must bring Christ to the task!

- **Acceptable offerings** – The offering that the Temple law required was a spotless lamb, the first and best of the flock. By its blood their sins would be forgiven forever, forgotten and never to be remembered. That blood covered their hearts so that the Law's penalties would be rendered powerless. This precious treasure literally bought them the privilege of access into God's presence, and the free flow of spiritual treasures from Heaven for their blessing. So why in the world were the Jews bringing another sacrifice to the Temple? Why were they not seeing the amazing mercy of God in this requirement of God's Law? Why were they satisfied with sacrifices far below God's standards of perfection when only perfection would do? They evidently considered the grace of God of little value.

  The same thing can be asked of modern Christians. Why in the world are they not bringing Christ – the Lamb, the Perfect One, the Firstborn – to the worship service? Why are they turning to other hopes? They should be focusing their attention on his saving work, his power, his wisdom, his Spirit that pours out the treasures of an opened Heaven into our starving hearts. Bring the Names of Christ, the works of Christ, the profound wisdom of Christ, the commands of Christ the King, the Kingdom principles and works that he is doing – these are the things that save us and bless us. To bring anything else but Christ to the worship service is putting our hopes in sacrifices that cannot help us. The requirement is to be Christ-centered, not man-centered.

- **Faithful priests** – The priests are supposed to instruct the people about the "weightier matters of the Law."

But you have neglected the more important matters of the Law — justice, mercy and faithfulness. You should have practiced the latter, without neglecting the former. You blind guides! You strain out a gnat but swallow a camel. (Matthew 23:23-24)

These "important matters" have to do with our relationships with God and man. In other words, sin – and the ways to cure that problem (righteousness). The purpose of the worship service is not celebrating, or telling people the things they must do to please God (moralisms), or entertainment, or the myriads of other themes that modern churches turn the service into. It's about getting real about one's heart before God and fixing what is wrong with us.

The priests (or leaders) must bring the Law to people's hearts. It's not an argument that we are no longer under Law but under grace; we wouldn't even know what sin is without the Law. The Law is the definition of righteousness; it's vitally important for all of God's people to know. By examining our hearts with the standard of the Law, we understand how far short we fall of the expectations of our God – we know how we have offended him. The leaders have to "put our noses in it" to keep making this point, or we wouldn't ever think about it.

Once we know how far short we fall, then it's clear what it will take to rescue us from our sin, to cleanse us so that we don't sin again – the entire ministry of Christ is all about that. So the work of teaching and preaching is about connecting people, with their sin and death, to the One who takes away sin with his power, wisdom, and spiritual resources, and gives us his righteousness. Leaders have an awesome responsibility to bring the remedy to the table and deliver the message of Christ to a people in great spiritual need of him.

- **Faithful worship** – God draws a parallel between the relationship with his people and the marriage covenant. A man who divorces his wife because he doesn't love her anymore is faithless to the covenant he made with her. His heart is false; he willingly throws the marriage and family away based on his emotional whims. Marriage is founded on a deeper basis than emotional whims, however; it's a commitment, a love that gives.

Our relationship with God is also a marriage contract. Through the prophet Hosea we learn that the Jews were God's wife, and his love for them made their punishment agonizingly painful to him – though they seemed to take their commitment to him pretty casually. Certainly they didn't understand the relationship.

And Paul says that Christ and the Church are in the same relationship. Let's think about that situation for a minute. If we come to church and we aren't the least bit interested in exploring the person and work of Christ, if we are self-centered and focused only on our own whims and desires, is that a healthy marriage? Wouldn't it show our faithlessness if we aren't focusing on him? Do we really desire Christ if we don't spend time learning about him, and coming to him, and worshiping him, and depending on him? If our sermons and lessons are all about "you must believe in Jesus" and yet there is nothing about Jesus that we focus on, is that a passion for Christ or a faithless prostitute more interested in herself and her own pleasures?

We really have to put it in these terms because God does. He doesn't take our casual attitude and lack of interest in him lightly – no more than a husband would who is being ignored by his wife. It's not just religious passion – it's a passion *for him*. The Song of Songs (though many feel that it's not about Christ, that's a serious mistake) teaches us how to love someone: we focus on who he is, and what he does. That's what gets our interest. But does the average Christian know enough about Jesus to love him and believe in him intelligently? That's why Paul prayed for our spiritual wisdom and insight "so that you might know him more."

- **Bringing the Tithe** – As we've seen already, food was the point of the tithe law. Now the obvious connection here for Christians is the Bread of life. That's the food that the Church feeds on for its life.

> I am the bread of life. Whoever comes to me will never go hungry, and whoever believes in me will never be thirsty. (John 6:35)

When the church gathers together, it's to feast on the Manna from Heaven; that's the only thing that holds us together. He's our life; he's our means of justification and sanctification. But there has to be real content – a meal is worth nothing if there's no food! The leaders have to present Christ in his fullness: his names, his works, his relationship to the Father, his Spirit, his many functions in the Kingdom. There has to be real information constantly given to the Church so that they can see him and submit to him and trust him for these very real things about him.

And we are also informed by the Apostles that it's not just the leaders who present this feast to the Church. We are all appointed as priests in the House of God.

> As you come to him, the living Stone — rejected by men but chosen by God and precious to him — you also, like living stones, are being built into a spiritual house to be a holy priesthood, offering spiritual sacrifices acceptable to God through Jesus Christ. (1 Peter 2:4-5)

Every true Christian is a priest in the Temple of God, assigned the duty to serve both God and man. Christ of course gave each of us the ability (power) and wisdom to do this spiritual task.

> But to each one of us grace has been given as Christ apportioned it. ... So Christ himself gave the Apostles, the Prophets, the evangelists, the pastors and teachers, to equip his people for works of service, so that the body of Christ may be built up until we all reach unity in the faith and in the knowledge of the Son of God and become mature, attaining to the whole measure of the fullness of Christ. (Ephesians 4:7, 11-13)

A spiritual gift is nothing less than the ability to make the person and work of Christ real to others, so that they can see and hear and feel the presence of the Lord and believe in him as a result. So the feast around Christ is something that we all share in; we all bring something to the table so that the entire family of God can enjoy Christ.

When this happens (and unfortunately it rarely happens!) "then all the nations will call you blessed, for yours will be a delightful land, says the LORD Almighty." (Malachi 3:12)

- **Fear the Judge** – We are so myopic – so self-centered that we can't see beyond our own little problems and pleasures. We forget too easily that this matter of our religion is not about us. But a clear vision of the risen Christ changes our whole world-view: in him we see that God is building an eternal Kingdom of which we are but a small part.

One of the favorite pastimes of our culture is to blame God for our problems. That's a sure sign that we are focused on ourselves, not on him. That is so far out of line in light of the Kingdom of God that he doesn't deem such an attitude worth taking seriously.

> Then those who feared the Lord talked with each other, and the LORD listened and heard. A scroll of remembrance was written in his presence concerning those who feared the LORD and honored his name. (Malachi 3:16)

God is leading his people to the Promised Land. Along the way he reveals his plans to them, plans to bless them and make them into a great nation. He fights their battles for them and destroys their enemies. He has the entire plan worked out ahead of time, even to the division of the land and who will inherit what. He has leaders chosen, a place of worship, the plans for the Temple – it's a great project in which he will get full glory and his people will live in peace and prosperity.

And what do his people do? They complain about little irritations all the way to the Promised Land!

> Today, if you hear his voice, do not harden your hearts as you did in the rebellion, during the time of testing in the wilderness, where your ancestors tested and tried me, though for forty years they saw what I did. That is why I was angry with that generation; I said, 'Their hearts are always going astray, and they have not known my ways.' So I declared on oath in my anger, 'They shall never enter my rest.' (Hebrews 3:7-11)

Christ is sitting on David's throne right now, putting his enemies under his feet, ruling over the nations with an iron rod, saving his people and bringing his enemies down in ruin. Anybody who doesn't see that is not living by faith in the Son of God. He *will* prevail; the book of Revelation is the encouraging promise of that fact.

Then why are we so focused on ourselves in worship? Why are we so myopic? Why do we complain to God in our prayers that he needs to give us more of what we "need"? Why are we so self-centered, with so little interest in finding out who God is?

A lack of faith in how the King is doing his work is an insult to his wisdom and power. Job found that out in a big way; Zechariah lost his voice because of his lack of faith; Jesus rebuked his disciples for theirs; the Apostles tried to encourage us to overlook hard times and trials for "the joy set before us." And in this passage in Malachi, it seems that answering the complaints of the unfaithful is beneath the Lord's dignity; he simply responds by promising a future Kingdom to those who *do* trust him. The events will be the clearest proof of God's power.

What gets us out of our self-centeredness (and the inevitable complaining that goes along with that) is to focus on *his* interests – the Kingdom that he's building. His project cannot fail. The more you get to know him, the more you will be convinced of that – and you'll learn how to put your little problems to the side in the interests of his Kingdom. His work becomes our work.

> So do not worry, saying, 'What shall we eat?' or 'What shall we drink?' or 'What shall we wear?' For the pagans run after all these things, and your Heavenly Father knows that you need them. But seek first his Kingdom and his righteousness, and all these things will be given to you as well. (Matthew 6:31-33)

> Therefore we do not lose heart. Though outwardly we are wasting away, yet inwardly we are being renewed day by day. For our light and momentary troubles are achieving for us an eternal glory that far outweighs them all. So we fix our eyes not on what is seen, but on what is unseen, since what is seen is temporary, but

what is unseen is eternal. (2 Corinthians 4:16-18)

Summary

Malachi's message is this: the people of God are worshiping God with less than the best. They're bringing sub-standard sacrifices, they aren't interested in God himself, they are focused on themselves and their own pleasures and desires, and they seemingly have little to no interest in God's Kingdom – just solving the problems of their own little world. In other words, they're going through the motions of worship, but God isn't in it.

The problem was that *they* thought they were doing it right. Malachi had to expose the simple but shocking fact that God wasn't there, and they didn't seem to care about that.

It's entirely possible, in fact it's much too common, for our worship to be centered on ourselves instead of on God. And when we do that, we can't see that we're doing it until a prophet points it out to us. True worship is bringing Christ to the front of the church, not ourselves, and taking from his hands the treasures of Heaven which will solve our spiritual problems.

THE OLD TESTAMENT – FATHER AND SON

The Jews consider the Old Testament to be a story between Father and son – the son, of course, being themselves, the people of Israel. Little do they know …

After I had been studying the Old Testament myself after twenty some years, it suddenly occurred to me what the Old Testament was about.

The Old Testament is the description of Christ and our relationship to the Father through him.

We've been looking at how much there is about Christ in the Old Testament, that the stories are actually clusters, as you will, of information about Christ that we have distributed across the entire book. To get the complete picture of who Jesus is and what he does, we have to gather them all together. And that's essentially what the Apostles do in the New Testament; they testified that this Christ predicted by the Old Testament is the man Jesus who came from Heaven in the flesh.

What we need to do now, however, before we lose the opportunity, is back up still further and look at the concept of the Son in the Old Testament. I realize it's probably easier to see what the Jews see, because the story is about a rebellious son, a wayward son, a son whom the Father had to correct and discipline and rebuke all along the way. It seems to fit their story better than it would Jesus. But we mustn't forget whom Jesus came to identify with.

> For what the Law was powerless to do because it was weakened by the flesh, God did by sending his own Son in the likeness of sinful flesh to be a sin offering. (Romans 8:3)

Jesus identifies with his people; he calls us brothers. He became one of us so that we might be with him in glory.

> In bringing many sons to glory, it was fitting that God, for whom and through whom everything exists, should make the pioneer of their salvation perfect

> through what he suffered. Both the one who makes men holy and those who are made holy are of the same family. So Jesus is not ashamed to call them brothers. (Hebrews 2:10-11)

Now it makes more sense. The Old Testament is about God dealing with a rebellious son – that's us. God, out of his love and compassion, delivers and redeems sinners – that's us. God brings us to himself as his Son – that's Jesus, *and* us because we are in him. Jesus' goal was to become one of us, in the likeness of sinful flesh, and then lead us out, step by step, through the process of salvation and redemption, to the Promised Land. In him is the way of escape for the children of God. And what is he leading us to? His Father in Heaven.

So the Old Testament is a story of God the Father delivering his Son from sin and death and making him ready to live with him in Heaven. There's the grand Mission of the Church, the Mission that we are all part of if we are truly children of God. And the entire thing takes place in, because of, through, and to the glory of Jesus, who is himself the Son of God come to take us home.

The Old Testament describes Heaven

I lately heard yet another preacher say that the Bible doesn't tell us much about Heaven, except for the last few chapters in the book of Revelation. That is so ignorant; it shows an abysmal lack of understanding of the Bible. As a matter of fact, the Bible describes Heaven so clearly that when we get there, we will recognize most of what we see there; it will already be familiar to those who have been studying the Bible. The description of Heaven is spread across the entire Bible, for those who have the faith to see it.

- **The glory of God** – All the Bible declares the glory of God in many ways. His many *names* tell us all sorts of things that he does, as well as describe his complex nature. The *ways* of the Lord show us the preferred ways he likes to do things, which are not at all the way we do things; the difference is that his ways work for what he wants to accomplish, and ours don't. God's *works* are the kinds of things that only God can do; necessary for our salvation, they are not things that we can do. God's *wrath* against the wicked is a real and terrifying aspect of God's nature, something that we may not have counted on in our dealings with him. God is *light*, which means he shines insight and revelation on everything – it's the way he sees things, not the way we see things, that is the truth. Warrior, Spirit, King, Creator, Deliverer – all these are characteristics of our God that many passages of the Old Testament reveal to us. We can hardly say, then, when we meet God on Judgment Day, that we haven't been exposed to a detailed description of the God we say we want to live with!

- **The House of God** – This theme actually starts in Genesis, not in Exodus with the Tabernacle. Remember that Jacob, in his dream, discovered that he was in the house of God.

> "How awesome is this place! This is none other than the house of God; this is the gate of Heaven." (Genesis 28:17)

Exodus and Leviticus are detailed explanations of what the house of God looks like, what the rules are, what it's like to live with God. He has his throne there; he rules over his people, and they submit to his rule over them. His throne is also a mercy seat where his people will find him a "compassionate and gracious God, slow to anger, abounding in love and faithfulness, maintaining love to thousands, and forgiving wickedness, rebellion and sin." (Exodus 34:6-7) There in his house is the eternal sacrifice that cleanses us so that we, who have sinned against him, might have the right of entry to his throne. God is the source of all good things for his people; it's in his house that we will find food and shelter and justice and peace and blessings. And in his house everything focuses on God; that is, in fact, what the word "holiness" means. Everything there is "from him, and through him, and to him." (Romans 11:36)

- **The Family of God** – When God called Abraham, he promised to give him and his family the terms of the Covenant. It was a family affair from the beginning. The promises did not go to Hagar's son, but to Sarah's son. I believe that we tend to forget this aspect of the story when we read the Old Testament. At no point do we find God extending this offer of salvation to "whosoever will" in the Old Testament. This was for the Jews only. If someone wanted in on the Covenant, they had to join the Jewish community. Otherwise they were part of the "goyim," the outsiders who were in the dark, "without hope and without God" as Paul describes them. Anybody who wanted anything from the Covenant had to prove that they were descendants of Abraham.

So the "whosoever will" of the New Testament can confuse someone who doesn't understand what's really going on. Yes, the Gospel is now offered to the nations. But as Jesus prayed, the Spirit of God is collecting the people of God from all around the nations, down through history – revealing who is in God's family.

> I have other sheep that are not of this sheep pen. I must bring them also. They too will listen to my voice, and there shall be one flock and one shepherd. (John 10:16)

Jesus surprised the Jews when he singled out some for salvation. For example, when he called Zacchaeus down out of the tree, his comment was illuminating.

> Today salvation has come to this house, because this man, too, is a son of Abraham. (Luke 19:9)

Not a child of Abraham by his DNA (though he was that), but by his faith. As Paul tells us, not every Jew is a Jew.

Jesus' parable about the banquet in Heaven also reveals the privacy of the closed community that Heaven will be.

> But when the king came in to see the guests, he noticed a man there who was not wearing

wedding clothes. He asked, 'How did you get in here without wedding clothes, friend?' The man was speechless. Then the king told the attendants, 'Tie him hand and foot, and throw him outside, into the darkness, where there will be weeping and gnashing of teeth.' For many are invited, but few are chosen. (Matthew 22:11-14)

- **The Altar and the Temple** – The Temple (and in earlier days, the Tabernacle) was the center of the Israelite community. It is also the center of Heaven.

> But you have come to Mount Zion, to the city of the living God, the Heavenly Jerusalem. You have come to thousands upon thousands of angels in joyful assembly, to the church of the firstborn, whose names are written in Heaven. You have come to God, the Judge of all, to the spirits of the righteous made perfect, to Jesus the mediator of a new Covenant, and to the sprinkled blood that speaks a better word than the blood of Abel. (Hebrews 12:22-24)

In the Temple in Jerusalem the functions of the Temple were ongoing day and night. There was always the *light* illuminating the way to God, because their need of him was continuous. There was always a *sacrifice* there, because we, being sinners, cannot come to God without it. There was always *bread* there, because God is literally our spiritual food without which we can't survive. The Temple was filled with gold, because every aspect of the Temple service is precious to us. The Name of God was there in the Temple, because whenever someone prayed they turned toward the Temple and called on that Name and God heard their prayer.

Follow the history of Israel and see how central the Temple was to the life of the Israelites. They couldn't survive without it. When they were forced to do without it (during their Exile in Babylon) they suffered as a result.

They couldn't wait to get back home, rebuild the Temple, and re-establish contact with their God.

Hebrews tells us that this Temple and its many aspects that the Old Testament describes to us is a shadow of the one in Heaven.

> They serve at a sanctuary that is a copy and shadow of what is in Heaven. This is why Moses was warned when he was about to build the tabernacle: "See to it that you make everything according to the pattern shown you on the mountain." (Hebrews 8:5)

We shouldn't be surprised, then, when we step into Heaven and see the Temple in the middle of everything. And the functions of the Heavenly Temple are the same as those in the earthly one. It's all described for us in the Old Testament.

- **The Kingdom of God** – This is the root of the solution for mankind's problems. And it's probably the one thing that will most offend sinners about Heaven.

We moderns don't appreciate the concept of a Kingdom, because we like to have a say in what's going on. We believe in the right to vote, to put in our opinion on things. We wouldn't have done well in the old days when the king's rule was the only law.

But from the book of Genesis on, we learn that this is exactly what God created – a Kingdom. In a Kingdom, only the opinion of the King matters. God is not interested in what we think, for the very good reason that our opinions are what got us into trouble in the first place! God's wisdom is perfect and profound; all he expects us to do is exactly what he tells us to do. Only in that way will this world of his be perfect.

Rebellion against God's commands (as we read in Genesis 3) only results in death, not life. For the rest of the Bible we read about God setting up a new Kingdom on the ruins of the first Creation, in which he intends to be

King over obedient subjects – or we're going to die. That's how kingdoms work.

Throughout the Old Testament we learn about how the Kingdom of God works. The Law of Moses (from Genesis to Deuteronomy) is the Law of the King; anybody who wants to be part of this Kingdom has to obey the Law completely, exactly, in the way that God wants to see his Law obeyed. Judges shows us Israel in chaos because they didn't obey God's Law – this is what happens when there is no king.

David set up a Kingdom in Israel that went back to the Law of Moses and re-established the kind of Kingdom that God wants to see over us. All the kings after him were expected to maintain that Kingdom – some succeeded, many failed. The Israelites finally rebelled completely against God's Law and was punished in Exile as a result.

When they came back home, they had learned their lesson: from now on, follow the King's Law! They tried, but again they showed that they were missing the point by the time Jesus arrived. He had to show them just how deep is the Law of God, how it reaches the heart, it requires an obedience that we can little imagine. The Kingdom of Heaven will be a Kingdom in which every thought, every action, every word will be obedience and service to the King. The wisdom and power of God will extend over all that is there, in every way – physical and spiritual. What was an unattainable goal in the Old Testament will finally become a reality in Heaven.

So we see that the Old Testament *completely* describes the world that we hope to be a part of in Heaven. And just to show you that the book of Revelation itself is actually a compendium of Old Testament themes, here's a list of images in chapters 21-22 of the book that are lifted directly out of Old Testament stories.

- The new Jerusalem
- the dwelling of God with men (described so fully in

Exodus and **Leviticus**)

- no more death or pain (**Isaiah**)

- the Bride (**Hosea**, **Ezekiel**, **Psalms** and the **Song of Songs**)

- gates representing the twelve tribes of Israel

- the angel with the measuring rod (**Ezekiel**)

- the nations and kings of the earth walking by the light of the city (so many of the **Prophets**!)

- the river in the city (**Ezekiel**)

- the trees yielding their fruit (**Psalm 1; Jeremiah**)

- even the Book of Life! (**Psalm 69**)

Obviously the Apostle turned to the Old Testament to describe the scenes of Heaven that he saw in his vision.

Metaphysically, there isn't much in the Bible about what Heaven will be like. The Apostles and Jesus give us a few clues, like being able to walk through walls and yet being able to eat a meal also. But as far as what is there, Heaven is fully described if you're willing to look beyond the narrow limits of Revelation and study the entire Bible.

Life with the Father

Jesus mentions, in his prayer in John 17, something of what his life with the Father had been like before he came to earth.

> And now, Father, glorify me in your presence with the glory I had with you before the world began. (John 17:5)

What *was* life with the Father like? The Gospels gives us many insights into this special relationship. Jesus is the beloved Son, who shares the nature of God and whom the Father loves deeply. Jesus shares in the Father's glory; he is the "image of the invisible God" and shines with the glory of God. Jesus shares his Father's throne, and is himself the King who rules over God's creation. Jesus knows the depths of the Father; only he can see the true God and knows the eternal nature of God. Jesus enjoys the fullness of the Father and is himself the Heir who receives all that fullness.

If we take all these things together, we see that Jesus is special – he alone is in the position to live with, and know, God. And for those who understand the immensity of this concept, Jesus therefore has the best seat in the house, so to speak. He has what no other creature in Heaven or on earth has privilege to – the fullness of God.

Now just imagine the staggering implications of what Jesus then says in his prayer about us.

> Father, I want those you have given me to be with me where I am, and to see my glory, the glory you have given me because you loved me before the creation of the world. (John 17:24)

Not where the angels are, not where the living creatures and other servants of God stand, but with Jesus before his Father. We will see and experience the same life of glory that Jesus himself does. He is the Son, and we are in the Son. The best seat in the house.

> His divine power has given us everything we need for a godly life through our knowledge of him who called us by his own glory and goodness. Through these he has given us his very great and precious promises, so that through them *you may participate in the divine nature*, having escaped the corruption in the world caused by evil desires. (2 Peter 1:3-4)

Commentators hesitate to give much credence to this comment from Peter, because obviously we don't believe that we will become God. But we will become one with the Son of God, through the mystery of the Incarnation, so that we will become children of God in our nature, and heirs of the Father as we are made one with the great Heir, capable of living the life that Jesus himself lives with the Father. We will not be standing before the throne of God with the rest of the servants; we will share the seat with the King himself, part of the family of God.

Does the Old Testament give us any preview of this? Well, it's hard to miss! The Old Testament tells us right from the beginning that this is going to be a family affair. And it's going to be the privilege of the ages as God prepares a people to live with him.

The heirs of the Promise. Christians will inherit the promises of the Covenant made with Abraham – the terms of the Gospel: the Heir through whom we will inherit the treasures of Heaven; the Land of Heaven; the family of God – the Church; and the blessing of freedom from sin, resurrection from the dead and eternal life.

The House of God. Christians will live with God in his house – with the right of access to God, with the privileges of status as God's children. Far from standing outside at the door (as the Israelites had to do), we will go in boldly and confidently and share the life of our Father in his own home. Everything he has will be ours.

What has to be done to us to come into this privileged status. The only way that Christians can have these amazing privileges and blessings is because of the price that the Son of God paid – his blood, his sacrifice, his power to cleanse the heart and mind of all of its sin and rebellion. We will always feel the presence of the Christ upon us making our life in Heaven possible, like a power surging in us giving us the spiritual life that helps us exist there. It's what Jesus talked about in John 6 – he is literally the Bread that gives us life.

The determination of God. God showed his amazing mercy and love to determined sinners; it's hard to reconcile that idea with any other concept except the way the Father deals with his son. Time after time the Israelites would turn away from God into idolatry and immorality, and God would continually send Prophets to warn them – and yet it did little good. Still, God stayed at it until even he had to draw the line and send them into Exile. But after the Exile he brought back the Remnant and started over with them.

There's something in the Old Testament that is inexplicable unless you see the point of the book as being about the Son – it's that God never gave up on the Jews.

The Jews were nobody special, as God himself testified in the Law.

248

> It is not because of your righteousness or your integrity that you are going in to take possession of their land; but on account of the wickedness of these nations, the LORD your God will drive them out before you, to accomplish what he swore to your fathers, to Abraham, Isaac and Jacob. Understand, then, that it is not because of your righteousness that the LORD your God is giving you this good land to possess, for you are a stiff-necked people. (Deuteronomy 9:5-6)

In spite of the fact that the Jews left an abysmal track record all through the history of the Old Testament, God was always faithful to them. He kept giving them a "second chance" long after the rest of us would have given up on them. From the sons of Jacob through the Wilderness wanderings through the period of the Judges through the rebellion of the kings of Israel, God preserved his people and kept giving them the promises of the Covenant, even though they didn't deserve a thing.

Scholars call this the principle of the *remnant*. Modern Christians give voice to this perplexing concept with the prayer, "Why me, Lord?" And David put it in poetic words.

> What is man that you are mindful of him, the son of man that you care for him? You have made them a little lower than the angels and crowned them with glory and honor. You made them rulers over the works of your hands; you put everything under their feet. (Psalm 8:4-6)

Hebrews has the answer to this question.

> In putting everything under them, God left nothing that is not subject to them. Yet at present we do not see everything subject to them. But we do see Jesus, who was made lower than the angels for a little while, now crowned with glory and honor because he suffered death, so that by the grace of God he might taste death for everyone. (Hebrews 2:8-9)

It's because the story is not about us; it's about the Son. God will never give up on his Son. The Father loves the Son; the Son lives forever in his Father's presence. The Son *will* enjoy the fullness of the Father; that's never been in question. And whoever is in the Son will experience this amazing faithfulness of the Father for themselves – not because of themselves, but because they are with the Son whom the Father will never turn away from or reject. The cry of Jesus from the cross – "Why have you forsaken me?" – was the cry of the Son to his Father, who answered by raising him from the dead. He will never forsake his Son, "who through the Spirit of holiness was appointed the Son of God in power by his resurrection from the dead." (Romans 1:4)

And that is why God never gives up on us; we are his children: we are "in the Son" and considered sons of God ourselves.

> Praise be to the God and Father of our Lord Jesus Christ, who has blessed us in the Heavenly realms with every spiritual blessing in Christ. For he chose us in him before the creation of the world to be holy and blameless in his sight. In love he predestined us for adoption to sonship through Jesus Christ, in accordance with his pleasure and will — to the praise of his glorious grace, which he has freely given us in the One he loves. In him we have redemption through his blood, the forgiveness of sins, in accordance with the riches of God's grace that he lavished on us. With all wisdom and understanding, he made known to us the mystery of his will according to his good pleasure, which he purposed in Christ, to be put into effect when the times reach their fulfillment — to bring unity to all things in Heaven and on earth under Christ. (Ephesians 1:3-10)

Even the punishment of the Jews in the Old Testament is what Hebrews calls "the discipline of the Father toward his Son." (Hebrews 12) Of course we know that Jesus didn't need punishment, though Hebrews also tells us that Jesus also "learned obedience." (Hebrews 5:8) But Jesus also took our sins upon himself (Isaiah 53); it's on his body that the punishment of the sins of God's people fell. What sins? All the sins that we read about in the history of the Jews. Here is a complete description of what sin is, how deeply it runs, how pervasive it is even among God's people. This is the black picture of humanity as Jesus finds it, and what the Law is talking about when it describes rebellion against God. And the sufferings of the Son is what it takes to purge us of *our* sin: the depth of the stain, the distance we have to go to get back to God, the pain and blood and suffering that it will take to restore our relationship to God. It's all the story of God's Son bringing the sinner – God's Son – back to God. The Prodigal returns home to the Father.

So the Old Testament is about the Father and his Son – the Divine and the human, the ups and downs, the perfection and the rebellion, the ideal and the failure, the Father making his Son ready for Heaven. This is our story, we who are the family of God. As Paul tells us in Ephesians, this whole thing was planned out in the very beginning – our destiny as God's children in Christ.

Summary

So the Jews were more right than they realized. The Old Testament isn't primarily about them as the son, but about Jesus as the Son and any (Jew or Gentile) who are, in Christ, part of the family of God.

But again we miss the point if we think it's all about us. It isn't. It's about Jesus the Son; he's the Heir of the Father with all the rights and privileges. We are only part of this story if we are part of Jesus. We share in his glory; the Father is graciously including us in if we want to be part of this kind of life with God. If so, we will all share in the Son's likeness as his story becomes our story.

MATTHEW – THE SON OF DAVID AND ABRAHAM

It should be obvious right up front what the Gospel of Matthew is all about. He tells us at the beginning.

> This is the genealogy of Jesus the Messiah the son of David, the son of Abraham. (Matthew 1:1)

He immediately connects Jesus with two of the great concepts of the Old Testament – the Covenant with Abraham, and the 5-Point Plan of David. But if modern preachers don't take the cue, it's probably because they don't understand those concepts and they fail to see how they get worked out in the Gospel of Christ. This is a perfect example of how much we need the Old Testament to educate us about Jesus. The data about Christ is in the Old; the Apostles rely on us to do our homework first in the Old before coming to the New. If we don't see that, we won't get the point – or we'll get the wrong point.

It's tempting to launch into a full-scale commentary on Matthew, because these two concepts enrich the book so much. But we will limit ourselves to a short summary of where to find examples of the Covenant and David's Plan in Matthew's account of Jesus' ministry.

David's Plan

Let's remind ourselves of David's Plan. There were five things that David had to do to pull the nation of Israel together and bring them back to God.

- **Capital City** – Here is where the throne of the King will be, as well as the Temple. It brought the nation together, and from here the King will rule over the entire nation.

- **Defeat the enemies** – David had to take care of this problem of their enemies once for all, because it was interfering with their life with God.

- **Back to God** – It was time to quit their idolatry and focus on God now, the source of all their blessings.

- **Government** – David set up a system by which his will – or God's will – would be distributed and maintained across the nation.

- **Build the Temple** – The Temple was where Israel's blessings all originated, and David set up a system that enabled the priests to serve both God and man.

This is the Plan that all of David's descendants were expected to maintain. Whoever sat on David's throne was responsible for the Plan; the nation depended on it. So we can expect to see Jesus, the Son of David, taking on the task of his father David.

Identity of the King

One of the problems that the Jews were to grapple with was Jesus' claim that he really was the Son of David. Such a claim carries a great deal of authority if true. So there were a number of times when not only Jesus laid claim to the title, but also others were enabled to see the truth of the claim.

- **Worship of the Magi** (Matthew 2) – These Gentiles knew who the King was when the Jews failed to identify their own.

- **Calmed the storm** (Matthew 8) – Showed his mastery over his Creation – the King rules the elements.

- **Transfiguration** (Matthew 17) – During his earthly ministry the King set aside his glory so that we could get close to him; but here we get a glimpse of who he really is. His is an inherent glory, not a glory of gold and robes and empty ceremony.

- **The blind men** (Matthew 20) – They could see the Son of David even though physically blind; faith showed them.

- **Jesus' authority** (Matthew 21) – He challenges the Jews to identify what gave him the authority to do his miracles and teachings – they didn't make the connection that he was the Son of David.

- **Son of David** (Matthew 22) – Again, he challenges the Jews to explain the concept of the Son of David; they couldn't see that the one fulfilling David's Plan would of course be the Son of David.

- **Signs of the end** (Matthew 24) – Jesus is warning his disciples not to be fooled by false Christs; at the second coming, the signs will be there that Jesus himself has come to take over his Kingdom.

- **Tenants** (Matthew 25) – A story about rejecting the rightful King – the Jews wouldn't have him.

- **Walking on water** (Matthew 25) – Proof that the Son of God has come, the Master of the elements.

- **Pilate and the King** (Matthew 27) – Pilate doesn't believe in the King because Jesus rejects a physical Kingdom.

- **King of the Jews** (Matthew 27) – An irony in which the truth is told through the unbelief of the Jews.

Capital city

Where the capital of the King is located determines what kinds of things can be done, and the nature of the entire Kingdom. Jesus sets his capital in Heaven; that means he has powers that no earthly king has (like judging hearts), and he distributes spiritual treasures, not physical ones.

- **Leper** (Matthew 8) – The leper discovers that the King is willing to give out the treasures of Heaven to those who ask.

- **Kingdom parables** (Matthew 13) – It's a spiritual Kingdom that Jesus is building, and it grows in ways that are contrary to the way we would think. We have to have eyes of faith to understand it.

- **Miracles** (Matthew) – The miracles that Jesus did are distributed all through Matthew. These are the good things of the Kingdom that the King pours out on his subjects. They are not only physical miracles, but spiritual too – this is the time of transition from the physical Kingdom of the Jews to the spiritual Kingdom of the Church.

- **Feeding 5000** (Matthew 14) – Jesus teaches the principle of pouring out Heaven's treasures on God's people – he first gives them to the Apostles, and they in turn give them to us.

- **Rich ruler** (Matthew 19) – Here is the Judge on his throne, analyzing the man's heart and correctly diagnosing his spiritual illness.

- **Triumphal entry** (Matthew 21) – Though the Jews were looking for a King, Jesus had no intention of setting up a physical Kingdom in Jerusalem. His was to be a spiritual Kingdom; so he appears now as a humble servant.

Defeat the enemies

There are particular enemies that Jesus is going to target: not the enemies that we might have, but enemies of God and those who want to destroy the spiritual Kingdom of God.

- **Temptation** (Matthew 4) – The "first blood" encounter with his great enemy Satan. Strike at the devil, and a major part of the battle is won.

- **Carrying the cross** (Matthew 10, 16) – One of our deadliest enemies – our own flesh – has to be destroyed if we are to be free of sin and follow Jesus to life.

- **Demons** (Matthew 8, 12, 17) – Jesus destroys the haunts of our spiritual enemies in all its forms and functions.

- **Paying the tax** (Matthew 22) – The Jews hated Roman rule and considered Caesar to be the enemy. Jesus seems to have no interest in fighting the Romans; he is targeting enemies of the soul instead.

- **Woes** (Matthew 23) – One of the tasks of the King is to confront and destroy the hypocrisy of the Pharisees, enemies of God's spiritual Kingdom, who themselves are the perfect examples of corrupted hearts and false leaders.

Back to God

There isn't anybody more qualified to bring us to God than the Son of God. Jesus knows the heart of God, the eternity and infinity of God, God's ways and works and glory. He knows how to strip away the superficial religion that we have invented and make us come face to face with the real God.

- **God with us** (Matthew 1) – No less than God himself has come to solve mankind's problems of sin and death. We can deal with him directly now.

- **The depth of the Law** (Matthew 5) – We can't continue to be satisfied with a shallow obedience to God; this God is unimaginably holy, and our service to him must come from a transformed and perfect heart.

- **I never knew you!** (Matthew 7) – Many are going to find out, too late, that their religion was missing one important part – God himself!

- **Taught as one with authority** (Matthew 7) – The Pharisees only taught *about* God; but Jesus *is* the Son of God – so his Word is truth, not man's opinions.

- **I know who you are!** (Matthew 8) – The demons do whatever they want with mankind until the Son of God shows up and strips them of their power.

- **They worship me in vain** (Matthew 15) – Empty worship full of ceremonies and traditions don't connect with the living God; true worship comes into his presence and receives Heaven's treasures as a result.

- **Love the Lord your God** (Matthew 22) – Here is the root of all true religion: to seek and find God, to find in him your "all in all", to forsake all else, and to enjoy the fullness and the glory of God.

Setting up a Government

Jesus intends to set up a perfect Kingdom, ruled by God's Law and filled with perfect subjects. One will reigns in this Kingdom – God's will. And he will organize his Kingdom into a hierarchy, a system that passes down the will of the King to all its servants. That means the ministry of the Word through the Apostles and Prophets, and then through pastors and teachers. The goal is peace, prosperity, life, joy and the fullness of God's goodness to all.

- **Wise men** (Matthew 2) – The Magi correctly identify the head of God's Kingdom and give him the honor he deserves.

- **Sermon on the Mount** (Matthew 5-7) – The Constitution, or by-laws, of Jesus' new Kingdom. Anybody who wants to be part of this Kingdom has to conform to his high standards.

- **Centurion** (Matthew 8) – A man under authority recognizes the Master's authority, through faith.

- **Laborers in field** (Matthew 9) – Jesus is calling for workers to help govern his Kingdom and take care of his subjects.

- **12 Apostles** (Matthew 10) – Jesus sends out the disciples as his first-level representatives, creating and maintaining his Kingdom around the world.

- **Sabbath law** (Matthew 12) – The intent of God's Law is for our good, for peace and prosperity and life – not for oppression by man.

- **Peter the Rock** (Matthew 16) – Not that Peter himself will be the Rock; but that through the Apostles Jesus will reign in his Kingdom, the Church, and those with the faith that Peter has (he sees the Son of God) will be part of this Kingdom.

- **Greatest in Kingdom** (Matthew 18, 19) – The point of Jesus' Kingdom is not to satisfy the King at the expense of his servants; it's to bless the entire Kingdom with the goodness of God. To that end, the King and all his counselors will work.

- **Unforgiving servant** (Matthew 18) – Again, the point of the Kingdom is not self-aggrandizement, but the blessing of all its inhabitants. Everyone has to understand this goal and help to advance it.

- **All authority** (Matthew 28) – The final command of the King while on earth: go build the Kingdom according to the principles that he taught us. It's time to carry out the Plan of David in the Church.

Building the Temple

The house of God is where God and his people will live forever in peace and blessing. Touching God is life, and that goodness gets spread around through the ministry of priests. So Jesus is making all of his people priests so that they will see and enjoy God directly, and pass on that richness to others. And there will be no slackers in God's house!

- **Gathering disciples** (Matthew 4) – The Apostles are going to be the foundation of the Church (see Ephesians 2:20) – their writings will be the rule for our faith and practice as Christians.

- **Judge a tree by its fruit** (Matthew 12) – The goal of every subject in Christ's Kingdom is that he/she bears spiritual fruit that will bless everyone else with the treasures of Heaven.

- **Brother sins against me** (Matthew 18) – There will be peace in the brotherhood, not war. That enables the work to go on in God's Temple. See Philippians 2.

- **Cursing fig tree** (Matthew 21) – Jesus really does mean what he says about bearing fruit in his Kingdom. Take warning.

- **Cleansing the Temple** (Matthew 21) – A symbolic act that shows Jesus is the Son of David: he will not have the house of God dedicated to man's greed or self-glory. His task is to set up God's eternal house so that all of God's children will do their duty and serve God and man.

- **Talents** (Matthew 25) – In God's house, everyone is a priest and everyone has spiritual gifts to minister the grace of God to all others.

- **Sheep and goats** (Matthew 25) – Service to God and man not only takes on forms that the superficial don't recognize – it's about true love, not one's glory – but it is also mandatory. Our eternal future depends on our service and whether we did what the King requires.

By doing these particular things, Jesus proved himself to be the Son of David. Not all the Jews liked what he was doing, though many did. But the Jews generally recognized what was going on, and the kind of claim that Jesus was making about himself.

> All the people were astonished and said, "Could this be the Son of David?" (Matthew 12:23)

The Covenant

David's Plan actually made it possible for the Jews to enjoy the blessings of the Covenant made with Abraham, which was the foundational blessing of the Jews. So let's review the Covenant's terms and see how Jesus honored and fulfilled that ancient agreement between Abraham and God.

- **The Son** – Abraham's heir – the "miracle baby" – will be the Executor of the estate through whom will come the blessings of the Covenant to all the other heirs.

- **The Land** – God would provide the Land of Canaan, the Promised Land, the "land flowing with milk and honey," for Abraham's descendants to live in.

- **The Nation** – Abraham's family would grow into a great nation – descendants of their father through their faith.

- **The Blessing** – Through Abraham's offspring would come the solution to sin and death, the overturning of the curse of mankind – resurrection from the dead.

We also saw that these Covenant promises had spiritual fulfillments in the Kingdom of Christ. In the Old Testament the Jews enjoyed the physical promises, but those who had faith could see that the real fulfillment was in the coming Messiah who would give them "a better country—a Heavenly one." (Hebrews 11:16) For example, there are a number of passages that testify that Abraham himself knew about this spiritual fulfillment in Christ (see John 8:56).

Now let's go through Matthew again and see how the author develops the idea of Jesus being the Heir of Abraham.

- **Out of Egypt** (Matthew 2) – From Joseph and the Israelites, through the history of the Jews in the Old Testament, and into the life of Jesus, we see the story of the Son who is destined to be brought out of bondage and into the presence of God to live with his Father.

- **John the Baptist** (Matthew 3) – The Jews thought they were the children of Abraham. But John tells them that God can make children of Abraham out of stones – which he has done with the Gentiles (see Ezekiel 36:26-27). The former heirs are going to be left out in the darkness.

- **This is my Son** (Matthew 3) – Here is God's designated Heir, the only Son who pleases his Father – the Righteous Son, the Son who knows the Father and shares in his glory. Here is the Executor of the estate of Heaven to whom the rest of us must go if we want anything from God.

- **Land of the Gentiles** (Matthew 4) – God's intent has always been to "enlarge the tent" of Israel to include both Gentile and Jew, to make Abraham's family out of all the nations of the earth.

- **Miracles** (Matthew 1-28) – Jesus spent his entire life handing out the blessings of the Covenant to those in need, to those who came and asked for them in faith. Their faith proved their descent from Abraham and therefore gave them the right to the inheritance.

- **Treasures in Heaven** (Matthew 6) – Jesus knows what the Covenant blessings are – they are not the treasures of this world. They are spiritual treasures, and he, as the Heir, has the key to the storehouse. He also knows how to get us in touch with them.

- **The Leper** (Matthew 8) – The leper discovers that the Executor of the estate is indeed willing to hand out the treasures of the Covenant to whoever will ask.

- **Children of Abraham** (Matthew 8) – Right now the entire family of Abraham is gathering in Heaven at their father's feet to get ready for the wedding feast – both Jew and Gentile, heirs with the faith of their father Abraham.

- **Jesus' family** (Matthew 12) – Jesus didn't have much hope that earthly families would be of spiritual benefit to us; he counseled us to focus on Abraham's family instead – our brothers and sisters in the faith.

- **The Kingdom of Heaven** (Matthew 13) – Jesus' description of Heaven shows us the spiritual nature of the Promised Land that God has for his people.

- **Lack of faith** (Matthew 13) – When people lacked Abraham's faith, Jesus did not do miracles among them. Those who are not spiritual heirs don't get the promises.

- **Canaanite woman** (Matthew 15) – Until she showed her true nature, Jesus couldn't give her anything she asked; she had no right to it as a non-Jew. But when she displayed the faith of Abraham, he was legally obligated by the terms of the Covenant to give her what she asked. She's part of the family.

- **Wedding feast** (Matthew 22) – Only those who have been covered with the righteousness of Christ will be allowed into the wedding as part of the family of God. This is the third and fourth promises fulfilled.

- **The Resurrection** (Matthew 28) – In himself Jesus fulfills the fourth promise of the Covenant, resurrection from the dead and eternal life with God.

Summary

Matthew gives us abundant testimony that Jesus was the heir of important Old Testament characters. As an Apostle, Matthew was given this clear vision of the Christ, and his job was to pass on that knowledge that he received to us. We also have to see Jesus as the fulfillment of the Abrahamic Covenant and as the Son of David working on his father's Plan. If we don't see that, we don't really understand Jesus – and therefore don't believe the truth about him.

ACTS – HOW TO PREACH CHRIST

The natural starting place to learn how to preach the Gospel of Christ is in the book of Acts, where the Apostles themselves carry the message of Jesus to the world. They were fresh from their own training: Jesus had lived with them and taught them for three-plus years; he was rejected and crucified by the Jews; after burial, God raised him from the dead; he gave last minute instructions to his disciples and then returned to his Father in Heaven. And at the beginning of the book of Acts, the disciples were filled with the Spirit and empowered to preach the Gospel of the One of whom they had such an intimate knowledge.

On the other hand, most people are *not* ready to run with the Apostles at this point!

That, I believe, is where the modern church is right now. Christians – in particular the leaders – think they are capable of understanding what the Apostles were doing and saying in their ministries, when actually they show themselves unprepared to handle the task. Proof? Our sermons about Jesus don't match the sermons of the Apostles! They are missing the data.

I made a chart that compares the modern Gospel with the Gospel that the Apostles preached in the book of Acts, and the differences are obvious. You can see from this chart that the Apostles focused on Old Testament themes to explain the Gospel of Christ. Modern preachers, on the other hand, focus on what we must do – there is nothing told us about who Jesus is. This new Gospel actually may qualify for what Paul condemns in Galatians as a "false Gospel"!

Apostles' Gospel	Modern Gospel
▪ The Creator	▪ God loves you
▪ The Covenant with Abraham	▪ You are a sinner
▪ Moses and the Law	▪ Jesus died for you
▪ David's Kingdom	▪ Accept Jesus as your Lord & Savior
▪ The Temple	▪ Come to Jesus
▪ The Prophets	▪ Believe and be saved
▪ The Jews rejected Christ	
▪ The Apostles' Testimony	
"If you do not believe that *I am the one I claim to be*, you will indeed die in your sins." (John 8:24)	Almost nothing said about Jesus – focus mainly on man.

The two Gospels don't match at all. Evidently modern preachers, when they preach through Acts, are looking at details in the text other than what the Apostles were actually saying. They do notice that the Apostles were preaching to Jews for the first half of the book, then to Gentiles (in Paul's ministry). They notice that the Apostles mention that Jesus fulfilled Old Testament prophecies. They can see that the Apostles believed that Jesus is the Messiah, the Christ. Other than that, they leave almost completely unexplored the points of the Apostles' sermons and limit themselves to preaching through the Apostles' missionary journeys.

And what do preachers actually say about the Gospel? They've filled in their own details on that score; they're not using the Apostles as their models. They're getting their information from our culture instead of the Bible; it's a consumer's market – they tell the paying crowd what the crowd wants to hear.

One of the primary purposes of the book of Acts was to be a model for Gospel preaching. These men were, after all, eyewitnesses of the Christ and specially trained in the Gospel. We're supposed to use their sermon points! But that requires a deep understanding of the Old Testament (as is evident in their constant use of that resource), which we for the most part are almost totally lacking. It's no wonder then that we don't appreciate what the Apostles were saying about Jesus.

Before we get into an analysis of the Apostles' Gospel preaching, let's notice one thing: never, in any of their sermons about Christ, did they ever say "God loves you." They never brought up the subject. That in itself is a major indicator of how badly we've twisted the message from its original content. I know that many preachers wouldn't think of leaving that out of the message, but it's not even the tradition of the church. It's a modern innovation that arose out of the theological upheavals that occurred in the twentieth century. And it's one of the main reasons that our message to the world has become enervated and powerless; witness how little effect the church is having on the world. We're preaching the wrong message.

So let's start over and faithfully follow the Apostles as they taught us how to preach the message of the Christ.

Acts 2 – Peter's Sermon

Although Peter, just weeks before this, showed a profound lack of understanding of Christ's purposes, here at Pentecost the light turned on for him. Suddenly everything became clear. The purpose of the Spirit's outpouring was so that the disciples could understand the spiritual truths of Christ's Kingdom.

Peter's first sermon can be outlined in this way:

1. Prophecy from Joel about the pouring out of the Spirit

2. The life of Jesus – good works, rejection and crucifixion, resurrection

3. David's prophecy of the Messiah

4. David's throne passed on to David's Son

5. Jesus now pours out the Spirit from Heaven's throne

6. Jesus is the Christ

7. Repent, believe and receive the Spirit

His quote from the prophet Joel sets the theme for the entire sermon. The Spirit of God is given to us *so that we can see the truth about Jesus*. The prophecy promises the Spirit to all of God's people – men and women, young and old. They will see visions and dream dreams. And they will see that they must call on the name of the Lord – in this case, the name of Jesus – in order to be saved. It's what they see in him that will prompt their prayers.

David saw the Christ – he could see that this Jesus would be the King that he himself couldn't be. The kind of Kingdom that God wants for all of his people is beyond David's reach; he died, but the son of David would be raised from the dead to carry on David's hope – David knew that.

Now that the son of David is sitting on the throne in Heaven (in the holy Jerusalem), he is pouring out his Spirit on any who turn to him in repentance. What will they see in the Spirit? That Jesus is the promised Messiah, the one who would fulfill the promises of the Old Testament and build the eternal Kingdom, the one who has forgiveness in his hands and yet rules over the nations in justice.

In other words, Peter is telling the crowd that, just as the Apostles now know who Jesus really is, they too can see the truth and apply for the treasures of Heaven. The Spirit gives that insight into the true nature of Jesus.

Acts 3 – Peter's Sermon

Peter's second message was on the occasion of healing the lame man at the Temple. People wanted to know what kind of magician Peter was, but he quickly dispelled that notion. This healing, he told the crowd, was a result of God's Covenant with Abraham. His sermon divides into two parts.

1. The God of the Covenant

   - The God of Abraham, Isaac and Jacob glorified Jesus

   - The Jews' treatment of Jesus

   - The risen Christ healed this man

2. The Prophets' message

   - The Christ must suffer

   - Repent and look to the Messiah's return

   - Moses' prediction of Christ the Prophet

   - All the prophets predicted these events –

   - The fulfillment of the Abrahamic Covenant

To the Jews, the Abrahamic Covenant meant everything. They knew that the only reason they could claim their privileges of being God's people was to prove their descent from Abraham, the father of their race. What Peter is doing here is connecting the ministry of Jesus with the fulfillment of that Covenant. The Jews rejected Jesus because they couldn't see the connection; they didn't understand that Jesus was the great Heir through whom they would receive their own portion of the Covenant blessings. Thinking that Jesus' claim was blasphemous and without merit, they got rid of him. Little did they know!

But the Prophets knew. Moses predicted the coming of Jesus when he saw that a "Prophet like me" shall come and do what no man before him could do. This was the Son, the Heir, who can hand out blessings both physical and spiritual to God's people, according to the terms of the Covenant. And when Jesus comes back from Heaven (in due time) he will bring "times of refreshing" as the Prophets described – a perfect Kingdom, the healing of all ills, justice and peace and righteousness. The Prophets gave us a clear picture of what life is like with the Messiah – they connected his ministry back to the promises given to Abraham.

It's all in the Prophets, Peter told them. And you haven't been paying attention to the Prophets but rejecting their testimony. It's time to repent, turn back to your God, and call on the Heir of the Covenant to give you treasures from Heaven.

Acts 4 – Peter's Sermon

Peter's next sermon was his defense (after being arrested for preaching the Gospel) before the Jewish leaders. It is very short – he may have said much more than this that wasn't recorded – but what he says here drives another point home about what the Gospel of Christ is.

1. The man that the Jews rejected, whom God accepted, healed the cripple.

2. Jesus is the stone that the Jews rejected.

3. God has made Jesus the capstone.

4. There is no other name but Jesus that saves us.

Notice that Peter calls the Jews "the builders." Modern students casually pass that idea off as a simple way of saying that the Jews weren't paying any attention to Jesus. Actually the idea is deeper than that. It's through the Jews that God revealed himself.

> He has revealed his word to Jacob, his laws and decrees to Israel. He has done this for no other nation; they do not know his laws. (Psalm 147:20)

It's what Paul refers to later in his letter to the Romans –

> … The people of Israel. Theirs is the adoption to sonship; theirs the divine glory, the Covenants, the receiving of the law, the temple worship and the promises. Theirs are the patriarchs, and from them is traced the human ancestry of the Messiah, who is God over all, forever praised! (Romans 9:4-5)

The truth about God, the way of salvation, the Kingdom of God, the answer to all of mankind's problems – all this was given to the Jews in their relationship to God. They had in their Scriptures the whole plan. The one thing left, as a crowning capstone to this magnificent and glorious House of God, was the one who can make the whole thing *work*. It was the only part they were missing. And they foolishly rejected it!

It takes faith to see that Jesus is the Heir of the Abrahamic Covenant, that he's the Righteous Man that the Law is talking about, that he's the Creator who is making the world to his own ends, that he's the great

268

Prophet who can uncover our hearts and cause us to hear the voice of God, that he's the High Priest who can bring us into the presence of God, that he's the Son of David who can successfully build his Kingdom according to plan and achieve an eternal Kingdom. Without that faith, Jesus appears as a mere man with grand claims and nothing more.

Salvation, then, is not just a shallow "I'm going to Heaven now" – the hope of immature souls. It's the capstone to the great system that the Christ has been working on throughout the Bible. He lifts us up from a system that is completely described (Old Testament) to that same system that works perfectly (New Testament). Salvation involves *all* the elements of the Old Testament system.

Acts 4 – the Apostles' Prayer

Prayer shows the state of our hearts like few other things do. How we pray, and what we pray about and for, reveal how little or how much faith we actually have in God.

When the Apostles returned from their first experience of persecution at the Jews' hands, they naturally turned to God in prayer. This is an outline of their prayer.

1. Prayer to the Creator
2. Prophecy of David
3. Their persecution by God's decree
4. Request for boldness and power through the name of Jesus

One thing I'd like to point out here is that they were using at least three Old Testament passages as the basis of their prayer. That's in direct contrast to our modern prayers, which hardly make any reference at all to God's Word, Old or New. Our agendas for prayer come from our personal desires, and from our personal opinions on what we think God should do. The Apostles, on the other hand, first studied the Bible to find out what God wants to do – and they made *that* the subject of their prayers.[18]

The name that they start out their prayer with – "Sovereign Lord" – is, in Greek, "despot", a singularly telling fact revealing what they were after here. They no doubt knew, based on their experience with Jesus' own ministry, that they would run into trouble with the authorities. Now they were experiencing it. And they knew two other things: only the power and authority of the King was going to give them success in their Mission. The "despot" who now sits on his throne is fully described in Psalm 2, which they quote from. Here is a picture of the Son of God ruling over the nations, raising up some and putting down others. He rules with a rod of iron; only those who repent and submit will find him merciful.

So the Apostles call on the King of kings to overrule the pettiness and shallowness and obstructionism of the Jewish rulers. And they call on the God "who made the Heaven and the earth" to do it with his Word, miracle, and command – in a way that nobody can stop.

So the Creator and the King will advance his Kingdom against all opposition. He intends to make a new Creation, and set up a new Kingdom that will completely replace this world. His disciples simply follow along behind endowed with his power and authority. The world can't stop the King and Creator, so it can't stop his messengers either – not when they are filled with his Spirit of power and wisdom.

Acts 7 – Stephen's Sermon

Stephen was a deacon in the early church assigned the task of taking care of the material needs of the believers, thus relieving the Apostles and elders of that task and letting them take care of the spiritual matters. But Stephen (as Paul tells us later) was a deacon who understood the deep truths of the faith. (1 Timothy 3:9) So he naturally shared what he knew of the Christ to others, and was immediately arrested.

---

[18] See the book *The Secret to Answered Prayer* for more on the kind of prayers that God answers.

In his defense to the Jewish leaders, he delivers a sermon that describes what he sees is the problem here.

1. The Covenant with Abraham – promised for the future.

2. Israel enslaved in Egypt.

3. God gives Moses to Israel – they reject him.

4. The God of the Patriarchs calls Moses to lead Israel out of Egypt.

5. The Prophecy of a Prophet like Moses.

6. The Israelites still reject Moses' leadership.

7. The Testimony of the Tabernacle – and their rejection.

8. The Jews still reject the Prophets.

This was not just a short summary of Israel's history. Stephen was pointing out the Jews' bad habit of rejecting the man whom God sends to save them. They almost always rejected God's messenger, and they are still doing it – they rejected the great Prophet who would be like Moses and build God's new House for his people.

But their rejection was not the real tragedy here; it's *what* they were rejecting. The Covenant with Abraham was the treasure of Israel. At different points in their history, that treasure was threatened by their enemies, and at those critical junctures the Lord sent a deliverer to rescue the Israelites and bring them back to the promises of the Covenant. So the crime of rejecting that deliverer was actually a crime of rejecting the treasure itself! In the very face of God's rich blessings they turned away. It turns out that its those treasures that the Jews don't want; that reminds us of Jesus' warning to the disciples that "If the world hates you, know that it has hated me before it hated you." (John 15:18)

People just don't see what they are hoping for in Jesus. They don't seem to be interested in adding data about Jesus to their religion. That takes all kinds of forms – including our modern sermons that tell us nothing of Jesus, and telling people that Christianity consists in what they have to do for God – a very superficial approach to worship.

Not only does Stephen have his theology down, but through faith *he* can see the Christ that the Old Testament describes.

> But Stephen, full of the Holy Spirit, looked up to Heaven and saw the glory of God, and Jesus standing at the right hand of God. "Look," he said, "I see Heaven open and the Son of Man standing at the right hand of God." (Acts 7:55-56)

God has rewarded his informed faith in Jesus with a vision of the glory of Christ in his Kingdom.

We are starting to see a pattern in the sermons recorded in Acts. Stephen hits the same point that the Apostles did before him: that the Jews, inexplicably, rejected the very man who can bring their system to a glorious perfection. If they would have just had faith (the ability to see God's spiritual world) they would have seen the Heir of the Covenant and come to him for what they were looking for.

Acts 10 – Peter's Sermon

God's revelation to include the Gentiles in the Church came as a real surprise to Peter. The Jews up to this point thought that the Gospel was only for the Jews; the Gentiles – well, they were just outside the pale. That means that the Jewish Christians still needed some correction in what the Gospel of Christ really is. As we see later in the book of Acts, they thought that every Christian had to follow the old Mosaic laws as well as believe in Jesus as the Messiah.

But God sent Peter to Cornelius the centurion with this message.

1. God shows no partiality.
2. Jesus performed his ministry filled with the Spirit.
3. The Jews crucified Jesus, but God raised him.
4. Jesus appeared to the disciples.
5. Jesus commanded them to preach about Jesus to the people.
6. The prophets testified to forgiveness in Jesus' name.

At first one would think that this is a simple run-down of the story of Jesus. But on closer examination, we notice that Peter leaves nothing to chance. He makes sure that Cornelius gets the story as God wants him to understand it. Every detail has a commentary attached that tells the "facts" from God's point of view. No doubt Cornelius had heard the story of Jesus from a Jewish point of view ("you yourselves know what happened throughout all Judea"), but Peter is now giving him God's point of view. For example, God may not be partial to any nation, but he does expect people to fear him and do what is acceptable in his eyes. Jesus was no ordinary preacher, but was anointed by God's Spirit and power to do his amazing works. He was opposing the devil's works with the power of God (a fact that would no doubt get past modern psychology). The Jews may have killed Jesus, but God raised him from the dead – an event only witnessed by the disciples. And they can testify that Jesus is indeed the Judge of all men (he can see into their hearts, they experienced that themselves), and that he forgives and cleanses the heart of its sin forever.

In other words, Cornelius heard that Jesus was no ordinary man. He was an extraordinary person, carrying out a mission from Heaven, and brings the blessings of Heaven to any who will call for them – be he Jew or gentile.

What we are witnessing is an Apostle telling someone things that only an Apostle has seen: the truth about this man Jesus. The only reason we can know these things for certain is because of the eye-witness testimony of the Apostles. And what the Apostle has seen is what our souls need. So, upon believing the message, the Spirit enters our hearts as well and gives us the same vision of the person and work of Christ that the Apostle told us about.

And we learn here that this Jewish religion is the hope of every child of God. Peter and the Apostles eventually learned that the Jewish hope is the Covenant to Abraham, and nothing less than that hope should be given to the people of God – Gentile or Jew. We are all children of Abraham if we have his faith; we all inherit the Spirit of God who brings the treasures of the Covenant to us from Jesus' throne in Heaven. Like Cornelius, it's time we started learning the depth of our hope in Christ by sitting at the feet of the Apostles as they teach us the real meaning of the Old Testament and how the Messiah fulfills it for us.

Acts 13 – Paul's Sermon

Paul's first recorded sermon about the Gospel has strong parallels to his later book to the Romans. It's obvious that, even at this early stage, Paul has a profound grasp of the essentials of the Gospel that people need to hear. It shows that his understanding of Christ is based on what he himself saw in Christ – the badge of an Apostle.

He and Barnabas went to a synagogue meeting in Pisidian Antioch, and he was invited to speak a few words. This is his message.

1. God chose the Jews and brought them out of Egypt to Canaan.

2. After the Judges (and Saul) God chose David to be King.

3. David did what God wanted done.

4. Jesus is David's descendent.

5. But John testified to Jesus' divinity.

6. God sent this Savior to his people.

7. The Jews rejected Jesus, but God raised him.

8. God has fulfilled his promises in Jesus, the Son of David.

9. Jesus will do what David could never do.

That's the main part of the message; then he adds this teaser at the end. [19]

10. Whoever believes in Jesus is justified from sins that the Law couldn't save them from.

The crux of this message as I see it is in verse 34: "I will give you the holy and sure blessings promised to David." This is a quote from the Prophet Isaiah, where God was promising to give them the blessings of the Davidic Covenant.

---

[19] I think he added that last point to pique their interest – and they responded by inviting him to come again and speak about more of these things – see Acts 13:42.

> Give ear and come to me; listen, that you may live. I will
> make an everlasting covenant with you, my faithful love
> promised to David. (Isaiah 55:3)

Now let's piece things together (following Paul is never easy, as Peter later testified!). The God of Abraham, Isaac and Jacob brought his people to Canaan to fulfill the terms of the Covenant. God chose David as "a man after his own heart" to secure those Covenant blessings for his people Israel. Then God made a covenant with David, that there would be a Son on his throne who would have an eternal Kingdom. Guess who? Jesus is that Son of David! And he of course is going to be "after God's own heart" as well, with the purpose of making sure the Kingdom of God is secure, peaceful, God-centered, rich with treasures of Heaven, and full of justice – so that the people of God will continue to enjoy the Covenant blessings. The fact that Jesus is doing that from Heaven means that we can enjoy spiritual treasures without fear of our enemies ever taking them away from us. After all, it *is* a spiritual Kingdom.

And one of those spiritual blessings is the forgiveness of sin through something that Jesus did, something that even the Law has no provision for and yet satisfied the Law completely. That is, if they're interested in coming back next week to hear about it! (No doubt they were going to hear next about the Covenant with Abraham and its blessings.)

Paul is describing the program of the Son of David – a far cry from many modern sermons that never even mention the program.

Acts 15 – the Jerusalem Council

We must make an aside here to notice an important point in the education of the Jewish Christians. Peter's experience with Cornelius, and Paul's successful missionary journeys, were throwing the Jews into confusion about what the requirements ought to be for the normal Christian life. They had been brought up in strict adherence to the Mosaic Law, and they couldn't imagine doing anything else if one wants to please God. But the Gentile converts didn't seem very interested in that side of the Old Testament; what was more confusing to the new movement was that Paul and others weren't pushing those requirements either. So they decided to hold a council on the matter.

275

As Paul and others described what was happening among the Gentiles, it became obvious that God was visiting these people as well with his Spirit. They couldn't very well deny what God was doing. So they decided to lay down a few rules against eating meat offered to idols, and eating blood (things that were heavily symbolic to the Jews) and abstaining from sexual immorality (an all-too-common characteristic in Gentile circles).

But what interests me most is the passage from the Old Testament (the prophet Amos) that they quoted from.

> After this I will return and rebuild David's fallen tent. Its ruins I will rebuild, and I will restore it, that the rest of mankind may seek the Lord, even all the Gentiles who bear my name, says the Lord, who does these things — things known from long ago. (Acts 15:16-18) [20]

It's a shame that we moderns have such a poor view of David. I've seen many a textbook on the Old Testament in which the author couldn't say anything good about David aside from the fact that he was a strong king who pulled the nation together. For the most part, they see him as an adulterer, murderer, poor father, and a general curse to the nation.

But the Prophets, and the Apostles, saw David as the model for the Messiah. What would the Messiah do when he came? He would rebuild David's Kingdom, along the plan of David – only on a higher level so that it can extend all around the world, include people from every tribe and nation, and last forever. The principles would always remain the same; the Messiah would succeed where David's successors failed.

By extension, then, what would the Apostles preach about Jesus? That he fulfilled the Davidic plan! Here we see that this is indeed their agenda.

---

[20] The way that the Apostles quoted from the Prophets shows that they thought deeply about these passages and saw the insights that the Prophets themselves had in the coming Messiah. These are not simply Christmas and Easter prophecies describing Jesus' acts in the Gospel history. They are principles of the Davidic Kingdom that the Messiah would deal with.

Acts 17 – Paul's Sermon

While Paul was waiting in Athens for his companions, he got into discussions with the Athenians about theology. They were intrigued and amused with this "foreign divinity" that Paul was always talking about. So they invited him to speak to them about it.

Being unknown to the "wise" Athenian philosophers, Paul decided to back up to the beginning and start with the basics. Gentiles know almost nothing about the true God (they never had the benefit of Jewish training in the Old Testament), and therefore they have to be taken back to the story of the Creation in order to lay down the right foundations; who is this God that we worship?

1. The Creator doesn't live in temples.

2. He doesn't need us – we need him.

3. God decides the circumstances of our lives.

4. Therefore, we should seek and find him.

5. But he isn't far off – there is hope in prayer.

6. God can't be represented by an image.

7. God commands everyone to repent.

8. Someday he will judge the world through his appointed Judge.

9. Jesus is this Judge – his resurrection shows that.

First things first: Paul has to straighten out their thinking about the nature of the true God. The Gentiles have come up with all sorts of gods that don't resemble the truth in any way. But rather than expound on how wrong they are, Paul simply announces the facts about the true God – that he's the Creator, and that he even created us to be what we are and live where we live. There's a purpose for Creation (remember the "command" aspect of Creation?) – God wants everyone everywhere to repent of their sins, and submit to his rule as King and Lord over them.

Paul follows through on the Creation formula: if God is King, and we are his subjects, and if he has given us rules to live by, then of course there's going to be a Judgment Day. God has to make sure we're doing what he told us to do. Paul reveals the identity of the Judge to us – it's going to be this Jesus whom God raised from the dead and seated on the throne of Heaven. Only from there can the Judge truly discern the truth of every man's heart and actions; only from there will come justice and a true standard of righteousness.

Now this is a sermon about Jesus to Gentile unbelievers. It has nothing of "love" in it; it's all about the Creator's standards that hang over the heads of all humanity. The news about Jesus is that he will penetrate "the thoughts and attitudes of the heart" and judge every person by the acts "committed while in the body." What is it about Jesus that shows us that this judgment is going to be fair and impartial and thorough? His position in Heaven: the doctrine of the resurrection was the door that Paul opens up to reveal the Judge of all the earth. There's nothing of salvation yet in this message; but it's all about Jesus and what we need to learn first about him.

Acts 28: Paul's sermons

Paul spent his last days in Rome under house arrest. While he was there, he invited the local Jews over for Bible studies – focusing, of course, on Jesus and the fulfillment of the Old Testament promises. We aren't given much of the text of his messages, but what little is given us is very suggestive of what he's been saying all along.

1. He explained and declared the Kingdom of God.

2. He attempted to prove that Jesus was what the Law of Moses and the Prophets were talking about.

By now we should be able to recognize Paul's themes. What other Kingdom would Paul be talking about except the Davidic Kingdom? And the Law of Moses, as Paul has reminded us many times, is about the Righteous Man, the Sacrifice for sin, the Temple that God is building for a testimony to him. Moses himself was a Prophet who predicted the coming of a Prophet like him. The rest of the Prophets predicted the Messiah who would rebuild the Kingdom of David along eternal lines.

In other words, Paul explained the Old Testament in depth to these people who thought they knew their Scriptures. The whole thing was about Jesus – the only man who could do what the Old Testament saints hoped in.

Now if this was the Jewish hope, why in the world would they turn down the only man who could give it to them? Why in the world would they turn away from the blessings of the Covenant and the peace and righteousness of the Kingdom when it is finally within their grasp? Such an unthinkable act could only be the hand of God, blinding the eyes of the obstinate.

> The Holy Spirit spoke the truth to your ancestors when he said through Isaiah the prophet:

> Go to this people and say, "You will be ever hearing but never understanding; you will be ever seeing but never perceiving." For this people's heart has become calloused; they hardly hear with their ears, and they have closed their eyes. Otherwise they might see with their eyes, hear with their ears, understand with their hearts and turn, and I would heal them. (Acts 28:26-27)

What is it that they can't see? They can't see the data of the Old Testament in Jesus. It's spiritual, for one thing; and they don't want to see it. So God won't show them. It's a fearful judgment that God brings down on the heads of those who reject the true meaning of Jesus' ministry.

Summary

Acts serves as a model for preachers and teachers as they take the message of Christ to the world. It isn't here that we learn the basics of Jesus; we get that from the Old Testament. It isn't here, either, where we learn about the life of Christ (that's in the Gospels) nor the glory of Christ (which is described best in the Apostles' letters, particularly Paul). The book of Acts is a homiletics class: what is it that constitutes a Gospel sermon? What should be our sermon points? What is the data that we have to get across to our listeners? The responses from our listeners will depend greatly on what we say to them. So if we want conversions, if we want people to believe in Jesus (which is our constant claim), then we have to tell them what the Apostles told people. After all, they were trained in this by the Master himself.

ROMANS – THE GOSPEL OF CHRIST [21]

There are all sorts of ideas about what the "Gospel" is in today's churches.   Leaving aside the Liberals' version of the Gospel, Evangelicals have also created various versions of their own.   This is perhaps due to two reasons:

- ▪ *First*, when people *want* to hear something, many teachers and preachers will alter the message to fit accordingly. Therefore we hear all sorts of messages like "Jesus wants to be your friend" to the lonely, and "Jesus will take care of all your needs" to the poor – and everything else that you can imagine to tickle people's ears.

- ▪ *Second*, preachers often pick out certain texts or ideas from the Bible and equate that with the "Gospel." So we hear Gospel messages exhorting people to "Just confess that Jesus is Lord!" or "Repent, and believe on the Lord Jesus Christ!" or "Come to Jesus and he will give you rest!" or "You don't need to know anything but Jesus Christ and him crucified!" All of these are true in themselves, because the Bible texts that they come from are true; but to equate a single verse to the Gospel is wrong and misleading.

You can get "conversions" – or emotional reactions – to just about any idea that you want to preach from the Bible. But the Gospel is a wide-ranging subject, and it requires the entire Bible to completely present and explain it. Not that a person has to master the whole Bible to become a Christian. But too often someone "believes" in Jesus too quickly; in other words, he or she heard some one or two things that are appealing about Jesus and jumped at the opportunity, without realizing that there's more to Jesus than a simple idea or two. That's why Jesus himself warns us that many at first will hear with joy, and then fall away when the temptations and trials of life come back and crowd out the initial interest in him. (Matthew 13:20-21) Too many people are

---

[21]   Taken from the book *The Gospel of Christ*.

going to discover, too late, that the Gospel of Christ was much more than they had bargained for: "Depart from me, you evildoers – I never knew you!" (Matthew 7:23)

I've been accused at times of not preaching the Gospel. In fact, some people have come to the church and then left again, claiming that they didn't hear "the love of God" in my messages. Others of my friends in the ministry have had the same kinds of accusations made against them, as if they didn't "show the love of God" to sensitive souls. I am not one to pass off such criticism lightly. If someone needs the Savior, it is my duty to present to them the truth of the Savior as faithfully as I can. But I also have learned not to accept everyone's opinions as the "Gospel" truth. My standard is the Bible. In fact, I have learned to adhere so closely to what the Bible tells me to believe, and how it directs me to go, that it often looks strange to others. They are so used to believing and acting as our modern culture dictates, that the Bible's way – even to so-called "Christians" – is actually a "smell of death," as Paul puts it.

> For we are to God the aroma of Christ among those who are being saved and those who are perishing. To the one we are the smell of death; to the other, the fragrance of life. And who is equal to such a task? Unlike so many, we do not peddle the word of God for profit. On the contrary, in Christ we speak before God with sincerity, like men sent from God. (2 Corinthians 2:15-17)

What does the Bible say?

When people's souls are at stake, my obligation is to do it the Bible's way. And one of the best sources of a balanced Gospel message in the New Testament is Paul's book to the Romans. So what we want to do here is take a careful look at how Paul presents the Gospel.

Remember that we can't approach this subject with our own preconceived notions. If we allow our definition of the Gospel to color the picture, we will most certainly miss what Paul is saying. It's time to let the great Apostle teach us. *This*, Paul says, is the Gospel that I preach. If your "Gospel" doesn't coincide with his, then of course it's time to take another look at what your understanding of the Gospel is.

I know that some will reject this approach because they don't want to change what they're doing, for one reason or another. But we teachers ought to fear for our souls: we who teach will be judged more strictly (James 3:1), because we of all people have to get the truth right. If we teach a different Gospel than the one that the Apostles passed on to us, we will be eternally condemned. (Galatians 1:8) So our duty as Christ's under-shepherds is not to put our heads in the sand and ignore Paul's instructions, but to learn and practice until we get this thing right. The sheep need the truth more than they need us; we can, and ought to be, replaced if we're not feeding Christ's lambs with the Word of Life.

The book of Romans is Paul's classic statement of the Gospel. We have the four "Gospels" heading the New Testament, but ("as one born out of time") Paul also wants to teach us the truth about salvation in Christ. He starts his letter by claiming to be set apart for the Gospel of God; the Gospel is his whole life. (Romans 1:1) He tells the Romans that he wants to visit them and preach the Gospel "also to you." (Romans 1:15)

Then he makes this famous summary statement of the Gospel:

> I am not ashamed of the Gospel, because it is the power of God for the salvation of everyone who believes: first for the Jew, then for the Gentile. For in the Gospel a righteousness from God is revealed, a righteousness that is by faith from first to last, just as it is written: "The righteous will live by faith." (Romans 1:16-17)

Then without missing a beat, he plunges into a letter-sized version of the Gospel for the Romans to study. For those of us who have the responsibility of teaching the "whole counsel of God" to Christ's flock, it is time to get out our notebooks and watch how this master presents the Gospel to the Romans. Paul expects us to follow his lead here; as he instructed Titus, every church leader must be careful to ...

> ... hold firmly to the trustworthy message *as it has been taught*, so that he can encourage others by sound doctrine and refute those who oppose it. (Titus 1:9)

An analysis of the Gospel of Romans

My approach has been to break down the letter to the Romans into its several parts. You might divide the letter in different places, but I don't believe the differences between your outline and mine would be significant. You will see the point that I'm trying to make once you see the analysis of the letter.

I counted the number of verses in each section, and then calcuated each section's percentage of the entire letter. In other words, how much time did Paul allot to each subject when he's presenting the Gospel?

So what I have in the end is not only *what* he discusses, but a measure of *how important* each idea is to Paul in his argument. This, finally, is a balanced presentation of the Gospel. It doesn't suffer from the distortions of our modern versions in that it is made up of *exactly what we need to hear* to understand the truth about Christ in a saving manner. Nothing important is left out of the Gospel.

Analysis of the Gospel of Romans

Sections	# Verses	% of total
Paul as Apostle		4%
Paul's authority	7	1.6%
Spreading of Gospel	10	2.3%
The Problem		**14.9%**
Broken Creation	15	3.5%

283

God the Judge	16	3.7%
Judges by the Law	21	4.9%
All are sinners	12	2.8%

Righteousness of Christ — 20%

Gift of righteousness - Intro	11	2.6%
Faith gets gift	25	5.8%
Christ reconciles us to God	11	2.6%
Death through Adam, Life through Christ	10	2.3%
Dead to sin, alive to God	14	3.3%
Slaves to righteousness now	15	3.5%

Motive power - Spirit — 13.5%

Can't be free on my own	19	4.4%
Power of Spirit makes it work	17	4.0%
Liberation of Creation	10	2.3%
We shall conquer	12	2.8%

Gospel of OT — 20%

Spiritual Israel	29	6.8%
Jews without faith	25	5.8%
Remnant among Jews	10	2.3%
Gentiles grafted in	14	3.3%
Israel will come back	8	1.9%

Life as a Christian 15.2%

You are holy	2	0.5%
Part of the Body	6	1.4%
Live like a Christian	13	3.0%
Submit to authorities	7	1.6%
Love each other	3	0.7%
Wake up	4	0.9%
Help the weak	30	7.0%

The Apostle to the Gentiles 12.4%

Gentiles included	6	1.4%
Minister to the Gentiles	8	1.9%
Mission plans	12	2.8%
Greetings to the saints	16	3.7%
Final instructions	11	2.6%
Total:	**429**	

The Love of God:	Romans 5:5	**Less than 1%**
	Romans 5:8	
	Romans 8:35	
	Romans 8:39	

A balanced presentation

What we want to do now is study this chart and find out *what* Paul is saying, and *why* he talks about it.

- **Paul's authority** – Paul starts out by claiming his authority to speak about this matter of the Gospel. Christ appointed him, Christ gave him the message, and Christ sent him out to the rest of us to tell us the Gospel.

  So, we learn what the Gospel is by listening to Paul's message. We can't change it or alter it, because that would be rejecting Christ who sent Paul out. And if we want to tell others the Gospel, we follow Paul's lead and tell them what he told us. By what authority would we change the message, or leave any of it out? The Apostle must be a faithful messenger, and so must we. He was the Witness; we are only permitted to pass on to others what he told us.

  Like the coolness of snow at harvest time is a trustworthy messenger to those who send him; he refreshes the spirit of his masters. (Proverbs 25:13)

- **The Problem** – The Gospel always starts out with a sobering analysis of our spiritual state. It is God's solution to our sin and rebellion against him – not to loneliness, or poverty, or sickness, or all the other ills that so many people want to be "delivered" from. Notice that there is no mention of these other "problems" in Paul's Gospel – only our sin.

  The problem has to be stated clearly and adequately. So he starts with Creation: we were not made to be the sinners that we are. God made a perfect world; we deliberately broke it. Paul covers all the kinds of sins that we immerse ourselves in – things that God thinks are sin, not what we might conceive as sin. The problem covers the entire human race. The Jews, though they were the people of God, also suffer from this spiritual blight as much as everyone else. (We will see the significance of this truth shortly.)

  How do we know what sin is? The definition is in God's Law. The Jews had to abide by it, and the Gentiles will be judged by it too. The Law is profound in its depth as well as its scope. Not only does it successfully convict us all of being sinners, but it is the only standard that God would use to consider anybody's claim to be righteous. We are not free to make up our own standards. So, God has us all cornered.

> Now we know that whatever the Law says, it says to those who are under the Law, so that every mouth may be silenced and the whole world held accountable to God. Therefore no one will be declared righteous in his sight by observing the Law; rather, through the Law we become conscious of sin. (Romans 3:19-20)

Here is the proper way to convict sinners – by using the Law of God. This discussion in Romans is an excellent example of how to "soften up" the ground with the plow of the Law, before sowing the Seed of Christ. It can't be done in any other way so effectively.

Notice too how much time Paul spends on this subject – 15% of the letter. The reason is that we will need a good deal of convincing that we are as bad as the Law makes us out to be! The hardest thing to convince a sinner of is that he *is* one. By the time Paul is done, none of us have an excuse and we are all condemned by the Law; we have no hope there. By the time Paul is done, we are all desperate (or should be!) to find an answer to this curse that is killing us.

- **The Righteousness of Christ** – Having closed the door to the Law being a way to our righteousness, Paul now turns to the amazing solution that God has provided – we can have Christ's righteousness as a gift. Notice that Paul isn't setting aside the Law's requirements (nobody gets into Heaven unless they are perfect!). He shows us that God provides *another way* to righteousness.

The success of our salvation depends completely on who Jesus is, and what he did. He is none other than the Son of God. This is important for two reasons: *first*, only he can become a man and actually achieve righteousness. Can you imagine God failing at his own Law? *Second*, as a man, he bought this crucial gift with his efforts so that he can make a gift of it *to us*. This gift completely solves our problem. Through Christ's work we are reconciled to God; the war is over. We are now God's servants; we are no longer his enemies. We are now fully righteous because we are *in Christ*, the righteous man, the second Adam, the beginning of a new race.

Faith is the key to this treasure. Living by faith is different from living by the Law; it's a completely different road to the same end – righteousness. God always did have this road in mind for his people, as Paul shows us in the story of Abraham. But faith is a special skill that only God's people know how to use – and our faith has to resemble Abraham's if we want to claim the inheritance that God promises us in Christ.

This is a difficult concept not only to understand but to accept. So Paul spends 20% of his letter on what receiving Christ's righteousness through faith means; he spends a great deal of his time discussing the Covenant with Abraham. We can't afford to get *this* wrong in any way!

- **The motive power** – So far, Paul has been using Old Testament doctrine to teach us. Righteousness, as the Law describes it, is the goal. Faith was a principle laid down to God's saints since the Covenant with Abraham. But how are we supposed to succeed when the Jews failed after 2000 years of trying?

  The answer is the Spirit of Christ. If Jesus has made available that righteousness that men need, how are *we* going to get it? Only if his Spirit lives in us. And that is the motive power behind the Gospel. The Jews couldn't do it on their own; we don't have to, either – not when Jesus makes a gift of it to us. The Spirit will *move* us to "live by the righteous requirements of the Law" (Romans 8:4) without any law-keeping on our own part. All we have to do is follow the Spirit, and we will be righteous – because we will be "in Christ" – just as the Old Testament predicted.

I will sprinkle clean water on you, and you will be clean; I will cleanse you from all your impurities and from all your idols. I will give you a new heart and put a new spirit in you; I will remove from you your heart of stone and give you a heart of flesh. And I will put my Spirit in you and move you to follow my decrees and be careful to keep my laws. (Ezekiel 36:25-27)

We are on the road now to restoring Creation. The power that Paul first mentioned in Romans 1:4 comes from Christ, who restores us to God, enables us to walk with God, and changes our natures to conform to his image – the image of God that man was supposed to be in the first place.

So now we have learned a key New Testament doctrine – we don't become righteous by our own efforts (as the Jews were obligated to do) but by what Christ does in us, and for us. This doctrine of the Spirit and his enabling power makes up 13% of the letter, and yet it's a subject that many preachers and teachers are afraid to spend time on because they themselves don't understand it.

- **The Gospel of the Old Testament** – Here is another area where modern Gospel preachers often fail. Christianity is not a new religion. It's the Judaic system "resurrected" to a spiritual level – point for point. Christianity isn't just a replacement of the Judaic system; it's the *power* that makes the Judaic system work.

Paul knows what God gave the Jews in the Old Testament. Yes, he gave them the Law, and yes, he expected them to obey that Law. But there was a deeper level in those OT lessons that the Jews should have seen – a righteousness by faith, the truth that he first taught Abraham. Their own system was designed to "lead them to Christ" if they had the faith to see it.

Christianity is actually first described in detail in the Old Testament. As Paul says to Timothy …

*... how from infancy you have known **the holy Scriptures, which are able to make you wise for salvation through faith in Christ Jesus**.* (2 Timothy 3:15)

I hope you realize that the "holy Scriptures," to Paul, was the Old Testament. The Old Testament is designed to describe Christ to us, so fully that there are only two new ideas left for the New Testament to cover. We Christians are living the Jewish system, from first to last. In the Old Testament we learn about the Kingdom of God, about God living with his people (a preview of Heaven!), about righteousness, about the Covenant promises that are fulfilled in Christ, about Creation (and therefore the second Creation), and many more fundamental doctrines of our faith in Christ. In fact, our future life with God in Heaven is almost completely described in the Old Testament.

The difference is that we now have the power to succeed and experience all this treasure, whereas before that was only a future hope for the Jews. "God had planned something better for us so that only together with us would they be made perfect." (Hebrews 11:40) Now, in the Church age, both Jew and Gentile have to become a Christian to enter Heaven; they must be filled with the Spirit of Christ to be part of God's eternal family.

Paul makes no bones about this issue when it comes to the Jews. They missed the point of Christ when he first came – they are guilty because they should have known all about him from their own Scriptures. They should have been ready to leave their physical model behind and step up to the new spiritual reality; he was making their hope real. So, the Gospel is going out to the Gentiles for now. But the day will come when the Jews will finally see their Old Testament God in Jesus – it will be a fitting end to the program that God had first begun with them.

Paul spends 20% of his time talking about the Jews in his Gospel, because their story, their doctrine, their life with God, form the very foundation of the Christian experience. All of *his* Gospel comes right out of the Old Testament.

- **Life as a Christian** – The point of Christianity is to make us *holy*. Again, we first learned what "holy" means from the Old Testament Temple and its service. Holiness is a way of life. And "without holiness," as the Scripture says, "no one will see the Lord." (Hebrews 12:14)

There seems to be a false notion going around that it's OK to have a little religion, but let's not get fanatical about this. But that's not Paul's message. To him, being a Christian is a 24/7 job. *Everything* comes under its power: the way we live, the way we deal with others, the way we worship God, the way we relate to those in authority over us, the way we deal with our fellow believers. We have no time off to ourselves in this respect, because (as we saw in Romans 6) we are God's slaves[22] now and live only to serve him. In this section, Paul makes it plain to us what that's going to look like on a day-to-day basis.

Notice that he spends 7% of his message just talking about our relationships with other Christians in church. We are priests now, serving God and each other with the spiritual resources of the Temple. Churches often fail right here, because they don't emphasize the fact that we are all at different levels of spiritual growth. It's going to take a lot of grace – a lot of the power of the Spirit changing our hearts – to willingly get along with each other, and meet the needs that we all have. Love – the family love that comes from the Father to his Son, motivates service. The goal is what Paul describes in Philippians:

> Do nothing out of selfish ambition or vain conceit, but in humility consider others better than yourselves. Each of you should look not only to your own interests, but also to the interests of others. Your attitude should be the same as that of Christ Jesus. (Philippians 2:3-5)

---

[22] The Greek word used in Romans 6 is δουλος, which literally means "slave."

Of all places to act like a Christian, we ought to in church – yet here we most often wage war with others! The Gospel is designed to solve this problem of divisive, warring church members and make them like "lambs lying down with lions," as the Prophets predicted. In other words, we should see the fruits of the Gospel first in the church, among the saints. The problem of sin gets solved here first, where the resources are.

- **The Apostle to the Gentiles** – Paul was there when the Jews rejected the Gospel of Christ. He knew what a significant event that was. It opened the door for letting the Gentiles into the church, and he went out with Christ's command to "go to the street corners and invite to the banquet anyone you find." (Matthew 22:9)

Christianity is not a new religion; it is Judaism lifted up to a spiritual level. But this means that everyone – including the Jews – have to be lifted up to that level in order to be a part of it. Paul gloried in the fact that Christ made the Gentiles every bit as much a child of Abraham as any Old Testament saint. Paul was a Jew, and a "Pharisee of the Pharisees." But these Gentiles were his brothers because they, as well as he, were part of the body of Christ. They were heirs of the Covenant of Abraham. Paul had to forcibly remind Peter of this truth once! (Galatians 2:11) And like Jesus, he was not ashamed to call them his brothers. (Hebrews 2:11) He loved them as his own family. This part of his letter shows his concern for them.

And the Apostles were eyewitnesses of the Christ – Christ revealed to them who he was, what he was doing here, and the importance of the whole situation for the Church. Their testimony forms the life of the Church – its doctrine, its life, its functions. And the Gentiles now can take part in this new Kingdom that God is making for his children.

A few closing observations

Paul was a master of the Gospel, and he was careful to lay "a foundation as an expert builder." (1 Corinthians 3:10) And so we can take this presentation in Romans as Paul's skillful work in laying out the Gospel for us.

Are there other topics in the Bible to teach and preach about? Certainly. Are they part of the Gospel too? Yes, as all roads in the Bible lead to Christ; "these are the Scriptures that testify about me." (John 5:39) But as a concise statement of the Gospel, as a presentation that gives us what we need to understand and close with Christ in a saving way, Romans is hard to beat.

As we step back and look at this book again, we can draw some conclusions about it.

- *Everything fits together, and everything is balanced.* If we leave any of this material out of our teaching, we won't get the whole truth that we need to be saved through Christ. Each point was important in Paul's presentation. If, for example, we leave out the section on the Jews and the Old Testament, we will mislead people and make them think that Christianity is a new religion. I've seen this done. Many churches and "Christians" actually brag about being "New Testament Christians!" But there is nothing in the Old Testament that we can afford to leave out. To properly present the Gospel to those who are perishing, we need to study and teach every point that Paul uses here in Romans. Anything less, and someone is going to suffer spiritually in some way.

- *The preacher has to have an extensive understanding of the Bible in order to present the Gospel as Paul did.* Paul learned the Old Testament as a Pharisee and a scholar; he learned its *spiritual* meaning when he became a Christian. He knew that it was the foundation lessons for even Gentile Christians in their spiritual growth (which is probably how Luke became so impressed with this idea). Yet the average preacher knows very little about the Old Testament; it's a confusing book to him. There doesn't seem to be much connection between the two Testaments that matters to a modern Christian. And it's embarrassing how Bible colleges and seminaries don't prepare ministers of the Gospel in this area. What we need are workers like Paul, who used the Old

293

Testament as his book of doctrine on Christ. He, unlike the Jews of his day, and unlike the so-called "Gospel preachers" of our day, saw Jesus everywhere in the Bible – and he preached it all. This gives true spiritual depth to the message. (For example, his reference to the "Son of David" in the first chapter is more profound than many might imagine!)

- ***The "Love of God" is not the only sermon to preach!*** Just as a last glance, I checked to see how many times Paul mentions the "love of God" in his book. There were only four times – less than 1% of his Gospel. And in those four places, God's love wasn't the point that Paul was working on; it was the reason he gave for *why* God did something else pertaining to our salvation. This isn't to say that the love of God isn't important to Paul. To him, however, it was the motive power behind *all* of the works of God in Christ. In other words, if every sermon is about the love of God, that's not preaching the Gospel the way that Paul did. That's a shallow and immature way of preaching; it will give you an emotional revival meeting, but it will also leave fatal holes in people's understanding of Christ and his work. Ironically, your hearers run the real risk of not being truly saved through such a version of the "Gospel."

HEBREWS: INTO THE TEMPLE!

Hebrews deals with contrasts. All through the book, the writer reviews the means that God used to deliver his truth to the Israelites in the old days: through angels, through Moses, through the sacrifices in the Temple. He compares each with Christ's ministry, which is designed to replace those old methods. Obviously Christ does what the old methods could never do – he changes the heart, whereas the blood of the Old Testament sacrifices only postponed the real cleansing.

> The Law is only a shadow of the good things that are coming – not the realities themselves. For this reason it can never, by the same sacrifices repeated endlessly year after year, make perfect those who draw near to worship. If it could, would they not have stopped being offered? For the worshipers would have been cleansed once for all, and would no longer have felt guilty for their sins. But those sacrifices are an annual reminder of sins, because it is impossible for the blood of bulls and goats to take away sins. (Hebrews 10:1-4)

But Hebrews never teaches that those old things were wrong, as if Christians needn't take them seriously. They were actually pictures, or lessons, teaching us what it's really like in Heaven now. The Temple in Solomon's day was a symbol of God living among his people, and their easy access to God for prayer and worship and blessing. This is what it's like right now in Heaven with all God's people.

> But you have come to Mount Zion, to the Heavenly Jerusalem, the city of the living God. You have come to thousands upon thousands of angels in joyful assembly, to the church of the firstborn, whose names are written in Heaven. You have come to God, the judge of all men, to the spirits of righteous men made perfect, to Jesus the mediator of a new Covenant, and to the sprinkled blood that speaks a better word than the blood of Abel. (Hebrews 12:22-24)

A tour of the Temple

The book of Hebrews actually takes the reader on a tour through the Temple itself. Remember that the Temple has four "courts" or areas in which different classes of people can enter. The Gentiles could come up close to the Temple – onto the Temple mount itself – but they couldn't enter the Temple where the Jews went in. The Court of Women and the Court of Men represented areas where the average Israelite was allowed to come in with his sacrifice. The priests would take the sacrifice and bring it into the enclosed Temple building and offer it to God. Finally, in the Holy of Holies, the High Priest was allowed to enter once a year (on the Day of Atonement – Yom Kippur) and offer a sacrifice to the Lord for the entire nation.

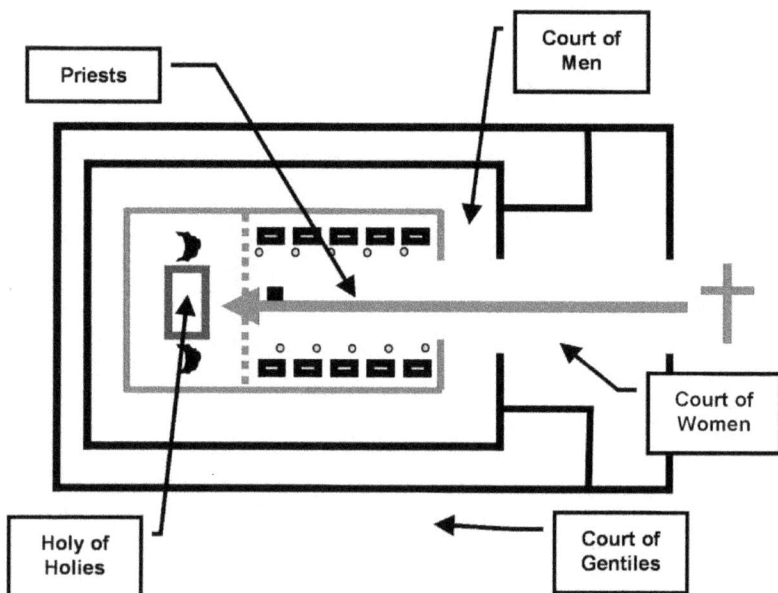

Depending on who you were, you were allowed in so far and no further. And if anyone was caught going in too far – going into a court that they had no right to be in – the temple guards would summarily escort you out and possibly execute you. God was very particular about who was allowed to do what. Read the story in 2 Samuel 6:6-8 to see how serious he was.

When you outline the book of Hebrews, it naturally falls into four divisions that correspond to this layout of the courts of the Temple. Here are the four main divisions.

Outline of Hebrews

The First Court	**Hebrews 1-2**	*All of Creation*
The Second Court	**Hebrews 3**	*The Israelites*
The Third Court	**Hebrews 4-6**	*The Priesthood*
The Holy Of Holies	**Hebrews 7-10**	*The Throne of God*

In each section, the author is going to show us 1) how the old system worked in the Old Testament; and 2) how it works now with Christ. The idea is to compare the old with the new. It's not that the new system is a new idea – it's that someone has come to take that same idea that was taught in the old and make it work, something that the people in the Old Testament couldn't do.

- **The First Court** – all of creation *(Hebrews 1-2)*

  The first courtyard at the Temple was an area which everyone was allowed to enter, even the Gentiles. This represents all of creation.

  Hebrews 1-2 discusses the role of angels in God's creation, and their responsibilities as God's messengers and workmen. Whenever God appeared in the Old Testament and spoke or did some miraculous work, he did it through angels. That's primarily because he was working in a physical world doing physical things; even the blessings given to the Israelites were physical blessings at that stage. And that's the kind of work that angels can do.

But now the time has come to work on a new world, and it can't be built through angels. The Son of God himself, who is in the image of God and has the fullness of God for resources, is the only one who can accomplish this great task. The world built through angels is destined to deteriorate and be destroyed; but the world put together by the Son will last forever – it will be made of spiritual stuff.

And one of the most important tasks at hand for the Son is to create a new race of humanity for Abraham's family. The first step was to become a man himself; the next step was to bring all of Abraham's descendants, either Jew or Gentile, around the world and down through all of history, into this new family. Jesus is the "second Adam," the first of a new race of men.

> If there is a natural body, there is also a spiritual body. So it is written: "The first man Adam became a living being"; the last Adam, a life-giving spirit. (1 Corinthians 15:44-45)

The question to ask at this stage is – do want to be part of this or not? It doesn't matter if you're Jewish or Gentile; the offer is open to all. But you have to come to the God of Israel's house if you want to be included in his Kingdom.

- **The Second Court** – the Israelites *(Hebrews 3)*

The second court was where the Israelites could go – the women had their court, the men had theirs. The Gentiles, however, were not allowed into this area.

The Israelites were special in God's eyes; they were the Chosen People, the descendants of Abraham, whom God delivered out of bondage in Egypt through Moses' ministry. At Mt. Sinai they were formed into a new nation with God's Law over them. They got their identity there.

Moses was key to this part of their history. And Hebrews puts both Moses and Jesus in the same class in chapters 3-4, saying that they both worked on the house of God, doing the same things – creating a new nation of God's people.

But where Moses put together a physical nation and took them to Canaan for the Promised Land, Jesus is putting together a spiritual nation and leading God's people to Heaven. Unfortunately both the Israelites and we Christians have some trouble accepting our destiny! Moses had to deal with unfaithful rebels on the border of Canaan; Jesus too deals with so-called "believers" who don't seem to get the idea that the *next* world is what they really want, not this world. But the Promised Land that Jesus is leading us into is far greater than Canaan ever was; and the nation that Jesus is putting together is going to be perfect, eternal, totally righteous and holy – an accomplishment that Moses could never reach in his ministry.

Here the question is this: did you bring the right Sacrifice that will get you entry into God's presence? Nobody comes in any further unless they bring the blood of the Lamb of God, because only that Sacrifice is acceptable to God. We must become children of Abraham, "true Jews" and heirs.

• **The Third Court** – the Priesthood *(Hebrews 4-6)*

The third court – actually the great room inside the Temple itself – was for the priests alone. The ordinary Israelite wasn't allowed into this room. But any Levite or priest who was ministering at the Temple came in here to do his work.

The role of the priest was critical for the life of Israel. He was the one who took the blood of the sacrifices that the people brought to the Temple and offered them to God. He was set apart for this holy task; he was anointed and ordained by God himself. No man took this job on his own authority; God ordained the descendants of Levi to work in the Temple. When others tried to do that special work, God struck them down. (See 2 Chronicles 26 for an example.)

The problem about the priests, however, is that they could only do so much for God and man. When they brought the sacrifice's blood before the throne of God, God sent them back out to the worshiper with a message of forgiveness. But that didn't change the man's heart; he went back home forgiven but completely unchanged inside. He was still a sinner.

The second problem was that not only were the Israelites, except for the priests, prohibited from coming before God, the priests weren't allowed to see him either! No man can see God and live; he's too holy to look upon sin.

So to really solve man's problems of sin and death, we need a new kind of priest – a priest like Melchizedek. And Hebrews talks a great deal about this new priest after the order of Melchizedek. Jesus isn't of the Levitical tribe, so he doesn't labor under the same limitations that the Levitical priests had. He's the priest of the Covenant with Abraham – the only priest who can actually put righteousness in our hearts and make peace between God and man.

Now the third question for those wanting to see God: are you ready to serve him? This is the point of the Law of God – love for God and love for man. No one is allowed to be part of God's house unless they are ready to be priests, Spirit-filled and set apart for the Lord's work.

- **The Fourth Court – the Throne of God** *(Hebrews 7-10)*

The fourth court, or room, was the Holy of Holies, the throne room of God. This is where God sat and ruled over his people; from here he blessed them with the promises of the Covenant.

But again, there was a major limitation in the Old Testament system. The only person allowed into the Holy of Holies was the High Priest, and he could only go in on one day of the year – Yom Kippur, the Day of Atonement. On this day it was his responsibility to take the blood of the sacrifice before God's throne and get forgiveness for the entire nation. But if anybody, including the High Priest, attempted to get behind the curtain on any other day of the year, they would be immediately struck down dead.

Hebrews now introduces a new High Priest, someone who gains permanent entry to the Throne of God with a sacrifice that will completely take away sin and guilt and change sinners hearts permanently. With this kind of Priest making our way plain, we can now come "confidently" into God's presence.

> Therefore, brothers, since we have confidence to enter the Most Holy Place by the blood of Jesus, by a new and living way opened for us through the curtain, that is, his body, and since we have a great priest over the house of God, let us draw near to God with a sincere heart and with the full assurance that faith brings, having our hearts sprinkled to cleanse us from a guilty conscience and having our bodies washed with pure water. (Hebrews 10:19-22)

Now we have come to the point of this whole exercise: are you ready to see God? From him and through him and to him are all things. Are you ready to be God-centered for the rest of eternity? To enjoy and worship him forever? That is the heart of Heaven, our joy and pleasure – to give him the honor and glory he deserves, and to know him and enjoy him as the Son of God does.

And that's why Hebrews encourages us about boldly coming before God in our worship. So the story line in the book of Hebrews is the spiritual journey from outside the Temple all the way inside to see God, step by step, accomplished by the work of the Son who can do what the Old Testament saints could not do.

But you have come to Mount Zion, to the city of the living God, the Heavenly Jerusalem. You have come to thousands upon thousands of angels in joyful assembly, to the church of the firstborn, whose names are written in Heaven. You have come to God, the Judge of all, to the spirits of the righteous made perfect, to Jesus the mediator of a new Covenant, and to the sprinkled blood that speaks a better word than the blood of Abel. (Hebrews 12:22-24).

Into the Temple!

But there is more. You have to realize that Jesus isn't going to break the rules; he loves his Father's house. He's going to do what God wants done in the Temple. So he isn't going to just drag whoever he wants inside. He first makes all of his brothers and sisters *priests* – so that we are allowed inside the Temple. Only priests are allowed in!

As you come to him, the living Stone — rejected by men but chosen by God and precious to him — you also, like living stones, are being built into a spiritual house to be a holy priesthood, offering spiritual sacrifices acceptable to God through Jesus Christ. (1 Peter 2:4-5)

The amazing thing is that he makes Gentiles priests, he makes women priests, he makes ordinary men priests – and then marches right into the Temple with his new family of priests and gets them started serving God in his house.

There is neither Jew nor Gentile, neither slave nor free, nor is there male and female, for you are all one in Christ Jesus. If you belong to Christ, then you are Abraham's seed, and heirs according to the promise. (Galatians 3:28-29)

Where did Jesus get the authority to do such things? How do we know that he can get God's approval for all these new changes? Because, as Hebrews has been telling us all through the book, he is the Son of God with all authority and power to build God's house the way it needs to be done.

This is what Jesus has given his people: they are called out from the world, cleansed and forgiven by his own blood, made priests to serve in

Heaven's Temple, and then brought into the presence of God to enjoy him forever.

Finally, Hebrews ends by telling us that, though this all may be a surprise for you, it was never a surprise to the saints of the Old Testament. They saw this spiritual progression long ago, before Jesus actually came and made the way open to God. They saw it by *faith* – the spiritual ability to see and live in the spiritual world of God.

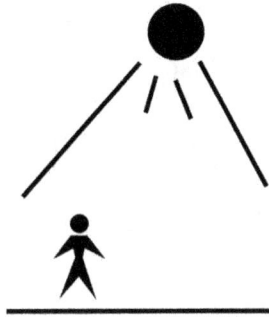

Faith: Walking in the light of God's World

So while they were serving in the physical Temple, while they were living in the physical land of Canaan and enjoying its physical blessings, those with faith knew about, and longed for, the day when "faith shall become sight" and these shadows would turn into reality.

> All these people were still living by faith when they died. They did not receive the things promised; they only saw them and welcomed them from a distance, admitting that they were foreigners and strangers on earth. People who say such things show that they are looking for a country of their own. If they had been thinking of the country they had left, they would have had opportunity to return. Instead, they were longing for a better country — a Heavenly one. Therefore God is not ashamed to be called their God, for he has prepared a city for them. (Hebrews 11:13-16)

The question is, do we see the same Jesus that they saw? They were ready for a new life with God in the Temple; are we ready for that?

REVELATION: THE REST OF THE STORY

The main point of the book of Revelation is given to us in the first verse.

The revelation of Jesus Christ, which God gave him to show
his servants what must soon take place. (Revelation 1:1)

We can avoid a lot of confusion while reading Revelation if we keep in mind that the book is about Jesus – it shows us things about him that we need to know. It's not primarily about end times, it's not about us, it's not mainly about the new world or how this world will be destroyed. These other subjects are discussed in the book, but the focus isn't there. We miss the point when we read the book apart from Christ.

For example, most of the things that happen in Revelation are from the hand of Christ. Revelation 5 shows us Christ on the throne, and he begins opening the seals of the scroll – and one of the seals involves blowing seven trumpets. What are we seeing here? If we remember that Jesus ascended to the throne of God, and he now lives and rules over the nations (see Psalm 2 for a complete description of his reign over the earth) then the pictures here in Revelation may very well be the ways he rules over us *now*. Plagues, wars, earthquakes are some of many ways he rules "with an iron sceptre" and dashes the nations to pieces. (Psalm 2:9) In other words, it's not a future sequence of terrifying events that we must fear, but a present King who will bring these things down on our own heads if we don't repent.

> Therefore, you kings, be wise; be warned, you rulers of the earth. Serve the LORD with fear and rejoice with trembling. Kiss the Son, lest he be angry and you be destroyed in your way, for his wrath can flare up in a moment. Blessed are all who take refuge in him. (Psalm 2:10-12)

That's not saying that there won't be future times of trouble as the end draws near, but it may be that we are so infatuated with the catastrophes planned for the end of the world and we're not paying any attention to our present standing before this King and appreciating his present rule.

The word "revelation" means to uncover and make visible. The thing covered was hidden completely from view, so much so that even educated guesses are a waste of our time. Man simply cannot know the truth about God until God himself makes himself visible to our minds. The entire Bible, for that matter, is a revelation of God to man.

In this book, we are given a revelation of Christ. Notice that John was "in the Spirit" when he received these visions. This is critical: the Spirit's job is to reveal the world of God to us so that we can see and understand what he is like.

> However, as it is written: "No eye has seen, no ear has heard, no mind has conceived what God has prepared for those who love him" – but God has revealed it to us by his Spirit. The Spirit searches all things, even the deep things of God. For who among men knows the thoughts of a man except the man's spirit within him? In the same way no one knows the thoughts of God except the Spirit of God. We have not received the spirit of the world but the Spirit who is from God, that we may understand what God has freely given us. (1 Corinthians 2:9-12)

From the day that man fell into sin and death, he has been completely blind to the world of God. He lost his ability to know God and relate to him. So if we would have any hope that our relationship can be restored, God has to make the first move and come out from behind the cover of darkness. He therefore sends his Spirit to pull the veil away so that we have a clear view of the world of God. The book of Revelation is nothing less than John entering into the halls of Heaven to see for himself what is going on there. What he finds is Jesus.

And what a view! John's vision shows him a King who is running a Kingdom that stretches from infinity to infinity. It's an extremely busy place. Angels and strange creatures, saints waiting for Judgment, orders coming continually from the Throne, powers and forces sweeping Heaven and earth as Jesus rules and reigns and forces all things into his will. Nothing is out of place, nothing is done apart from his will, nothing prevails against the King's power, everything is orderly and right on schedule. What a contrast to the seeming confusion of earth! Most people conclude that Jesus has very little to do with earth, even with the affairs of the Church, when everything in life is in chaos and nobody knows what's going on. In Heaven, however, we see the other side of the tapestry that Christ is weaving through history. All the loose ends and chaotic patterns of this life that we see confuse us; in his hands, however, they are all part of the overall project and make perfect sense. We just needed to see it from his perspective to understand them.

On the other hand, Revelation isn't a series of exact photos of Heaven. Any time you explore the world of God you are immediately immersed in mystery. God's world isn't like our world; he is Spirit, and "the Most High does not live in houses made by men." (Acts 7:48) He is not part of his Creation, nor does he need his Creation. So we can expect to encounter a strange world when we come before God. The Spirit will show us what it's like there, but only by using familiar images to describe the indescribable. "Streets of gold" and "each gate made of a single pearl" and a "sea of glass" are symbols that try to convey special spiritual truths about God.

And we're not going to be told everything that Jesus is up to. For that matter, God only shows us what he wants us to know; he limits the visions to those matters that will promote our spiritual growth. "The secret things belong to the LORD our God, but the things revealed belong to us and to our children forever, that we may follow all the words of this Law." (Deuteronomy 29:29) In other words, there are a few more matters about Jesus Christ that we need to know for our salvation. Therefore, for a short time, God brings us into his eternal world to get that precious information. That's the purpose of Revelation.

Filling in the picture

When we study the Gospels, we get a definite picture of who Jesus is. He is the fulfillment of Old Testament prophecy; he's the Messiah, our Redeemer, the Suffering Servant who takes upon himself the sin of the world. He is wise enough to handle the opposition of the Pharisees and teachers of the Law. He is tender to the poor and oppressed. He's the leader of the disciples. He opens up the Scriptures to us so that we can understand their true meaning.

But we didn't get a complete picture of him in the Gospels. We see the Son of Man there, the fulfillment of the Prophets – but, concerning the King, we only get the assurance of his royalty. He actually refused to put himself on a throne, claiming that the time had not yet come. When his enemies challenged him and finally laid hold of him to kill him, he didn't raise a hand in self-defense. Though he claimed to be setting up a Kingdom, it certainly did look as if it failed completely when the Jews and Romans crucified him and his disciples scattered across the country.

If the Gospels were the only accounts that we had about Jesus, we would have a skewed and off-balance picture of him. But this is not the only view of Christ. During his life on earth we didn't see him in his full glory. He had set his glory aside, we are told in Philippians 2:3, to assume the humble role of a servant. Little did people realize that they were looking at the King of kings in the humble carpenter's son!

Revelation shows us another side to the Gentle Savior, the Lamb crucified. Without it people would think things about Jesus that simply aren't true – as is the case with modern unbelievers. Revelation is going to correct those misconceptions.

For instance, here are some contrasts between the stories of the Gospels and the vision of Christ in Revelation:

In the Gospels	*In Revelation*
Jesus was a **servant** – as he demonstrated when he washed the feet of his disciples	Jesus was a **King**, as we see him sitting on the Throne of Heaven about to send forth judgments on the earth – Revelation 5
Jesus was **humble** – as he stood before the Sanhedrin, about to be crucified	Jesus **reigns** in power, as we see him sitting in judgment over the whole world – Revelation 6 & 20

Jesus seemingly **lost** his battle when his enemies crucified him	Jesus will **win** the battle when he rides into battle with his host of Heaven – Revelation 19
Jesus **forgives** even the worst sinners – as he did for the woman caught in adultery	Jesus will issue **justice** to the nations and punish the wicked – Revelation 20
Jesus was born a **man**, and was an infant in Mary's arms	Jesus is **God** in all his infinite and eternal glory – Revelation 1
Jesus was a man of **peace** who prayed for his enemies and refused to call down fire from Heaven on those who rejected him	Jesus is the Captain of **war**, leading the hosts of Heaven in battle against the earth – Revelation 19
Jesus was **lonely**, rejected by all – even by his own disciples	Jesus is the **Lord of Hosts**, surrounded by worshipers – Revelation 14
Jesus was **shamed**, spat upon, and struck by his enemies	Jesus lives in **glory** far above all principalities and powers – Revelation 19 & 20
Jesus got no credit or **glory**, even from his own hometown	Jesus will get all **glory** from every creature in Heaven and on earth – Revelation 5
Even during Jesus' life **the wicked prospered**	Jesus will **destroy the wicked** – Revelation 20

As you can see, the two accounts are very different. Revelation gives us "the rest of the story" about Jesus. In fact, without this new information we would definitely get the wrong idea of who Jesus is by reading only the Gospel accounts. No wonder, then, that the saints in John's day, who were asking tough questions about whether this Jesus really did come to set up a new Kingdom, needed to hear these truths about their Savior!

There are a lot of aspects of our Christian faith that would remain mysterious to most people if it weren't for this Revelation of the glory of Christ. God in his mercy occasionally gives his people crucial insights to strengthen their faith, restore their hope, and encourage them to persevere. For instance, David almost lost hope when, as he struggled with the trials and burdens of life, he noticed that the wicked were "always carefree, they increase in wealth." (Psalm 73:12) How could a just God give the good things in life to people who don't deserve it, and require his own people to struggle on through problems?

> When I tried to understand all this, it was
> oppressive to me till I entered the sanctuary of God;
> then I understood their final destiny. (Psalm 73:16-17)

From high above the world, in the halls of the Temple of God, one can see what's really going on in the earth. The wicked aren't going to get away with a thing. It's the righteous who have blessings, not the rebellious. All the wealth of sinners is going to weigh them down to the grave and destruction, and all the trials of the righteous are earning them a reward in Heaven. Everything becomes clear and easy to understand in the presence of God.

In the same way, the book of Revelation answers many of our questions. If we go by our physical senses, none of Christianity makes sense, nor does it seem to work out well in this world of ours. But with faith we can see that Jesus put us in a perfect position to succeed in eternity; we just need that Heavenly perspective to see the whole picture. Revelation is the great "Aha!" of the Bible, clearing up our misconceptions and filling in the holes in our understanding.

- **<u>What happened when Jesus left this world?</u>** We are told in Acts that he ascended into Heaven, and the Epistles tell us a little bit about Jesus on the throne ruling over the world. But Revelation opens the doors of Heaven so that we can see the Lord Jesus – and he's on a throne! Multitudes are worshiping him and giving him the glory he deserves. The Father has given control of all the earth to him, which he is exercising in the judgments he issues from his throne. Angels serve him, await his Word, and carry out his orders on earth. He is comforting his people who have already died. He continually examines and judges the Churches, and promises rewards, issues threats and warnings, and sends spiritual resources to them in their need. He marks his people with his protective Name. Revelation is full of information on the works of Christ which are going on in Heaven and earth right this minute. Phase II of God's plan of salvation didn't end with the Gospels, and there is more coming even after this age of the Church that we're presently in.

- **Why did he set aside his glory when he came to earth?** In God's schedule there's a time for salvation, and there's another time for judgment. Right now it's the time to repent and come to him pleading for God's mercy. Sinners will find the doors of Heaven open to them – as they found Jesus ready and willing to welcome them into his Kingdom. While he was on this earth he wanted to show the love of God toward sinners, not chase them away with his overwhelming justice. Jesus will not always leave the doors of mercy open, though – the time will come to wrap up the affairs of earth, judge those who refused to repent, wage war against his enemies and destroy them, and set up a righteous Kingdom that will last forever.

- **Is there any justice for the persecuted?** There certainly is! He promises eternal life, a place in God's eternal city, the Name of God on their foreheads, an inheritance, and the privilege of ruling with him over the universe. Not only are the persecuted comforted with these promises, they will also have the pleasure of seeing their former oppressors so thoroughly destroyed that the smoke of their destruction will ascend into Heaven forever. God's revenge will be pleasant to all those who have longed to see the glory of God and the destruction of the enemy.

- **What is the Church?** The Church is a great multitude, of such a number that can't be counted. It comes from every tribe and nation of the earth. They are dressed in robes of white – the righteousness of Christ. The Church surrounds the thrones of God and of Christ, and it worships and glorifies them with praises about the works they received at God's hand. The Church is the very bride of Christ, made beautiful in holiness and inner perfection. The Church is the house of God where he will live with his people forever. The people of God are marked and preserved by God. Revelation shows us a protected and special people, and Jesus works diligently for their eternal salvation and blessing.

- **<u>Is there really a war going on?</u>** Without eyes of faith we can't see the spiritual conflict between Heaven and earth. We know about war only too well – wars between men and nations. But behind the scenes, over our heads so to speak, rages a spiritual battle in which our souls hang in the balance. Satan leads the forces of darkness, destroys multitudes in his fury, and yet gets thrown back before the superior forces of Heaven. Jesus himself leads the Host of Heaven in the assault on earth. Angels, the "winds and fires" that God sends out to do his work on earth, wage battle in great power all over the world. They use overwhelming weapons that strike terror in the hearts of men and nations. We cannot successfully resist them. The final battle will clear the earth of all sin and death, and Christ in victory will set up an eternal Kingdom in Heaven and on earth to replace the kingdoms of darkness that have existed too long among us. If only our history books had taught us about this continual war that has raged around us, we would have had a much better understanding of human history.

- **<u>Will there ever be an end to sin?</u>** Sin *will* be destroyed eventually. We get a preview of what happens to sinners when John gets his first glimpse of Christ in Revelation 1 – he falls at the feet of this utterly holy God as though he were dead. Jesus has come to destroy the works of the devil, and the first terrible work that the devil performed on this earth was to lead mankind into sin. Starting with the Churches, Jesus examines the hearts of his people and roots out the problem of sin and rebellion. In the visions of his warfare against the wicked of the

311

earth, we see a determined foe of sin as he destroys all traces of rebellion – in fierce wrath and power – so that the earth is cleansed by fire, swept clean of all its filth. Finally the Church is cleansed completely like a bride in her purity, ready for a holy God to take up his permanent residence among them. There's no question that there will be an end to sin; it's been God's goal since the beginning of time.

- **What is Heaven like?** The book of Revelation shows us a busy place surrounding the throne of God. Praises continually go up to the Father and the Son; considering the fact that the wisdom and majesty and power of God are infinite, eternity won't be long enough to fully explore and admire the excellence of the Lord. There will always be more things to discover and ponder about God's nature and works. And Heaven has a very full population with its creatures, elders, saints in white robes, and angels. Heaven is also a high vantage-point over the Creation. From the throne of God one can see all the nations, the hearts of men everywhere, the judgments of God being carried out all over the earth, the prayers of all the saints. In Heaven we see the Temple of God and the sacrifice that opens the way to access to God, even to sinners. That way is busy night and day as God's people take advantage of their close relationship to their Father. And God is preparing his home in Heaven where he will live in the midst of his people; he loves his family, and he intends to bless his children forever with the riches of Heaven.

- **Is it worth it to deny oneself and carry the cross?** Sin can be very appealing at times. "Stolen water is sweet," (Proverbs 9:17), and one wonders whether it might be better to throw off the restraint of Christian morals and enjoy life as the wicked do. It seems as if being a Christian gains us nothing but pain and hardship as we put aside this world's pleasures for future promises of things that we can't see. So Revelation shows us the rewards for being holy. Jesus tells his saints in the

312

Churches that, if they remain faithful to the end, there will be great reward and honor in God's courts. Those who were persecuted for their faith will receive many times more than what they lost in this world. The precious nature of the treasures of Heaven – shown by the imagery of gold and gems – is eternal wealth, which should encourage anybody to leave behind the temporary riches of a world destined to be destroyed. Not only will the saints receive in Heaven much more than they had to give up on earth, they will receive great satisfaction in God's judgment on those who made their lives miserable here! They will rejoice over their enemies when the smoke of their destruction rises to Heaven.

• **Are the wicked going to get what they deserve?** Revelation is also full of promises of what God intends to do to the wicked. It won't be pleasant. Chapter after chapter is filled with curses, death and destruction, trials and terrors. Nobody will escape the wrath of God; the entire earth will be laid waste by degrees until every single sinner is rooted out and punished. At the end of time, all flesh will be brought to God's Judgment Seat and everyone will have to face the record of their sin and rebellion. The final punishment – the second death in the lake of fire – is an *eternal state of misery* for God's enemies. If nobody believed Jesus' threats of Hell in the Gospels, here at least is the visible picture of the damnation of the wicked in colors that nobody can mistake.

Summary

We don't (or won't!) know the interpretation to everything in the book of Revelation, but we are shown what's important to know. Maybe if we focus on what's important, God will reveal more about the rest. At the very least we ought to take John's introduction seriously and learn more about Jesus. This is going to be critical for our life of faith while in this world.

THE NEW TESTAMENT: TWO NEW CONCEPTS

Most Christians believe that the New Testament is their book, whereas the Old Testament is the book for the Jews. In fact, many of them call themselves "New Testament Christians". It's in the New Testament that their faith is finished, perfected, culminated. To them, the New Testament is more important for their faith than the Old.

What worries me about that is their faith becomes *limited* to the New Testament for the most part. Everyone knows that our Christian faith has Old Testament concepts that it grew out of – the Passover, King David, the sacrificial system, for example. But to say that the clear, full, and adequate explanation of our faith is exclusively in the New Testament without necessarily turning to the Old is really missing the mark. The New cannot stand on its own; it's more like one leg of a four-legged chair. Any Christian who limits their understanding of the Gospel of Christ to just what they learn from the New is going to seriously misunderstand the Gospel; they will be trying something that even the Apostles dared not attempt.

Let's go over again what the purpose of the Old Testament is. We've seen that God distributed information about Jesus throughout the Old Testament; we call this "Distributed Revelation" because we have to go from passage to passage to put the entire picture together. Each cluster of data fully explains a single aspect of Christ; put them all together, and you now know who Jesus is – or will be. [23]

The limitation of the Old Testament was that these lessons were learned in context of the physical – the people and events were the means by which God taught them about the Messiah, but nobody was equal to the task of lifting these concepts up to their perfect form. They knew what things *should* be like in God's Kingdom, but nobody could get there on their own.

---

[23] See the chapter above entitled "General Principles" for an explanation of Distributed Revelation.

The concepts were explained so clearly, however, that we don't need them explained again in detail in the New Testament. The Apostles had another goal in mind in their letters; if their students needed more training in the basics, they sent them back to the Old Testament for further study.

What the Apostles did was add two new concepts to finish the picture.

The New Testament shows us the New Man and what we have to do to become one with him.

The *first new concept* of the New Testament is the Incarnation. The idea of God becoming man was a staggering idea, and one that God decided not to burden the Jewish mind with at the beginning. It was enough to wean them away from worshiping idols and staying with the true God. They would not have understood the concept of the Trinity, though there were hints in the Old Testament of such a thing. But the time had finally come to introduce them to it, because there are several concepts here that are critical to our salvation.

Jesus came as a man, as one of us, so that the Law of God will finally be kept as a man – something that God has wanted to see from the creation of the world. Someone had to keep this Law! Now that it's been done, we have a righteousness here that is perfect, a righteousness earned by a man that satisfies God's requirements of man. None of us could do it, but Jesus could and did.

Now Jesus has a man's righteousness that he can give to us – as a gift. He doesn't give it to all, but only to those who come and ask for it in repentance and humility and faith. We take on his righteousness like a robe covering our hearts and lives, and now the Law has no more quarrel with us, no more than it does with Jesus.

So the main idea of the Incarnation is that Jesus came to do what man must do in the eyes of the Law – for the sake of the rest of us. Nothing new here – it's all described in the Old Testament – but it is new that the Son of God himself would do man's part of the Covenant agreement (though it was hinted at). Only the Son could have done such a thing – he had the power and wisdom of Heaven to bring to the task.

The **second concept** that the Apostles introduce to us is our union with Christ. We learned from the Old Testament that the central theme is the Son living with the Father. Well, that's our goal – we want to see God. But how can we, being the sinners that we are, not to mention that we are only flesh and blood? Is our destiny only to look at God from a distance like the angels and the rest of Creation? If so, that would be blessing enough; but that's not the theme of the Bible. The goal is that we might see God as his children, not simply as servants.

The only way to do that, however, is to make us one with the Son of God. And here we get into the second mystery of the New Testament – the special operation of the Holy Spirit who unites us with Christ, fills us with the presence of Christ, and changes our natures so that we all become the Body of Christ. And this too is a staggering concept. We may feel that God really didn't have to honor us in such a way, but here is the guiding principle of the Bible from beginning to end. We were never meant to be restored to simply the level that Adam and Eve enjoyed. We will approach God in Christ, come into the Trinity, before the presence of the Father and will know the Father as Jesus the Son knows him. What Jesus is and has, we now have. We have become children of God in every full sense of the idea.

These two concepts are so amazing, so complex, so mysterious that the Apostles spend their whole time in the New Testament explaining them to us. As they develop these ideas, they keep reaching back to the Old Testament themes to explain what they're talking about. The Incarnation and the Union with Christ makes us part of the system that God has been developing over millennia since the time of Genesis. The Old Testament system is now ours, only now on a spiritual level. The physical limitations have been erased by using these two new concepts; and now all of God's people, Old and New Testament, receive the same hope. "Only together with us would they be made perfect." (Hebrews 11:40)

Physical versus spiritual

One of the most important aspects of the Bible is how the physical and spiritual levels interact with each other in the timeline of God's works.

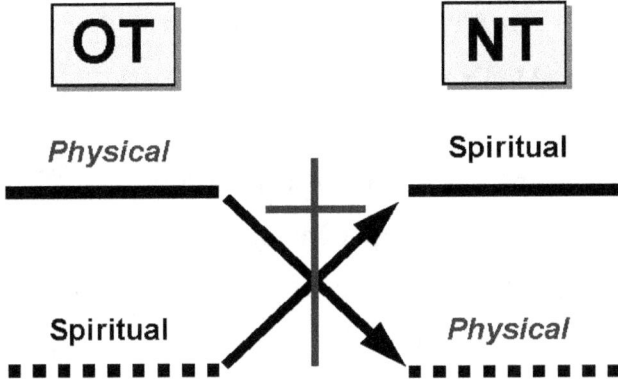

Figure 8 – Physical versus Spiritual

• In the **Old Testament**, the *physical* level predominates. We see animal sacrifices in a physical Temple. We see the children of Israel settling down in Canaan. We watch David pulling the tribes together and defeating the Moabites and Philistines. Just about everything we read about is something that we can see, feel, or hear with our physical senses.

God did this for a reason. Since the solution to mankind's problems of sin and death is so complex – and since the ultimate solution is a spiritual one which nobody can see – he started out by teaching us the answer on a level that we could easily grasp. It's amazing how much children can learn if you make your point in the form of stories and pictures.

So to teach us lessons of his spiritual world in terms of which we cannot mistake the meaning, he used stories describing his works in the lives of real people in real places. The point is there for anybody to see; a child can understand the story; and if we read and believe what God is saying, we can be saved.

Some of the important stories of the Bible include the following:

317

The Creation of the world

Abel's sacrifice

The Flood

The Covenant with Abraham

The Blessing of Jacob

Deliverance through Joseph

The Exodus

The Promised Land

David and Solomon

The Divided Kingdom

Punishment and Exile

Rebuilding the Temple and the walls of Jerusalem

We miss the point, however, if we think that these events (and many others) were merely physical events that happened for the benefit of the Old Testament saints only. The Bible was written for all of us; the whole Church is the recipient of God's letter. The physical events recorded in the Old Testament describe the same things that happen in God's spiritual world *in all ages*.

Though the physical level predominates in the Old Testament, we can catch a glimpse of the spiritual just behind the physical, right underneath the surface, if we have the eyes to see and ears to hear. Passages like the following show us that God always did consider the physical level to be temporary and not the ultimate point:

> "The multitude of your sacrifices – what are they to me?" says the LORD. "I have more than enough of burnt offerings, of rams and the fat of fattened animals; I have no pleasure in the blood of bulls and lambs and goats." (Isaiah 1:11)

Didn't he tell the Israelites to bring these sacrifices to him at the Temple? Yet here he is claiming that he hates them! The point is that they were hiding behind the animal sacrifice as if that would buy them a reprieve from the condemnation of the Law, and then going right back into their sin. This is not the way to worship God! The sacrifices were designed to teach us how terrible is the effect of sin. We're supposed to stop our sinning. If anything, the sacrifice would point up the need for something more permanent that would change the heart, so that we wouldn't sin anymore. The sacrifices of the Temple were an embarrassing reminder of the weakness of the system. (See Romans 8:3 and Hebrews 10:1-4 on this point.)

Paul also gives us clues revealing that some of the Old Testament saints understood the ultimate goal of a spiritual Kingdom.

> A man is not a Jew if he is only one outwardly, nor is circumcision merely outward and physical. No, a man is a Jew if he is one *inwardly*; and circumcision is circumcision of the *heart*, by the Spirit, not by the written code. Such a man's praise is not from men, but from God. (Romans 2:28-29)

> The LORD your God will *circumcise your hearts and the hearts of your descendants*, so that you may love him with all your heart and with all your soul, and live. (Deuteronomy 30:6)

It was always understood, by those who had the faith of Abraham, that the physical symbols were lessons pointing to the spiritual realities in God's Kingdom.

• In the **New Testament**, the *spiritual* level predominates. The situation flip-flops, so to speak. Now instead of a physical Temple, we learn of the Temple in Heaven that we must come to. Now instead of a physical

319

land of Canaan to inherit, we inherit Heaven. David sitting on his throne in Jerusalem turns into the Son of David sitting on his throne beside the Father. The Philistines aren't a problem to us anymore, but our sins and the "spiritual forces of darkness" certainly are.

Of course the situation in the Old Testament was also spiritual, but they were required to learn and work things out through the physical means that God gave them. Only by faith would they realize that a more permanent solution from Heaven would eventually come to light on earth. Now, however, the veil has been taken away, the time has come; the eternal solution has been revealed to us.

> These were all commended for their faith, yet none of them received what had been promised. God had planned something better for us so that *only together with us would they be made perfect*. (Hebrews 11:39-40)

The Gentiles need to learn the lessons of the Old Testament so that they can understand their faith. The Jews need to graduate from their physical system so that they can finally enjoy the spiritual reality of God's salvation. Either way, we don't need the physical anymore. It has served its purpose; the lessons are now recorded in the Old Testament for all to learn. Those lessons are a stepping stone, a primer to something better. Why long for the shadow when you can have the real thing? That's why the Apostles urged us to leave the physical behind and, through faith, reach out for the eternal realities:

> The blood of goats and bulls and the ashes of a heifer sprinkled on those who are ceremonially unclean sanctify them so that they are outwardly clean. How much more, then, will the blood of Christ, who through the eternal Spirit offered himself unblemished to God, cleanse our consciences from acts that lead to

death, so that we may serve the living God! (Hebrews 9:13-14)

We do have a few minor physical aspects to our religion, however. We gather together in church buildings, we are baptized with water, we eat bread and drink wine at the communion service, we have preachers and teachers who train us with the Word of God. But we understand (or we're supposed to!) that these can't touch the soul like the Holy Spirit can. The reality isn't in the things we use in our religion; those are "vessels" through which God touches us with the treasures from Heaven. We know now that we can pray anywhere, not just in Jerusalem – because the Spirit lifts us up to the Throne of Heaven.

> Believe me, woman, a time is coming when you will worship the Father neither on this mountain nor in Jerusalem. You Samaritans worship what you do not know; we worship what we do know, for salvation is from the Jews. Yet a time is coming and has now come when the true worshipers will worship the Father in spirit and truth, for they are the kind of worshipers the Father seeks. God is spirit, and his worshipers must worship in spirit and in truth. (John 4:21-24)

The list of physical concepts that God used to lead Israel is still important to us, but now on a spiritual level.

Physical	Spiritual
The Creation of the world	*The New Creation*
Abel's sacrifice	*The sacrifice of Christ*
The Flood	*This world will be destroyed*
The Covenant with Abraham	*The Gospel of Christ*
The Blessing of Jacob	*Treasures in Heaven*
Deliverance through Joseph	*Deliverance through Christ*
The Exodus	*Leaving the world behind*
The Promised Land	*Heaven*
David and Solomon	*King Jesus*

The Divided Kingdom	*Division in the Church*
Punishment and Exile	*Discipline of God's people*
Rebuilding the Temple and	*Rebuilding the Church*
the walls of Jerusalem	

Remember that this is a short list; there are so many lessons to be learned in the Old Testament and they all have spiritual counterparts in Christ's Kingdom. God's Kingdom used to be on earth, among the Jews, and they first learned what it's like to live with this God. Now the Church is living with him, and they too must learn the same lessons. We are all in training for living with a spiritual God that we can't see or touch.

The role of the Apostles

The act of making us one with Christ is a mystery indeed; nobody can understand how it works or how to make it happen. (See John 3:8 on this.) But the Creator who made the world knows how to recreate us in his image – a second Creation, not able to fall into sin and death again but able to live in the presence of God forever. Making the Son of God a man was the open door for humanity to live with God. The way that you and I can take advantage of this new opportunity is to become one with Christ, the righteous Man, through the Spirit.

If you think that these are difficult concepts to grasp, you're right. Even the angels long to look into these things! And since God knew we would need help understanding the mystery of the Gospel, he gave us Apostles to explain it to us. You will also notice that they don't spend much time on the basics – they're too busy explaining the new material, which is difficult enough to understand. They assume that the reader has done his homework already in the Old Testament.

We have much to say about this, but it is hard to explain because you are slow to learn. In fact, though by this time you ought to be teachers, you need someone to teach you the elementary truths of God's word all over again. You need milk, not solid food! Anyone who lives on milk, being still an infant, is not acquainted with the teaching about righteousness. But solid food is for the mature, who by constant use have trained themselves to distinguish good from evil.

> Therefore let us leave the elementary teachings about Christ and go on to maturity, not laying again the foundation of repentance from acts that lead to death, and of faith in God, instruction about baptisms, the laying on of hands, the resurrection of the dead, and eternal judgment. And God permitting, we will do so. (Hebrews 5:11 – 6:3)

The disciples of Jesus (who were later the Apostles – the "ones sent out") were hand-picked eyewitnesses who spent three years with Jesus. They saw his works, they listened to his lessons, they pondered over the events surrounding the life of Christ. But even they had little idea of what was happening ... until the Spirit of God filled them at Pentecost. Then the mystery was made plain to them and they had supernatural ability to carry the *right* message to the nations. They saw the truth about **the nature of Christ** and they knew the steps that one should take **to become one with the Son of God**. The data was the same as before; but now they became the teachers of the Church. We understand the true nature of Christ and his work through their teachings.

> Consequently, you are no longer foreigners and aliens, but fellow citizens with God's people and members of God's household, **built on the foundation of the apostles and prophets**, with Christ Jesus himself as the chief cornerstone. (Ephesians 2:19-20)

Since the Spirit of Christ is the key to being one with Christ, the Apostles explain difficult but critical concepts like being filled with the Spirit, walking in the Spirit, not grieving the Spirit, and bearing spiritual fruit.

They also teach us a great deal about the New Creation. They don't want us to make the same mistake that the Jews made, thinking that the old physical system is God's ultimate goal for his people. The Epistles of the New Testament contrast the old world with the new world; they show us Heaven, and the glory of God in the Church. They press upon us the need for conversion of the soul, not just outward conformity to the Law. Of course all this was taught in the Old Testament, but now the time had come to cut the cord with the physical and implement the spiritual Kingdom.

And speaking of the Jews, one point that the Apostles were careful to make clear is that anybody can come to Christ for salvation and the New Creation – not just the Jews. The promise was always there in the Old Testament that God would eventually extend his plan around the world; the Jews were the first to learn about his Kingdom, but they are not the *only* ones allowed into God's Kingdom! It was always predicted that the Gentiles would eventually come into the family of God; but the Old Testament never fully explained how that was to happen. The reason for that is that it requires an understanding of the second mystery that the Apostles revealed to the world: that to become spiritual children of God, we must become one with Christ. In other words, it's not enough to be a Jew, but you must become a Christian – and both Jew and Gentile must do that to be an heir of Abraham.

> His purpose was to create in himself one new man out of the two, thus making peace ... He came and preached peace to you who were far away and peace to those who were near. For through him we both have access to the Father by one Spirit. Consequently, you are no longer foreigners and aliens, but fellow citizens with God's people and members of God's household. (Ephesians 2:15, 17-19)

The Apostles were actually interpreters of Christ. Like the Pharisees, it was entirely possible to look at Jesus of Nazareth and miss the point about him. Because he came as a man, it was easy to miss his true glory. Only by faith can we see the Son of God in Jesus and his work. But just in case we missed the point in the Gospels from Jesus' teaching, the Apostles also focus on that point in their letters. There should be no mistaking their message: the Messiah has come to gather his people to himself and take them to Heaven. The old promises that God made to his people are true; but the *way* he plans to fulfill them is completely unexpected – this time it's going to work.

324

Section Three: Miscellaneous

TEN KEYS THAT UNLOCK THE BIBLE

There comes a time when every student of the Bible has to move from the beginner's level to the intermediate level. At first we all have to spend time learning the data: times and places, people and events. Once we get the big picture of what's going on in both the Old and New Testaments, then we have to start learning principles of interpretation.

A *principle of interpretation* is a concept you use to get the right meaning out of a passage. All of us use some sort of concepts to filter the Bible stories through as we read them; but not all concepts are valid or useful. For example, a lot of people think that the Old Testament is strictly for the Jews, and the New Testament only for Christians. That's a principle of interpretation that they're using to judge what to believe about the text. (It's also wrong!)

There's a whole science about principles of interpretation, and most preachers training for the ministry have to take a course or two in the subject. After all, they have to give the right meaning to their congregations when they preach.

Ten Keys to the Bible

There are some systems of interpreting the Bible that are definitely wrong; you should do some research before you believe anything that's out there. We're going to look at one system here that's safe, because it uses simple ideas that occur throughout the Bible over and over again. If these ideas are so pervasive in God's Word, they must be important to him – and therefore should be important to us.

There are ten major themes that run across the entire Bible that are characteristic of the way God is building his Kingdom. These Keys are so integral to the story of the Bible that you can use them like keys in a door – they will open up just about any passage and show you what's really going on there.

The reason these concepts are important to God is because the Keys get us away from a man-centered interpretation of a text, and make us look at God in the text. These ideas bring God to the forefront and show us what he's like and what kinds of things he does. And the Keys also keep us from wrong interpretations: for example, I already mentioned that interpreting the book of Genesis without coming to grips with the Abrahamic Covenant is missing the entire point of the book. Time to start again!

But keep in mind that this is a second-level approach to the Bible. This isn't your ordinary Sunday School material; you will have to work at mastering these concepts. Not only will you need to study them thoroughly to properly understand them, but also you will need to be skilled at spotting them in the text. The Apostles were skilled at this; we already saw an example of their insights in the passage from Acts when they used three different OT passages in their prayer. And another example we've already seen: we interpreted Genesis 18 not as the proper way to get a believing spouse, but the beginning of the fulfillment of the third promise of the Covenant. Seeing the right key at work is the goal of Bible study.

With these concepts in the back of your mind, and some practice at seeing them in the text, you can tackle just about any passage in the Bible and pull out at least the beginning stages of its proper meaning. [24]

• *Revelation*

Revelation means "to uncover", to make something visible that was hidden. And in God's case, we really need revelation if we are to know who he is. Since God is the Creator, he has to show himself to his creation if we're to know him; we can't go the other way and probe into God's divine nature. We simply don't have the tools for such a thing.

That's the purpose of the Bible – to reveal God to us. From beginning to end, God shows us who he is, and what he does, so that we can make informed decisions. There is no other revelation of God (though nature, which Paul tells us about, shows us his "invisible

---

[24] For a complete discussion of the Keys, see the book *Ten Keys to the Bible*.

qualities" to some extent – Romans 1) that we have. The libraries are full of books about God, yet unless they got their information from the Bible they are only opinions and guesses and (at worst) lies about him. The Bible is our only true source of information about God.

Now let's look at that idea from another angle. If we look for God when we're reading the Bible, we're using the book in the way that God intended. And if we don't look for God in every passage, then we are misusing the Bible. That means that people who use the Bible for moralisms and social theory and political programs and all kinds of things that people use it for are abusing the Bible. It's true that the Bible talks about all aspects of human life; but that's not its primary purpose. It is revealing God to us. Once we see clearly who God is and what he does, then we can start learning our appropriate responses to him.

The Bible doesn't show us everything about God, however. God is limitless; he's eternal; his glory can't be measured or fully grasped by the human mind. God is only going to show us what we *need* to know about him. Remember that he's the King, and the Creator made a Kingdom at the beginning with the intention that his servants obey him and serve him. We will need truth if we're to do our duty in the proper way – and **truth** is *revelation of the way God sees things, the way he wants us to see things*.

Science can uncover how this physical world works, but it can't help us at all in seeing and understanding God's spiritual world. At Creation, God made a combination world – the physical inside the framework of a spiritual world. You have to be able to see both to be a responsible citizen in God's Kingdom. So the Bible uncovers that spiritual world so that we can see God in his glory, we can see the basis for morality and ethics, we can see the worth of the human soul, we can see what obedience and rebellion really are, we can see the remedy for sinners and the way to God's throne in worship and repentance and life. All of these things are uncovered for us in the Bible so that we can live in these two worlds at the same time.

As we work through the Bible, then, we have to keep alert to what it is showing us about God and his special world. Creation shows us the two worlds being fit together. Abraham saw the promises to him and his descendants. Moses and the Israelites heard the voice of their God and followed him out of bondage into the Promised Land. David followed God's Plan and brought Israel back to God. The Prophets took the Word of the Lord to the Israelites in an attempt to bring them back to their God in humility and repentance. This very spiritual God destroyed Jerusalem and punished the Jews in Exile for their sins against him. And once we get into the New Testament, God himself comes into the form of a man and rescues his people from their sin, gives them a way of escape from the dangers of this physical world, and gives them a hope of an eternal Promised Land – the Apostles were witnesses of these events.

All these realities are normally hidden to the eye of flesh; but through eyewitnesses, and their testimony, we now have vital information that will greatly affect our lives if we act on that information appropriately. That is what it means to live by faith – to live according to the revelation that we receive about God in his Word.

• *Miracle*

We discussed miracles in the Creation chapter, but let's review the details.

A miracle is something that only God can do. God does something in our physical world that we would like to see happen, or that we really need to happen – but we can't do it ourselves. Give us the time, and tell us the steps to take, and we may be able to do some of these same things ourselves; for example, we can make wine too if we go through the steps and take enough time doing it. But when Jesus made wine, he skipped the steps and made it instantly; the wedding guests didn't have months to wait for it.

So by definition a miracle is something that science will never be able to explain; it lacks the steps, and the time, that it requires to duplicate it. And some miracles that God does simply can't be done by science, no matter how brilliant the scientists are or how many resources they have at their disposal. We will never be able to raise the dead, for example, or cast out demons from someone's soul. There are some things that only God can do.

That means that every miracle that is recorded in the Bible is something that we can't do ourselves, for some reason, and yet God decided that someone really needed this to happen.

Miracles don't happen all through the Bible. They occur in clumps, so to speak. Creation of course was the first great miracle; the next miracles we read about are in the ministry of Moses, then a few during the period of the Judges, then during the time of Elijah and Elisha, and then it jumps to the miracles of Jesus' ministry and the ministries of the Apostles. "Minor" miracles happen along the way, but these are the major groups of miracles recorded in the Bible. But in general the miracles were limited to the inauguration of the three great categories of Scripture: the Law, the Prophets, and the Messiah.

The reason for miracles is because something must be done that this physical world doesn't have the resources to do, or the structure for. God's Kingdom requires a step that the physical can't provide. So the Judge steps in, the Creator steps in, the King steps in with the necessary spiritual push that steers the Kingdom of God in the right direction. Without that miracle, the situation would have proceeded strictly along natural lines – which wouldn't have answered the needs of God's Kingdom.

There were two kinds of miracles in the Bible: physical and spiritual. It's easy to find the physical miracles, but it's not so easy to appreciate the spiritual miracles. For this we need the idea of revelation, because here we learn that God changes the heart of the sinner from a stone to living flesh (Ezekiel 36), that God gives repentance (Luke 4), that God shines the light along the path to his Throne (Acts 9). Conversion is a true miracle, because (as we learn from Jesus and Paul) a sinner is, naturally speaking, dead to God and incapable of even knowing God, let alone repenting and obeying him. (See Ephesians 2:1-3.) The Spirit of God has to come into the heart and make us alive to God so that we, like newborn babies, can see and know God and start living in his presence. This requires the hand of God – in other words, it's a bona-fide miracle.

We will never understand how miracles happen, but we can appreciate the need for them – and live in the realities that God has created around us.

You were taught, with regard to your former way of life, to put off your old self, which is being corrupted by its deceitful desires; to be made new in the attitude of your minds; and to put on the new self, created to be like God in true righteousness and holiness. (Ephesians 4:22-24)

• *Faith*

The idea of faith fits right alongside that of Revelation. If we can give a short definition to it, **faith** is *living in the light of God's world.*

Faith is not what a lot of people think it is. Many think that faith is simply a list of doctrines that we believe in. Or that faith is a hope, a wish, that something will turn out true in the end. Actually faith is a *certainty* – it's not a hope, but a knowledge based on personal experience.

Now faith is confidence in what we hope for and assurance about what we do not see. (Hebrews 11:1)

The first necessary step to faith is that God must turn the light on. He does this in many ways – the primary way he works now is through his Word, as the Spirit opens it to us. When God opens our eyes to the reality that the Bible is talking about, that's what "turning the light on" means. A bright light from Heaven is shining into your mind and heart now, and you can see things you couldn't see before.

Is this possible, to see the invisible God? We can't live by faith unless we do. The author of Hebrews tells us that the saints of the Old Testament lived by that kind of faith.

By faith he left Egypt, not fearing the king's anger; he persevered because he saw him who is invisible. (Hebrews 11:27)

That light from Heaven enables us to see all sorts of things that are still invisible to the unbelieving. We can see who God is now, and why we need to fear him and worship him. We can see the true nature of the world around us and why we need to get away from here. We can see our own hearts and the kind of trouble we're in. And we can see Jesus, the solution of our problem, and the way of escape through him. All of these things are designed to save us, to bring us to eternal life; without faith, we have no hope of any of this.

Faith takes two to work: you and God. You can't make yourself see the invisible God; only he can show himself to you. That's the first step of faith (though many don't appreciate the dynamics at work here). The second step is that you start living in light of those spiritual realities that you see. God does his part, we do our part.

It's not only seeing God's world, it's living according to what we see. The author of Hebrews (Hebrews 6:4-8) rebukes those who have seen the Lord's glory, have tasted the goodness of the world to come, and yet went back to their old lives and rejected Christ's salvation. That's not faith. Faith is walking in the light, as we learn from John.

> But if we walk in the light, as he is in the light, we have
> fellowship with one another, and the blood of Jesus, his
> Son, purifies us from all sin. (1 John 1:7)

So the person of faith walks in two worlds at the same time. He lives in the physical world with his physical senses, and he can take advantage of the world around him. But he also lives in God's world and takes advantage of what he sees there too. The person who has faith will do things that are unaccountable to the unbelievers, because he's listening to a different tune than they are. He moves this way when they are moving that way, and they don't understand his rationale. He can see what's killing them, and they can't see what's saving him. But in the end, even they will see why he lived like that – only it will be too late for them.

> They are surprised that you do not join them in their
> reckless, wild living, and they heap abuse on you. But they
> will have to give account to him who is ready to judge the
> living and the dead. (1 Peter 4:4-5)

But did the Old Testament saints live by faith? Certainly! They saw the same God that we see. They could see Jesus himself in his glory. It's a mistake to think that they had a crippled view of Jesus, whereas we have a full view. If you think about it, some of those people saw astounding things about Jesus in visions and dreams that we can only read about – we've never seen his glory as they did.

> Your father Abraham rejoiced at the thought of seeing my day; he saw it and was glad. (John 8:56)

> In my vision at night I looked, and there before me was one like a son of man, coming with the clouds of heaven. He approached the Ancient of Days and was led into his presence. He was given authority, glory and sovereign power; all nations and peoples of every language worshiped him. His dominion is an everlasting dominion that will not pass away, and his Kingdom is one that will never be destroyed. (Daniel 7:13-14)

God is building a new world to replace the first, fallen Creation. But we would have no idea what is going on if we didn't have some spiritual skill to follow what he's doing. That's the purpose behind faith – it enables us to see, understand, and participate in this new project that God is working on, his eternal Kingdom. Even the Old Testament saints understood that this new Kingdom was necessary, that the physical system that they were working with was only a shadow of the real one in Heaven – necessary to teach them the principles, but soon to be replaced with spiritual realities.

So as we read the stories in the Bible, if these people got anything right about God it's because they saw the reality of God, they saw his spiritual world; it wasn't hearsay or tradition, but personal experience of the living God. In other words, they lived by faith.

> For in the gospel the righteousness of God is revealed — a righteousness that is by faith from first to last, just as it is written: "The righteous will live by faith." (Romans 1:17; see also Habakkuk 2:4)

• *Ways*

When we speak of "ways", what we mean is this: the *road* that we take to reach a goal, or the *method* that we use to achieve a certain end. It isn't the goal or the end that we want to look at here, but the *means* of getting there.

The Bible says that God has ways of doing things. In fact, it's one of the more important things to know about God – we are told that if we don't know his ways, there is no way we are going to get into Heaven.

> That is why I was angry with that generation; I said, 'Their hearts are always going astray, and they have not known my ways.' So I declared on oath in my anger, 'They shall never enter my rest.' (Hebrews 3:10-11)

The Bible actually says a lot about the ways of the Lord:

> *As for God, his way is perfect.* (Psalm 18:30)

> *The way of the LORD is a refuge for the righteous.* (Proverbs 10:29)

> *Show me your ways, O LORD, teach me your paths.* (Psalm 25:4)

> *As the heavens are higher than the earth, so are my ways higher than your ways and my thoughts than your thoughts.* (Isaiah 55:9)

God has unique traits that distinguish him from everyone else. He has opinions about things that explain why he does things the way he does. He uses certain methods for achieving his goals, for doing his works. We ought to be able to see these kinds of things about him when we read the Bible, since he wants to make his ways known to us.

But this knowledge also comes from living with him. For example, if you knew someone's name and address you could say that you knew something about that person. But if you went and lived with that person, then you would, over time, learn much more about them than just facts! You could observe them in action, how they arranged their home, what they liked and didn't like. You would get to know them well enough to predict what they would do in a particular situation. In fact, if you lived by the rules of the house, you would probably have to change your ways and preferences to get along with them in their house.

When you study God from the standpoint of his ways, you are going to find out these kinds of things about him. Suddenly you begin to see patterns in his works, common elements across all the stories that show you the same traits over and over. You begin to see that God prefers certain ways of doing things. It is also obvious that, being the

335

Master of the house, he expects everyone to do things his way. You can see then the importance of learning what his ways are so that you can get in step with him.

Knowing his ways gives you a deeper understanding of God than just knowing doctrines about God. The doctrines are good, and you must know who he is so that you don't mix him up with false gods. But knowing his ways means you are getting close to him, you are living with him, you are walking with him and working with him. This comes from an intimate acquaintance, not just textbook learning.

Where will you learn his ways? From the Bible! The Scriptures show you his ways in action. It won't always be spelled out in so many words, but you are supposed to dig deeper than a superficial level. After a long string of lessons in the desert, for example, the Israelites were supposed to understand the way God liked to do things. Anybody with spiritual insight would have begun to see patterns in the work he was doing. Did they?

> Do not harden your hearts as you did in the rebellion, during the time of testing in the desert, where your fathers tested and tried me and for forty years saw what I did. That is why I was angry with that generation, and I said, "Their hearts are always going astray, *and they have not known my ways.*" So I declared on oath in my anger, "They shall never enter my rest." (Hebrews 3:8-11)

Let's look at what happened when they didn't know God's ways. When they arrived at Canaan they still didn't understand the way God does things, even though he had been teaching them his ways; they rebelled at his command to go in and take the land. So instead of letting them into the Promised Land, he turned them away at the edge of Canaan and sent them back out into the desert for another 40 years *to die there.* It was that lack of understanding that so angered God. You can read about it in Numbers 13-14.

Notice too that the New Testament repeats this warning. That means that we Christians are supposed to learn his ways! He will keep *us* away from the Promised Land too, if we are so ignorant as to miss the lesson in the stories that we have recorded for us in the Scriptures.

So we must learn his ways: they will be life to us, the key that unlocks the power in following God as he leads us through this dark world. Those who walk in the ways of the Lord will succeed against impossible odds and against all conventional wisdom.

It would be nice to take the time here to examine his ways, but we don't have the space. What we can do is mention some of his ways so that you can study this subject further on your own. The Bible is full of examples of each of these ways. The problem isn't that we don't have enough material to study this, but that it's so hard for us to see the point. We are often just like the Israelites who lived with God for years in the wilderness and yet never learned the lesson.

- **He works through his people**. There are two kingdoms in the world right now: man's kingdom, and God's Kingdom. Most people are busy working to build up this physical world and keep it running, but there are a few people who can see God's spiritual Kingdom and are spending their time and energy working to make that grow. At the end of time we will all realize that the spiritual Kingdom was the one that God was really interested in throughout history, and the "little people" that we haven't paid much attention to were actually master craftsmen who were building the Eternal City. All the work of this world will be destroyed, but as the saying goes, "what is done for Christ will last."

- **He uses time to ripen**. We either love time or we hate it: we either want it to hurry up so that we can get where we want, or we want it to slow down or stop to prevent something from happening. We are an impatient people. But God purposely works through periods of time to do his works. He will often work on a single project across several generations, for various reasons. We have to learn this tendency of his to stretch things out over time and not get impatient or lose our faith in him when things don't work out on our own schedules.

337

• *He wins by losing.* We don't like to lose at anything. In fact, we will do anything to keep from losing! Losing shows weakness; it means that we can't have what we want. But God will deliberately put us through failure, heartache, loss, suffering, setbacks, and other painful experiences – for which there will not be an escape – in order to achieve deeper spiritual victories. Perhaps the greatest example of this way of God's is the crucifixion of Christ: Jesus had to die before he could live; the death had to happen before there would be life for all of us. Our death is also necessary sometimes; our faith has to learn to accept the failure from him, not reject it, so that we will be ready for the resurrection.

• *He uses a little to accomplish a lot.* We are easily impressed with big things. We love to look at mountains; we fear the massive power of the atom bomb. But we are almost never impressed with little details. God, however, is a master at using little things. He can use little people to accomplish great works. He will stop us at the throne of grace and refuse to listen to our worship because of a sin in our hearts that we thought was too little to pay attention to. He will reward the cup of cold water given in his name. He takes the mustard seed and grows it into a great tree, of benefit to all. Little things give lots of room for God to do miracles and get more glory.

• *He works through his Spirit.* The ways of God are mysterious and hard to understand, and perhaps this is true all the more because he prefers to work through his Spirit. If God would come down in a fiery chariot and take over down here on earth, we would find it easier to see and understand him. But when he sends his Spirit instead – invisible and not detectable by our senses – then we just don't know what to make of what he's doing. But the Spirit is the foundation that the entire universe depends on for its existence. And by working through his Spirit, God is deliberately enforcing the principle that we believe and trust in him *not by*

sight but by faith, which is the only faculty of our souls
by which we can know him.

God has many more ways of doing things, though we don't have
the time and space here to explore them all. For example, keep your
eyes open for these kinds of things: he uses our faith to do big jobs; he
builds up instead of tears down; he uses man; he keeps things simple;
he keeps things in balance; he uses variation and creativity; he loves
tradition and ceremony (his own!); he hates pride. The more you learn
about the way he does things, the better you will know him personally
and start working with him instead of against him.

• *Works*

We understand the concept of work because we all do some form of
work every day. We use materials and procedures to accomplish a task
or reach a goal. And even though we may have been aware that God
does work too, we may not have thought it through very well. The
point of God's works is that they are unique to him.

There are certain things that only God can do. We've already seen
many of things – like miracles, and revelation, and the creative
command. Situations come to a point where we really need help, and
we can't do it nor can anybody else. Most people sense when that
point is reached, and they start praying because they know that only
God can help at a time like that. So far so good. But what do they ask
for? Is it something that only Israel's God can do, or is it something
that they could get from someone else – the world, a false god, a
political party, the supermarket? In other words, their prayer reveals
whether they really understand what the works of the Lord are.

God can certainly make what we could get from the supermarket –
Jesus made bread and fish to feed thousands of people. But those
prayers only get answered in certain situations; if you'll notice, many
of the prayers that ask God for material things often get answered by
our parents or the Salvation Army or some government agency, or
maybe not at all. It would be hard to prove that God actually answered
such prayers. But ask God for the kinds of things that he wants to give
us, and now you have an answer that can't be accounted for by any

other means but the hand of God. Those kinds of answers glorify him; those are the works of the Lord.

God's works can be broken down into seven categories.

- **Creation and Providence** – The first great work that God did was to make the universe, and we saw that only God could have done such a miracle. This world is not only put together in the way that God wants it to operate, he makes sure that along the way we will have the resources we need to obey him as his servants.

- **The making of Israel** – God called Abraham, made a Covenant with him and his descendants to start a family, a nation in which the solution to mankind's problems of sin and death would be solved. The Old Testament is the story of how God put together this system that forms the substance of the Gospel. God adds to Abraham's family and includes them in the Covenant; as John the Baptist once said, God can make children out of stones!

- **Judgment** – God alone can see our hearts, and he alone knows what we are and how to judge our actions. We don't even know ourselves that well! God does this because, as Creator, he will judge how well we fit into his Kingdom and what place, if any, we have in its future.

- **The Coming of Christ** – The work that Christ does for his people was planned long ago, before the foundation of the world. It involved the entire sweep of Old Testament events, and the system was nearly complete when Jesus showed up in the flesh and added the finishing touches. The project is huge; but it fulfills and finishes the system that the entire Bible describes, and it produces a finished salvation in Heaven.

- **Building the Kingdom** – We saw that God set up his creation to be a Kingdom; unfortunately man rebelled against God and threw everything into chaos. God has not forgotten his original plan, however; this new Creation that he is working on is going to be a perfect, eternal Kingdom in which we will all have our places under his will, and we will all perfectly obey the King – not because of his tyranny over us, but because only God's will is going to give us the peace, joy and fullness that makes life good. He is building this Kingdom one soul at a time; all are going to "bend their knee" to the King in the end.

- **The Last Day** – There are a lot of unanswered questions left over from history. What has God been doing? What did man do wrong? What is useful to God in man's works, and what is not useful to him? There are all sorts of things that either we've been completely mistaken about, or we've invented lies to replace the truth. Well, on the Last Day all that will be straightened out – the righteous will get their final reward, the wicked will get their final punishment, and God will get all the glory that is due him. This must happen for justice's sake, so that we will all finally know the truth about God and ourselves. God plans to show us the truth about everything that happened in history.

- **The Scriptures** – Though there are those who believe that the Bible is the work of men, that's actually not true at all. God could never judge us based on the opinions of men. The Bible is the Word of God, given through the Prophets and Apostles, given to us to teach us the truth about God and his spiritual world. It's all God's revelation to us showing us things that we need for our salvation. We can depend on it being the truth.

The Bible tells us many times that we must learn what the works of the Lord are:

> For you make me glad by your deeds, O LORD; I sing for joy at the works of your hands. How great are your works, O LORD, how profound your thoughts! (Psalm 92:4-5)

> Great are the works of the LORD; they are pondered by all who delight in them. (Psalm 111:2)

341

They have harps and lyres at their banquets, tambourines and flutes and wine, but they have no regard for the deeds of the LORD, no respect for the work of his hands. (Isaiah 5:12)

LORD, I have heard of your fame; I stand in awe of your deeds, O LORD. Renew them in our day, in our time make them known; in wrath remember mercy. (Habakkuk 3:2)

And we know that in all things God works for the good of those who love him, who have been called according to his purpose. (Romans 8:28)

For it is God who works in you to will and to act according to his good purpose. (Philippians 2:13)

Great and marvelous are your deeds, Lord God Almighty. Just and true are your ways, King of the ages. (Revelation 15:3)

There are at least two reasons for this. *First*, God's works differentiate him from all other gods. No other god can do the special kind of works that he does for his people. No other god wants to do these things. The Israelites knew better than to ask Baal to save them from sin; it was Baal who tempted them to sin! Israel's God, however, forgives and forgets and delivers us from those sins. These are the very things on God's agenda to do, because these are the things that accomplish his great task of building an eternal Kingdom.

Second, once we know what it is that God does, that tells us what we should be asking for in our prayers. Why go to God for something that we can get from our neighbor? Why waste the opportunity of a lifetime and ask God to tie our shoes when we can do it ourselves? Instead, we need to ask the King for what only the King can give us. We need wisdom; so we ask the God of truth to give us wisdom in his Word. We need salvation from sin; so we ask the God of Abraham to give us the Covenant blessing. The works of God help us focus on the kinds of things that will help us spiritually, the things that the Church needs to accomplish its Mission. The other side of that coin is that you will also find that these are the kinds of prayers that get answered; God is very focused on what he wants to do in your life, and he expects you to be just as focused on them. Don't waste your energy worrying about minor issues, particularly since he told us that he'd take care of them for us.

So we are obligated to learn the works of God. As you will find in the following list, the more we know of what God does, the wiser we become and the more useful we will be in the Church.

- ***Test someone's claim.*** "Dear friends, do not believe every spirit, but test the spirits to see whether they are from God, because many false prophets have gone out into the world." (1 John 4:1) When you know what the God of the Bible does, you have the necessary knowledge to test whether he is at work in a particular situation. People will make all kinds of claims so that you will follow them; they aren't all right, however! Perhaps they are trying to deceive you. Maybe they don't know themselves that God isn't behind what they are doing. You, however, don't have to stay in the dark about it. The simple thing to do is to check what is going on against what the Bible says God actually does.

- ***Work with God, not against him.*** "Since we live by the Spirit, let us keep in step with the Spirit." (Galatians 5:25) When two work together, and one person tears down what the other one is building up, they aren't a very efficient team, are they? Yet that's exactly what we end up doing when we don't know what God is doing and we are busy doing what we want instead. There must be communication between us. And he isn't going to change his plans: *we* must change, and we must conform to what he wants done. But if we know what he wants to do then we become valuable servants to him. He entrusts us with more work, more responsibilities, more opportunities, because we "have in mind the things of God." (Matthew 16:23)

- ***Praise him.*** "Declare his glory among the nations, his marvelous deeds among all peoples." (Psalm 96:3) The Lord not only does wonderful works, he wants everyone to know about them. You are his "advertising agent", so to speak: through your testimony of his works others will hear about him and come to him for the same things. When your neighbor sees that God made such a difference in your life, he will either be turned off (his sin won't let him approach the God who did these things to you!) or become interested in the Lord himself. This means that you have to change what you talk about to others: instead of directing their attention to you, you must start talking about what God did for you. After all, though others may be interested in you as a person, it's what God did for you that is going to help them. All that you have is a gift from God.

• *__Let him do his work — you stick to yours.__* This is the hardest part about learning God's works. It may come as a surprise that some things that you thought *you* were responsible for in your salvation were really God's doing. Don't take God's glory away from him; only he can do certain things for you. If necessary, make a list of the things that only God can do and make another list of the things that he expects of you. (Be sure to get your list from clear statements in the Bible!) Then **wait** on him to do his part, and you stick to your list. Your waiting on him proves that you are really convinced that this is God's job, not yours.

• *__Pray for these things.__* "LORD, I have heard of your fame; I stand in awe of your deeds, O LORD. Renew them in our day, in our time make them known; in wrath remember mercy." (Habakkuk 3:2) When you learn what God does, by reading the record of what he has done in the past, ask for the same things. This pleases the Lord; it means that you are getting the point. Prayer means asking God for what you read in his Word. "Do good to your servant according to your Word, O LORD." (Psalm 119:65) This shows him that you liked what you saw and value them above what your heart would want. And you ask for these special works of God because you see that only they will solve your spiritual problems.

- ## *Glory*

Glory, in the Old Testament, had at least two meanings. The first meaning is "to be heavy" – like gold is heavy, therefore it is glorious. With God, that means that he has a presence that is overbearing; he's majestic, he humbles us in his presence, he overcomes us with holiness. In fact, when Solomon built his Temple, the priests directly experienced the presence of God at its inauguration ceremony.

> Then the temple of the LORD was filled with the cloud, and the priests could not perform their service because of the cloud, for the glory of the LORD filled the temple of God. (2 Chronicles 5:13-14)

And that's why the Apostle John couldn't stand in the presence of Christ, when he had his vision of Heaven.

> The hair on his head was white like wool, as white as snow, and his eyes were like blazing fire. His feet were like bronze glowing in a furnace, and his voice was like the sound of rushing waters. In his right hand he held seven stars, and coming out of his mouth was a sharp, double-edged sword. His face was like the sun shining in all its brilliance. When I saw him, I fell at his feet as though dead. (Revelation 1:14-17)

The other meaning of "glory" is this: *who gets the credit?* When someone does something good, he generally likes to get credit for it. He wants others to know that it was he who did it. So we put our names on books that we write, or we tell others what grades we made in school, or we receive awards for a job well done. We even put our names on our gravestones because we don't want history to forget us – we think we are important.

God is the same way, but not for the same reason. He doesn't try to get credit because he is proud or wants to prove how much better he is than we are. He wants credit because it's a *testimony* of what he can do for anybody who comes to him for help.

God is the source of all good things; being the Creator, he of course made our world, and everything in it is because of him. We wouldn't be anything without him. He gives us the food we need, shelter, friends and family, jobs, communities, pleasures and protection – he is literally our support in every way.

The whole task of mankind is to glorify God; that's what we were made to do. The Westminster Catechism says it best: "The chief end of man is to glorify God and enjoy him forever." This means that, if we do what we were made to do, we will turn to God and he will be the center of our lives. We will come into the presence of, and get hold of, the divine power and wisdom of God, and that will be the source which supplies all of our needs. God will be our life.

Israel got the first chance to learn the glory of God. And they experienced the richness of God in all of its forms and functions. Every human need found its fulfillment in the God of Israel. He covered all the bases, so to speak – he gave them purpose and meaning, he gave them salvation from sin and death, he gave them wisdom and insight, he gave them miracles and power to solve their problems. By the end of the Old Testament we know that "there is no other god like the LORD." That gets him the glory he deserves.

And addressing the second meaning of "glory," we will worship him as God. Praise (and prayer) is acknowledging and appreciating what he is to his face. He likes that – by that he knows we understand how fundamental he is to our lives. Again, not because he is proud, but because he is in fact what he claims to be; and when we believe that then we experience the pleasure of the goodness of God. That gives him pleasure.

The Bible is where we learn about God's glory. For example, the following Scriptures teach us important things about his glory:

- His Names show us his glory, especially the Name that is arguably the most important Name in the entire Bible. *(Exodus 33:18-19)*

- God's glory filled the Temple so overwhelmingly that the worshipers couldn't go in. (*2 Chronicles 7:1*)

- The heavens declare his glory to us. (*Psalm 19:1*)

- We are supposed to glorify the Lord because of what his Names teach us about him. (*Psalm 29:2*)

- The whole earth is filled with the glory of God. (*Psalm 72:19*)

- God gets himself glory through his works. (*Isaiah 26:15*)

- God refuses to let others get the glory that should be his alone. (*Isaiah 42:8*)

- The Lord is going to send his people all over the earth with news of his glory. (*Isaiah 66:19*)

- When God's glory left the Temple, that was the worst thing that could have possibly happened to the Israelites. (*Ezekiel 10*)

- When God's glory came back to the Temple, that was the best thing that could have possibly happened to the Israelites. (*Ezekiel 43*)

- We have seen the glory of God in Christ. (*John 1:14*)

- Jesus glorified the Father in everything he did. (*John 17:4*)

- God is behind everything (except sin), and therefore he deserves glory for it all. (*Romans 11:36*)

- Christians are to reflect God's glory in their lives. (*2 Corinthians 3:18*)

- Christ is the radiance of God's glory — which means that we see the glory of God best in him. (*Hebrews 1:3*)

- Heaven is a place where people continually give God glory. (*Revelation 4-5*)

As you can see, the Bible is full of the glory of God. No other book gives God the credit that he deserves. That's not surprising, because the Lord was behind the writing of the Bible and he *made sure* that he would get proper credit for what he did. It would be a shame if we read it and missed the point — unfortunately, that does happen. Some people are so blind that they can't see the glory of God in the very thing that glorifies him the most!

God is behind all that happens in this world (except for sin – that's our fault). And yet did God get credit for any of this? Did you read in the news today that God took care of billions of people all around the world? Or that he brought nations down, and lifted other nations up? Did you see that God passed judgment on the wicked and gave them what they deserved, and vindicated the righteous? Probably not – the crime of history is that God doesn't get any credit at all for what he does in our world.

God richly deserves glory. The problem is that he usually gets no credit at all for being what he is. He ought to get lots of glory, but he doesn't. We are strangely reluctant to give God the credit he deserves. God has been the most misunderstood being in history! People have claimed to know all about him, when really they didn't know a thing about him; they describe him in ways that completely contradict the way the Bible describes him. The things that people say about God borders on the absurd. In fact, that's the reason we have so many other gods in our religions: everyone has their own idea of who "God" is, and usually no two people are agreed on it.

When we look around for someone to save us, we *don't know* that God can and will save us if we go to him and ask for it — in other words, we don't give him the credit for being the Savior. When we need an explanation for why circumstances turn out the way they do, we *don't know* that God was behind it working out his purposes — and we come up with nonsense trying to explain the way the world works. So, God is like an expert that we should be using but nobody knows about. The Lord gets no credit at all for being what he is, and we continue to shuffle along without him. Most of the time we act as if he wasn't even real.

The result is that "my people are destroyed from lack of knowledge." (Hosea 4:6). This confusion can't continue; the Lord wants everyone to know the truth about him. He wants a Kingdom in which all eyes are on him and he does everything for them that they need. He wants a people who trust in him completely. He wants sinners to fear him. He will be pleased only when we start to take him seriously.

• *Name*

The Name of the Lord is a critical concept in the Bible. Not only does God have many names – the Father, Son and Holy Spirit all have multiple names – but each of the names is our guide to God's nature and the kinds of works he does.

A name describes something. We can usually tell by the name of something what that thing is, or what it's made of, or what it does. A "subway" has within its name the idea of traveling underneath the ground. We use that word instead of "bridge" to distinguish one manner of travel from another.

We also use names for people so that we can get their attention. If I want to talk to Bill, I don't call on Mary. And Bill hears his name and turns toward me to listen.

God's names are used in the same ways. His many names describe the kinds of things he does; in fact, by using these names, he's either telling us that he's the best of something, or he's the only source for something. For example, God is Light, and no other god that we invent can show us the Truth like Israel's God. We may find deliverance in earthly forts and castles, but only in God is the kind of Fortress we need from our spiritual enemies.

God is so rich and full that we start learning his many names right at the beginning of the Bible. He is called the God of Abraham, Isaac and Jacob because he's the God of the Covenant. He's the LORD (capital letters), which represents his special name that he taught the Israelites – it's defined for us in Exodus 34. And over their history they learned the depths of this Name.

> Then the LORD came down in the cloud and stood there with him and proclaimed his name, the LORD. And he passed in front of Moses, proclaiming, "The LORD, the LORD, the compassionate and gracious God, slow to anger, abounding in love and faithfulness, maintaining love to thousands, and forgiving wickedness, rebellion and sin. Yet he does not leave the guilty unpunished; he punishes the children and their children for the sin of the parents to the third and fourth generation." (Exodus 34:5-7)

It's so important to understand the purposes of his Name that we have many Scriptures teaching us how to use it. For example, the Fourth Commandment warns us not to "misuse" it or "use it to no purpose". Yet how many people use God's Name for a curse word or an empty interjection ("O my God!) and have no intention on calling on God by his Name?

When Solomon built his Temple, he understood the true purpose of the Temple.

> But will God really dwell on earth with men? The heavens, even the highest heavens, cannot contain you. How much less this temple I have built! Yet, LORD my God, give attention to your servant's prayer and his plea for mercy. Hear the cry and the prayer that your servant is praying in your presence. May your eyes be open toward this temple day and night, this place of which you said *you would put your Name there*. May you hear the prayer your servant prays toward this place. Hear the supplications of your servant and of your people Israel when they pray toward this place. Hear from Heaven, your dwelling place; and when you hear, forgive. (2 Chronicles 6:18-21)

So God wants us to call on his Name; he hears, he answers, he gives according to the Name that we use in our prayer. That is in fact what Jesus meant when he said we aren't using his Name in our prayers – or, we could say, his many Names. We aren't seeing who he is and calling on *that* God for help.

> Until now you have not asked for anything in my Name.
> Ask and you will receive, and your joy will be complete.
> (John 16:24)

Unfortunately the Jews made a stupid rule late in their history, between the time of the Exile and the coming of Christ. They decided they would take the Law of God seriously from now on, and of course when they came to the Law about not taking the Name of God lightly they wanted to review that as well. They felt that even pronouncing God's special Name – Yahweh – would be to shame and defile the Name, since they were sinners. So they made a law prohibiting the use of the Name in any way. Even during their worship services, they would replace the Name Yahweh with the word Adonai, which means "lord" or "master". They thought they were being extra holy, but what actually happened is that they cut themselves off from their only hope of salvation.

> And everyone who calls on the Name of the LORD [*in Hebrew, "Yahweh"*] will be saved. (Joel 2:32)

No wonder, then, that when Jesus arrived with his special Name ("Jesus" means, in Hebrew, "the LORD saves") the Jews turned away from him and refused God's offer of salvation in him. Their hearts were already hardened against their God.

One wonders, however, if modern Christians have the same fatal characteristic – they too fail to call on, and utilize, God's special names in their prayers.

• *Prophecy*

We already looked at the subject of Prophecy in an earlier chapter, so we will simply review its most important aspects.

- • *First*, prophets only showed up when there was trouble. People were not following the Law of the Lord, so it was time to send them a harsh warning.
- • *Second*, the Prophet knew exactly what to tell the people. God showed him what was in their hearts. That meant that the message was straight from God, and it hurt – it was dead-on accurate.
- • *Third*, the message was always the same: repent or perish! If they didn't turn away from their sin and come back to the Law of Moses, God was going to send an army to destroy them. He was not playing games.
- • *Fourth*, for this reason, nobody liked prophets. Their message was uncomfortable; it uncovered the sin under their hypocrisy, and it threatened punishment. So the people usually either ignored the Prophet or got rid of him. Persecution of prophets is proverbial.

All the prophets had this kind of ministry and message. The two greatest prophets, Jesus and Moses, were assigned the task of setting up the Kingdom of God and its government. But they too had the same elements in their ministries that the rest of the prophets had, with the same results. People were just as uncomfortable around them, and rejected them, as they did the rest of the Prophets.

• *Deliverance*

Christians are so used to using the word "saved" that I'm afraid it doesn't mean much of anything anymore. It seems that a person can be "saved" simply by feeling depressed about the problems in their lives, then hearing and believing a Gospel message like "God loves you, come to Jesus!", then eagerly start going to church looking for a new life. It's obvious that the church is filled with people like this right now, because they haven't been saved from anything that Jesus came to save us from.

To help us get the true meaning of this concept, let's switch to a different word – *delivered*. And the best story to illustrate this is the deliverance of Israel from Egypt.

The descendants of Abraham had been in Egypt since the days of Joseph, and after 400 years came to number in the millions. But they were slaves of Pharaoh. The time had come to get them out of there and fulfill the Covenant made to their forefathers. So God raised Moses to take on the task and lead them out of bondage.

You probably know the story; the Jews celebrate it every year at Passover. Through a series of miracles, the Lord not only broke the back of their Egyptian overlords, he got them out of the country, across the Red Sea on dry ground, and safe at Mt Sinai.

Now let's look at something very obvious here: nothing short of getting them out of the country would do. If Moses had told the people, "Take heart, the Lord cares about you; just keep trusting him!", that wouldn't have been any help at all. They wanted an end of their slavery; they wanted their own land, where they could worship God freely as they ought.

That's the core idea of deliverance. The goal is to *get you out of danger and into a safe place.* Salvation doesn't mean a thing if it doesn't mean that. And the only one who can deliver you is God himself; you are helpless in the enemy's power until God works a miracle with his power and gets you away from there.

Notice that the final step of deliverance was to take them to Mt. Sinai – now that he has delivered us, we belong to him now. We have been delivered to serve our God in holiness and righteousness.

We've already seen, in the chapter on David, who our enemies are – the world, the flesh, and the devil. We have formidable enemies who know how to destroy us easily, and we can do little about it. We need God to deliver us from these enemies. Being "saved" means being delivered; the words are synonymous. That's why I don't think many people understand what conversion really is, because these so-called Christians are still in the grip of the enemy. They haven't been saved from anything; all they did was join a club.

This formula for deliverance – slavery under the enemy, getting us away from the enemy, living with God – is all through Scripture. Deliverance means nothing if not this. God delivered the Israelites from their enemies under David's rule; God delivered Lot from the destruction of Sodom; God delivered Hezekiah and Jerusalem from Sennacherib; God delivered the Apostles from their persecutors.

If we take such a "low road" approach to salvation as to tell people "Just believe in Jesus and you'll be OK!" then the church is going to fill up with unsaved sinners. Salvation has to mean being delivered from sin, from our enemy the devil, from the world and the weakness of our own flesh. If all we have are cheap, superficial conversions, I'm afraid that what Jesus said will come true.

> When the unclean spirit has gone out of a person, it passes through waterless places seeking rest, but finds none. Then it says, 'I will return to my house from which I came.' And when it comes, it finds the house empty, swept, and put in order. Then it goes and brings with it seven other spirits more evil than itself, and they enter and dwell there, and the last state of that person is worse than the first. So also will it be with this evil generation. (Matthew 12:43-45)

- ### *Covenant*

Again, we already looked at the Abrahamic Covenant; so let's just summarize its main points here.

- **The Son** – Abraham's heir – the "miracle baby" – will be the Executor of the estate through whom will come the blessings of the Covenant to all the other heirs. If anybody wants anything from God, they must come to the Heir.

- **The Land** – God would provide the Land of Canaan, the Promised Land, the "land flowing with milk and honey," for Abraham's descendants to live in.

- **The Nation** – Abraham's family would grow into a great nation. They would be distinguished by their father's characteristics: for the Jews, their DNA; for the Christians, their faith.

- **The Blessing** – Through Abraham's offspring would come the solution to sin and death, the overturning of the curse of mankind – resurrection from the dead.

The entire Old Testament works this Covenant out in detail. The Jews found out that they were the **Chosen People**, the one race on earth through whom would come the Covenant blessings. They were to be a testimony to the world, and through them the Lord world bless the nations of the earth. At least that was the theory – in spite of their special calling, they were often a great disappointment, because they couldn't get their own relationship with God straightened out, let alone be a blessing to the rest of the world.

The **Land** – the Promised Land of Canaan – would have been a blessing to them, but over time their sins against God put this promise in jeopardy too. At first the entire land was given to them and sectioned out to the Twelve Tribes; but due to their rebellion, pieces of the land here and there were taken from them, until the Exile when they lost everything. Even after the Remnant was allowed to return, they came back to only a small percentage of what they used to own.

The **Nation** was at first all of Abraham's offspring. No Gentiles were allowed to take part of this Covenant, unless the alien was willing to become Jewish by the Law. But so many Israelites showed their true colors when they turned away from God and took up idolatry, immorality and immersion in the world. The Northern Tribes were wiped out by the Assyrians, and Judah was reduced to a remnant of her former glory, and no king.

And the **Blessing** to the nations – in the form of the Temple and the sacrifice that took away sin – came and went also. The Jews were on their third Temple by the time of Jesus; it had been destroyed and rebuilt over the centuries as God punished his people for their sins instead of redeeming them. By Jesus' day, the Holy of Holies inside the Temple was missing some key elements – the Ark of the Covenant, and the Law tablets from Moses' day.

That's why we should be looking for a replacement for the physical side of this Covenant by the time we get to the New Testament. And we learn from Paul (Galatians 3:8) that the Covenant is actually the Gospel of Christ. God gave everything back that they had lost – only now on a spiritual level, in a form that we can't lose. **Jesus** becomes the Son, the great Heir of Abraham, the Executor of Abraham's estate who will not only live forever, but he will also hand out the spiritual treasures of Heaven to God's children. God intends to give **Heaven** to his people, a Promised Land that will be an eternal joy and pleasure with peace and justice that this world has never seen – again, an eternal promise that will not be taken away from them. The **Church** has replaced the Jewish people with their DNA claims back to Abraham; now membership in Abraham's family, claiming a spiritual inheritance, is based on faith – the universal family characteristic of all of God's people. And the Blessing is **resurrection from the dead** – not symbolic this time as it was in Isaac's reprieve from the death sentence, but a real resurrection to an incorruptible body with no sin.

Conclusion

The Keys are useful, first of all, to focus our attention on God. When we analyze a passage in the Bible using these Keys, they naturally bring God to the forefront because they target something about who he is and what he does. That is in fact the point of the Bible – to teach us about God. So that's the necessary first step to take in any Bible study; the Keys will help you do that.

The next step, of course, is to see what these Keys show us about Christ himself. Because he is the Son of God, the "express image of God", and he does the same things that his Father in Heaven does, we should expect that in Jesus also we see many examples of the Keys in progress.

For example, Jesus *revealed* the Father to us; he did *miracles*; he won battles by losing (the *ways* of God); he taught his disciples (one of the *works* of the Lord – the Bible); he claimed *credit* for being the King; he insisted that people use *faith* to understand him; he revealed God's *Name* to his disciples; he *delivered* people from their sins; he honored the *Covenant* promises by handing out treasures to Abraham's descendants. He did all the things that God does, according to what we learn from the Old Testament.

So what does all this tell us? That Jesus and the Father are one, and that the work that Jesus does for us is nothing less than the hand of God doing what we need and yet can't do for ourselves. What Jesus did, God has been doing from the beginning of time for his people. Our God never changes.

FROM MORALISMS TO CHRIST

There are certain passages in the Bible that are almost always turned into moralisms. The story focuses on someone so completely that it seems obvious to us, and natural, to draw the conclusion that it's teaching us the kind of behavior that God wants to see from all of us.

A unbeliever creates a religion that makes sense to him in light of the fact that his god is a creation of his imagination; once he decides what he wants his god to be, then he invents appropriate behavior so that he can get his god's approval. Their moral system is completely rational and fits right in with the way their world works.

But Christians "live by faith, not by sight." God reveals himself to us, and only then do we know how we have to act toward him. His revelation is always unexpected, and we don't know what he expects of us until he reveals himself. There are always two sides to this equation of morality, and we're not getting the whole picture until we see God.

When we read the stories of the Bible, therefore, we can't be satisfied with just focusing on people's moral actions. These people saw God; what they saw made them act the way they did. If we could see what they saw, the reasons for their actions would become plain to us. But without that insight of theirs, we are probably going to badly misunderstand their actions.

In fact, faith is being able to see the spiritual world of God. With faith we can see realities in God's world that absolutely demand certain actions from us; if we don't take appropriate actions, we're going to suffer in this world, or miss out on the treasures of Heaven, or (what's far worse) end up being punished by him for our sins. The people in the Bible learned this. The God of Israel is different from any other gods, and following him will mean taking new roads and putting your mind and heart on things not in this world. In a sense, none of God's requirements will be predictable – we have to carry our cross to be saved, and we have to leave this world behind if we want the next one.

So we shouldn't be too quick to gravitate to morals when we read about the stories of the saints in the Bible. They were enabled to see

357

God; that's what we need to see also. We're going to look at some of the stories and passages that seem to badly confuse modern readers; they want to apply a moral to the story when really it's a huge revelation of our God.

A wife for Isaac

Genesis 24 tells the story of how Isaac found a wife – or rather how the Lord found him a wife.

This was the problem: while Abraham was living in Canaan, he was a "stranger and alien" and didn't have a place to call his own. And he certainly felt out of place among the Canaanites who worshiped other gods besides the Lord. As far as he was concerned he could live with that; he just stayed on the move through the land.

But the time came when he had to find a wife for his son Isaac, and now he had a problem. He couldn't allow his son to marry one of the pagan girls; she would be certain to steer his heart away from the Lord and the Covenant, and that would be unacceptable. So he sent his servant back to the rest of the family in Haran to find a girl there who knew of Abraham's God. The chapter goes on to describe how the servant put the situation in the Lord's hands, and he was guided directly to the right girl.

So the lesson for most students has been – what else? – how to find a godly wife!

There's no denying that this was in Abraham's mind, but there's something far bigger than that going on in this story. It's all about the third Covenant blessing.

Let's review the Covenant with Abraham. The Lord agreed to do four things for Abraham and his descendants. He told Abraham he would give him a son who would be his heir, the heir of the Covenant itself. That's Isaac. Then he told him that he would give the land of Canaan to Abraham's offspring. That hadn't happened yet, but Abraham was living in the land and learning about it.

The third promise was that God would make Abraham into a great nation. But the only way that one man will turn into millions is if his son finds a wife and starts having children! Abraham himself had no idea who God would have in mind for his son's wife, but then he didn't have to: the Lord had already promised that he would keep this Covenant for Abraham.

So the Lord guided Abraham's servant back home, right to the doorstep of the girl that God had in mind as the fulfillment of the third promise. The fact that Rebekah agreed to go to Canaan with this stranger and marry someone she had never seen before showed that the Lord was directing this whole situation to his own ends.

So the story isn't primarily about finding a godly wife; actually there is very little in it that parallels our modern romances. It's about the Lord faithfully fulfilling the third promise of the Covenant to Abraham *by a miracle,* and starting his family that would eventually grow into millions. Isaac and Rebekah had Jacob, and Jacob had twelve sons who became the patriarchs of the Twelve Tribes of Israel.

Joshua – be strong and brave

When the Israelites were about to cross over into Canaan, they lost their leader of forty years – Moses died on Mt. Pisgah and was buried there. Hs second in command – Joshua – was assigned the task of taking the Israelites across the Jordan River and conquering the Canaanites.

This was no small task. The Lord had promised Abraham that he would give his descendants the land of Canaan, but it was filled with determined pagans who had no intention of just moving over and letting the Israelites in! There was going to be war. But the Lord was not only ready for battle, he plainly told the Israelites to have no mercy – they were instructed to kill every single Canaanite in the land and take their homes and fields as their own. It was to be total annihilation.

Seeing Joshua facing this monumental task, the typical preacher naturally focuses on this encouraging line in the first chapter of Joshua.

Be strong and courageous! (Joshua 1:6)

The Lord himself tells this to Joshua twice, and the Israelites repeat the encouragement as they promise to follow Joshua into battle.

What preachers don't seem to see, what they hardly ever mention, is that Joshua has good reason to be strong and courageous. He's going to follow the Lord into battle and therefore he can't lose!

Life is hard, and we all have our battles to fight. But when we are feeling very alone, being told to be "strong and courageous" is no help. When there's no light, no hope, no direction and no idea of what to do with our problems, we have every reason to be in despair.

Now Joshua not only had his instructions on what he had to do, he had the Lord's promise that God himself would lead the way into battle. All that Joshua had to do was to follow the Lord. As it turned out, this is exactly what Joshua did, and miraculous things happened. Their first success was the complete destruction of Jericho after the Lord made the city walls collapse. After that it was one victory after another as the Lord gave each city and tribe over to them to destroy.

So what exactly was Joshua's hope? It was that God would do the hard parts for them. Joshua's courage wasn't going to win this fight; it was the Lord's right arm. Surely God's command to "be strong and courageous" brought some critical events to mind – for example, when Moses told the Israelites "the LORD will fight for you; you need only to be still." Then the Lord split the Red Sea apart and led his people across on dry ground. Moses knew his God; that was the basis of his confidence.

And God made the same promises to Joshua.

> I will give you every place where you set your foot, as I promised Moses.

> No one will be able to stand against you all the days of your life. As I was with Moses, so I will be with you; I will never leave you nor forsake you.

> Do not be afraid; do not be discouraged, for the LORD your God will be with you wherever you go.

If you're going to preach about Joshua's courage, then you must also preach about Joshua's God; because the Lord's power and wisdom was the source and foundation of Joshua's courage.

David and Goliath

The story of David and Goliath is probably one of the most misunderstood passages in the Bible. No doubt most everyone knows the story; so we won't go over all the details here. You can read the story in 1 Samuel 17.

The Philistines were threatening the Israelites again; they were a perpetual problem to God's people, and there weren't many valiant heroes who knew how to solve this problem once and for all. During this particular battle, Goliath – a giant man – mocked the Israelites with an offer for a man-to-man fight that would determine the outcome of the battle. Nobody was so foolish as to take him up on his offer.

At least that's how the troops saw it. David, however, just a shepherd boy in from the fields to watch the battle, offered to fight Goliath. Armed with only a few pebbles and a slingshot he brought the giant down and cut off his head. It shocked everyone, including his fellow Israelites.

Now the moral of this story is – fill in the blank! Preachers have had a field day with this passage. Moralisms abound: we are told to have the courage of David, the faith of David, the skills of David. We are told to face our problems like David did, and the Goliaths of our lives, no matter how big, will fall down at our feet as we "fight the good fight of faith."

What's ironic is that this is what the Israelites themselves thought was necessary, and that's why they couldn't defeat the giant!

David saw a completely different point.

> Who is this uncircumcised Philistine that he should defy the armies of the living God? (1 Samuel 17:26)

> Your servant has killed both the lion and the bear; this uncircumcised Philistine will be like one of them, because he has defied the armies of the living God. The LORD who rescued me from the paw of the lion and the paw of the bear will rescue me from the hand of this Philistine. (1 Samuel 17:36-37)

> You come against me with sword and spear and javelin, but I come against you in the name of the LORD Almighty,

the God of the armies of Israel, whom you have defied. This day the LORD will deliver you into my hands, and I'll strike you down and cut off your head. This very day I will give the carcasses of the Philistine army to the birds and the wild animals, and the whole world will know that there is a God in Israel. All those gathered here will know that it is not by sword or spear that the LORD saves; for the battle is the LORD's, and he will give all of you into our hands. (1 Samuel 17:45-47)

How often does the man have to say something before we get the point? Goliath wasn't in a fight with the Israelites, but with the God of the Israelites. David wasn't going to destroy Goliath; God was going to destroy him. This is God's fight! David was just the means that the Lord would use to bring Goliath down. And because David could see this critical point, the Lord used him instead of the others.

When we are following Christ, we are not going to win the battles – he is. The world hates *him*; it only hates us because we are with him. And the Lord takes his war against his enemies very seriously; he would never leave us alone to fight these battles. Walking in faith means that we know he will fight his own battles, and he graciously lets us participate in the victory with him. There is nothing in our walk of faith that is the least flattering concerning our abilities, because we have none – at least anything that would get us anywhere with our enemies. He does it all for us.

Proverbs – rules to live by

Proverbs – the classic book on do's and don'ts. It's filled with moralisms across all thirty-one chapters. It's probably a difficult thing for most preachers to try and fit these into the context of God.

But again I've always been uncomfortable just teaching the Proverbs without direct reference to something about God. If we do that, what difference is there between Proverbs and, say, the works of Confucius? Or the moral code of most any religion? If we preach through the Proverbs as simply moral principles that we ought to live by, what would we say that a Jewish rabbi or a secular psychologist couldn't have told us? That doesn't say much for the divine nature of the book.

FROM MORALISMS TO CHRIST

Like any difficult passage (difficult only if you're serious about finding God in it) we have to first start looking around at the context. We will find a significant revelation at the beginning of the book.

> The fear of the LORD is the beginning of knowledge,
>
> but fools despise wisdom and instruction. (Proverbs 1:7)

This oft-quoted verse has more significance than most people realize. Let's begin with that little word "LORD." By using this particular name of God, Solomon puts us before Israel's God, not just any god. Israel's God had a special name that he wanted to be known as. And that Name (in Hebrew it is *Yahweh*) is clearly described in the Law.

> Then the LORD came down in the cloud and stood there with him and proclaimed his name, the LORD. And he passed in front of Moses, proclaiming, "The LORD, the LORD, the compassionate and gracious God, slow to anger, abounding in love and faithfulness, maintaining love to thousands, and forgiving wickedness, rebellion and sin. Yet he does not leave the guilty unpunished; he punishes the children and their children for the sin of the parents to the third and fourth generation." (Exodus 34:5-7)

Think about that passage for a little bit, and you can understand why Solomon recommended fearing this God. He isn't playing around with us. He is an amazingly forgiving and gracious God – but only to those who come to him for salvation. The ones who don't will find that he's a jealous God, a righteous God, a fearful Judge who rejects the wicked and even their descendants. In other words, the LORD really, really wants you to quit sinning against him! He is doing everything possible to make that happen, and he is angry with those who aren't interested in working on it. Sin is the big issue with this God.

In light of that, we can go back to Proverbs and understand more clearly what these principles are focusing on. The context is our relationship to God's Kingdom, in which we all live. We are all subjects of the King (remember the Creation principle?) and duty bound to serve him in all that we do and say. A King's realm operates under Law and justice; woe to that man or woman who steps out of line with the Law! The calling is glorious, the stakes are high, the goal is

God's glory, the punishment is fierce – like it or not, we live in a Kingdom that *will* advance until it covers all the earth. God himself is seeing to it.

So the Proverbs *are* telling us how to live, but the context is what gives it depth and meaning. We obviously can't forget the larger context that we learn from the entire Bible: remember that Jesus also talked about setting up this Kingdom in the Sermon on the Mount, and we learned there that any imperfection will never be tolerated. We learn from Paul that we are sinners, whether we admit it or not, and we will never get along with the Law's requirements unless we find the way of escape from the Law's judgment on us. And we learn from the Apostle's letters that the Spirit of God is actually conforming us to the righteous requirements of the King to make us fit into his Kingdom and be the righteous subjects that he expects us to be.

The more we study, the wider the scope that the book of Proverbs takes on. It's a replay of what we saw in Matthew 5-7 – the description of model citizens in the LORD's Kingdom, and also describes the ones who don't belong there.

The Sermon on the Mount

The Sermon on the Mount is loaded with instructions on how to live our lives. If there's anything in the Bible that's a garden of moralisms, this passage must be it. I have to admit, for a long time I approached this passage in that way. It seems very obvious that Jesus expects us to do this and this and this.

And yet that interpretation always felt unsatisfying to me. The reason I was uncomfortable with it is because the things that Jesus is telling us to do are way beyond our reach. He may expect us to be perfect, but we are never going to reach that goal – and I expect he knows that far better than I do!

His goal is our absolute perfection.

> For I tell you that unless your righteousness surpasses that of the Pharisees and the teachers of the Law, you will certainly not enter the Kingdom of Heaven.

> Be perfect, therefore, as your Heavenly Father is perfect.

364

Now if he doesn't mean *perfection* here, then I don't know what he does mean. It's very simple language.

And when he exposes our hearts with the spiritual level of the Law – like adulterous thoughts and murderous thoughts – I'm sure we all cringe inside with guilt. It's too late to save us because of our sinful past; and it's no use to get our hopes up with the kind of hearts we have now. We will never measure up to these expectations.

Jesus is dealing with the Law of God here – the Law found written in the books of Moses. Most Christians stay away from the Law because of Paul's statement about it (Romans 6:14), but that's not how Jesus looked at it. The Law is actually describing how we should act toward God and man; if we would all follow the Law to the letter, we would actually be nice people.

> Love the Lord your God with all your heart and with all your soul and with all your mind.' This is the first and greatest commandment. And the second is like it: 'Love your neighbor as yourself.' (Matthew 22:37-39)

On the other hand, though it describes a perfect person, we are so far away from obeying all the intricacies of the Law of God that we are without hope of pleasing God with our behavior. We don't even know what most of the Law says. Jesus knows, though, and he knows what the Law is really after – perfection of the heart. Everything that Jesus says in this sermon is such a high standard that whoever fools himself into thinking he's got it is actually blind and dead to the real God. Jesus was severe with the rich young man who thought he was following God's Law.

> If you want to be perfect, go, sell your possessions and give to the poor, and you will have treasure in Heaven. Then come, follow me. (Matthew 19:21)

If we could see the real God in his glory, we would instantly understand how far short we fall of that glory. Man's pride only thrives in ignorance of God, never in his presence.

Once we come to grips with the fact that we can't do what Jesus is telling us in this Sermon, then we can start asking some intelligent questions that should have occurred to us in the first place. First, who is speaking in this passage? He's not your ordinary man, or even a wise teacher like so many other teachers claim to be. These aren't just good ideas of his; they aren't proverbs or sayings that will make our lives more comfortable if we follow them. Jesus is different from all the rest of the wise teachers in history: he's the King, setting up his new Kingdom.

Now every kingdom or nation has a set of laws that it goes by, a constitution, if you will. And anybody who wants to be a citizen in this kingdom has to agree to its constitution. Jesus' Kingdom is no different. In this Sermon, he's setting out the high standards of citizenship in his Kingdom. He will have nothing less than perfection in his Kingdom! There will be no more sin, and as a result no more suffering and death. He's once and for all going to solve the problems of the human race with a perfect world. Remember David's Plan?

How is anybody going to be a citizen in this perfect Kingdom? Well, we have to turn to other passages in the Bible for that answer; we know what Jesus has in mind for our salvation and sanctification. He has to buy our forgiveness, cleanse our hearts, and fill us with his Spirit to make us ready to live in Heaven. But if anybody is interested in living in this kind of Kingdom (that's what he's aiming at in the Beatitudes – these are the marks of those who are truly interested) then he tells us, in this Sermon, what to expect to see if we ever get there.

So the point is not that we should go out and be this kind of person. The point is that, if we're interested, he will make us this way so that we can live in his new Kingdom. The King will have no other kind of citizens living with him.

> But when the king came in to see the guests, he noticed a man there who was not wearing wedding clothes. He asked, 'How did you get in here without wedding clothes, friend?' The man was speechless.

> Then the king told the attendants, 'Tie him hand and foot, and throw him outside, into the darkness, where there will be weeping and gnashing of teeth.'

> For many are invited, but few are chosen. (Matthew 22:11-14)

The Rich Young Ruler (Matthew 19)

The story of the rich young ruler illustrates the tendency of not looking deep enough into the layers of the story. I recently heard a teacher give the standard interpretation of this passage.

A young man came to Jesus asking for counsel. He evidently had heard a great deal about Jesus' teaching, particularly what people needed to do if they wanted to be part of God's Kingdom. So he wanted to know what more he needed to do to qualify. When Jesus told him that the Law of God is the door into the Kingdom, the man answered that he did keep the Law – ever since he was a boy. Jesus' answer was that there was one more thing he lacked – sell all that he had, give it to the poor, and then follow him. That the man couldn't do; he loved his riches too much.

This teacher's interpretation of this passage was that the young man was so close – but he made his money his god, and that kept him out of the Kingdom of God. If he could have let it all go and done what Jesus said, he would get in. The love of money was his one remaining sin.

I'm afraid this teacher was missing the point. Jesus saw a much deeper problem in this man's heart. As usual, Jesus works on a deeper level than we do, and he probes the depths of the heart in ways that we can never go. But he does it so easily! In a few words, he uncovered the young man's heart so that everyone could see the problem. Everyone, that is, who knows anything about the Old Testament and the Law.

The Ten Commandments (which is what Jesus and this ruler both quoted) can be found in Exodus 20 and Deuteronomy 5. The Ten can be separated into two groups: the first four deal with our relationship with God, and the last six deal with our relationships with other people. In fact, you will often find them separated like this in pictures of the two stone tablets that God gave Moses.

This neat arrangement lends itself to Jesus' summary of the Law of God.

> 'Love the Lord your God with all your heart and with all your soul and with all your mind.' This is the first and greatest commandment. And the second is like it: 'Love

367

your neighbor as yourself.' All the Law and the Prophets hang on these two commandments. (Matthew 22:37)

Love God, and love your neighbor. Now take this summary back to the story of the rich young ruler. Jesus' prescription for his soul was to:

- *Love your neighbor* – sell all that you have, and give it to the poor.

- *Love God* – follow me.

The man could do neither. The man thought he was obedient to God's Law; but Jesus very easily showed him that (in the spirit of the Sermon on the Mount, where he reveals the true depth and meaning of some of the Law's commandments) he wasn't following the Law at all, not in the way that God wanted to see. He had no intention of following it. He loved neither God nor man as the Law requires. So it wasn't a single issue that was the problem; it was his entire outlook on the Law of God.

In just a few minutes he was stripped of his pretense of following the Law and shown for what he really was: a sinner in need of salvation.

The point of this passage is not how close the man came to his goal, but how fearful a thing it is to bring our religion to Jesus for his approval. What will we do when we find out that the very things that we thought we were doing right are of no use to him? And instead of encouraging us to try to do more, he insists that we give up what we have been trusting in and go a whole new direction; if we don't, he'll let us walk away unsaved. Because, you see, we must be perfect according to the Law, as God sees perfection.

> Not everyone who says to me, 'Lord, Lord,' will enter the Kingdom of Heaven, but only the one who does the will of my Father who is in Heaven. Many will say to me on that day, 'Lord, Lord, did we not prophesy in your name and in your name drive out demons and in your name perform many miracles? Then I will tell them plainly, 'I never knew you. Away from me, you evildoers!' (Matthew 7:21-23)

Our superficial morality is of no use to God; he requires more than we can do. Our righteousness "is as filthy rags" to him. Even if we try to please him, we don't come any where close to the true depth of the intent of his Law.

When things look this bleak about what Jesus expects of us, we begin to think that maybe it's not in what we do, but what Jesus can do for us. When we get to that point, we're ready to listen and accept his grace, instead of depending on our works, to get to Heaven.

Salt of the earth (Matthew 5)

There's a passage in the Sermon on the Mount that preachers and teachers love to work with, yet I seriously doubt they've thought through the implications of what Jesus is saying there.

> You are the salt of the earth. But if the salt loses its saltiness, how can it be made salty again? It is no longer good for anything, except to be thrown out and trampled underfoot. (Matthew 5:13)

The usual approach is to talk about salt and how useful it is to make food enjoyable. So far so good. Then they go on to draw the parallel – we Christians are made to be salt by Jesus, so that we will be a good influence – a spiritual influence – on that part of the world that we live in. The idea is that maybe we can help turn a bad world into a nicer place. Again, not bad.

But that's where they stop. And that's fatal to the message of the Gospel. The reason we can't stop there is because we've still not discovered what it is about us that would be so useful to the world. And what exactly makes us "salt" in God's eyes? There's too much data missing from this picture; we need to dig deeper. I have met many "Christians" who were most definitely useless in the part of the world that God put them in.

If we back up and look at the bigger picture, it isn't hard to fill in the necessary details. The only thing we have to offer the world that would be of any help at all is Jesus – not ourselves. Jesus is the Savior, he is the Creator, he is the King, he is the Judge – these are all vital functions of the work of Christ as he saves people from sin and death. So if we are interested in his program – saving people from sin and death – then we have to start with bringing Christ to the table.

But even this isn't good enough; many Christians think they are capable of confronting unbelievers with the Gospel of Christ, when actually they don't know much about it at all. It takes years of study, meditation, and experience walking with the Lord before we start getting skilled at applying Christ's medicine to the ills of men. The disciples studied with him for three years before they were ready.

And we've seen that a good grasp of the Old Testament is necessary to truly understand who Jesus really is, and what he has come to do in this world. Paul says about even the deacons of a church that they need to be proficient in the "deep truths of the faith" (1 Timothy 3:9) to carry out their duties over the physical needs of the church.

What all this is leading us to is this: when we walk with the Lord, and learn from him, and obey him in all things, and practice our faith – *then* we will become like salt to others. We have learned to tap the resources of the Messiah. We do not automatically become like salt when we get converted. And we are not going to be like salt if we don't spend our time with the Lord – in prayer, deep Bible study, meditation on his Word, fellowship with the saints.

So I believe that people who are salt in the earth are the ones with spiritual degrees from Heaven, the ones who have fought the good fight of faith and come back from the front with ribbons, the ones who have suffered the cross and rose up victorious, the ones who have labored much in the field and have lots of profit to show for their hard work. Those are the kinds of people who will be useful to others in their need.

Instructions to Timothy (1-2 Timothy)

We should make a quick note about the letters that Paul wrote to Timothy. At first glance we have a long list of requirements and standards that Timothy was supposed to oversee in his church. Choosing elders and deacons, instructions on worship, seeing that each group in the church is behaving itself and helping others, being careful to teach sound doctrine – all these are housekeeping matters in every church. It looks rather mundane on the surface.

But the picture suddenly becomes clearer – it takes on color, so to speak – when we remember who is the Lord of the Church. The Church is not a democracy; it's a hierarchy, with the Lord Jesus on the top. Since he is King, he issues commands for his people to follow. These are not just good ideas; they are his published will. If you'll notice, Paul instructs Timothy to deal summarily with people who refuse to cooperate – this is the kind of thing you would find in a Kingdom, not a democracy.

> As I urged you when I went into Macedonia, stay there in Ephesus so that you may command certain people not to teach false doctrines any longer or to devote themselves to myths and endless genealogies. (1 Timothy 1:3-4)

> Keep reminding God's people of these things. Warn them before God against quarreling about words; it is of no value, and only ruins those who listen. (2 Timothy 2:14)

These are not suggestions, they are instructions to command and rule. This authority that Paul and Timothy have comes from the top. That's why they had confidence to act like this in the church, and they really expected people to respect their authority and do what they said. After all, it's not Paul and Timothy that we are obeying, it's the Lord Jesus himself.

Christ's commands to the Church are for its good – it's not tyranny. Obedience to the King results in life for everyone, peace in the Church, rich spiritual blessings as we follow his leading. So the books of Timothy (and Titus and James and the others) aren't really the words of men, or suggestions or opinions that we can follow if we feel like it. This is what the King wants his Church to look like.

Doers of the Word (James 1)

There's an interesting passage in James that preachers use with great effect in their sermons. It almost always makes people feel like they're not doing enough for God.

> Do not merely listen to the word, and so deceive yourselves. Do what it says. Anyone who listens to the word but does not do what it says is like someone who looks at

371

his face in a mirror and, after looking at himself, goes away and immediately forgets what he looks like. But whoever looks intently into the perfect law that gives freedom, and continues in it – not forgetting what they have heard, but doing it – they will be blessed in what they do. (James 1:22-25)

James is most definitely one of the books in the Bible full of things that we must do. In fact, it's well-known that some the teachers in church history felt that James may not even belong in our Bibles. It feels so out of touch with Paul's message of the free grace of God in Christ.

Without tackling the whole book at this point, let's just focus on this particular passage. It's plain that James is telling us that we have to do what the Word says. But let's remember what the Word is telling us. Hebrews gives us insight on this.

For the word of God is alive and active. Sharper than any double-edged sword, it penetrates even to dividing soul and spirit, joints and marrow; it judges the thoughts and attitudes of the heart. Nothing in all creation is hidden from God's sight. Everything is uncovered and laid bare before the eyes of him to whom we must give account. (Hebrews 4:12-13)

God sees things in us that we can't see – or worse yet, things that we don't want to look at. He measures us by his high standards. He looks for a spiritual foundation – resting on Christ, remaining in Christ, calling on Christ (not just our trying to connect with him, but actually finding Christ built into our lives in real ways). God sees the lack of spiritual treasures in us; he sees too much of the world, a shallow heart satisfied with outward trappings of religion without the reality of Christ. He sees our attitude toward the King, whether we are submissive or not, whether we honor him or not. He is the great Prophet who has been speaking his Word into our hearts and minds for years, and he knows whether we're listening and taking him seriously.

It's all in the Prophets. If you read through their books, you'll see the same close examination, the same holding to God's high standard. The Israelites were never allowed to examine themselves; they would think themselves good people and forget about God! We too are never allowed to decide for ourselves whether we measure up to Christ's standards. He will do that for us, through his Word. And you can count on it, you are far short of the mark.

But the Prophet also holds out hope for us. Even though we are sinners and helpless, the Word offers a way of escape – what Jesus has done and is doing for us. There are treasures available for us, spiritual helps that the Word describes to us. The way to life and Christ is plainly marked in the Word for all to see. Christ has a program already outlined for our salvation, and he laid it all out in the Bible.

In fact, there's an enormous amount of material in the Bible that we may or may not be taking advantage of. The typical churchgoer has a wonderful way of sitting through a sermon and forgetting all about it by the end of the day. He's the kind of person who James is talking about in this passage. It takes a dedicated Christian to dig into all this and start taking advantage of it. The Bible has a wealth of information about God and his plans for us – it requires years of work to master and use skillfully.

The way we use the book of James, then, is not just to get busy with our religion. We have to get busy interacting with the Word, which faithfully examines and analyzes our hearts and tells us what we need from God. We've been looking too much at one side of the equation and not looking at the other side – which was James' very point. It's what we see in God and his Word that we must take seriously, not just ourselves.

Walk in the Light (1 John)

I should make a quick reference to the passage in 1 John that talks about walking in the light. This too is a favorite of preachers who only look at one side of the equation.

> But if we walk in the light, as he is in the light, we have fellowship with one another, and the blood of Jesus, his Son, purifies us from all sin. (1 John 1:7)

Many a sermon has encouraged us, nay commanded us, to "walk in the light." But those same sermons have told us almost nothing about the light itself. Again, we like to emphasize what we need to do, and for some strange reason we are reluctant to fill in the blanks about what God is. We are quite content to tell each other to "walk" and "believe" and "trust" without explaining anything at all about the obvious – who is it that we are believing in?

John discusses the concept of light further in his Gospel. The light is the light that shines on the world that the Logos made.

> In the beginning was the Word, and the Word was with God, and the Word was God. He was with God in the beginning. Through him all things were made; without him nothing was made that has been made. In him was life, and that life was the light of all mankind. The light shines in the darkness, and the darkness has not overcome it. (John 1:1-5)

The Logos is the wisdom of God, through whom all the universe was made. He's the one who made the world to be structured and run by law, and he also made us capable of seeing and understanding what we see so that we can take advantage of it. The Logos makes it possible for us to see and know the world we live in.

John of course was setting us up for the next step in his argument – that this same Logos has come back to make a new world, a spiritual Kingdom, which at present we don't have the capability of seeing or living in. The Gospel is actually a call from the Logos to follow him into this new spiritual world. Along the way, he's going to open our eyes to its realities, and he's going to empower us with his Spirit to live in this new world. How does he do this? Well, he gives us his Word (the Bible) where he lays the whole thing out and describes it to us; and he gives us his Spirit, which enables us to see beyond the physical and the words and perceive the spiritual world behind it that it's talking about. In other words, God will become real to us; we will be living in two worlds at the same time.

The Logos continues to shine the light on his people as they walk in faith from day to day. The key is to keep walking in that light that he's shining on us. If we stray away from him, his Word, his Spirit, we end up in darkness – confusion, loneliness, and without God. Get back on the path, put yourself in the light (the Word and the guidance of the Spirit) and you will start seeing what you need to see again.

This is what John is referring to here in his first Epistle. Again, we see the emphasis is not on what we do, but on what Christ is showing us about himself. Stay in *that* light.

Conclusion

We could spend much more time on this here, but I hope you have seen my method. There are many passages in the Bible that, at first glance, lend themselves ideally to a moralistic sermon. But looking at them in that light is much too narrow a view, and it misses the true scope of the passage.

Develop the habit of looking for God in every passage. Remember that the Bible's purpose is to reveal God to us. He's there, everywhere you go, if you know how to look for him. He's intimately involved in every part of Creation. And he's intimately involved in every aspect of the revelation of Christ – the Bible – which is going to prove our salvation.

Be wary, therefore, of jumping straight to the application when dealing with a text. Look around in the context and ask yourself, "Where is God in this passage?" You may have to back up and look at the entire book; you may have to focus on a single word for the clue – like the example of the word "LORD" in Proverbs. But every application in the Bible is a *response* to what we see in God; otherwise it would be no different from other religions who don't know God and don't care to know him.

POSTSCRIPT

Hopefully you have seen in all this that the Bible is rich on information about Christ. If our modern generation's sermons are impoverished, it's mainly because preachers and teachers haven't been able to see the data in the Bible. That's what I've tried to do here – show you where Jesus is in Genesis, in Leviticus, in Matthew.

The reason we have to focus on Jesus is because he is our lifeline to Heaven – he's the reason we have a relationship with God. The Bible makes Jesus and his work on our behalf very plain to us, so that we can walk in faith with the Son of God. Any religion that isn't focused on Christ is not Christianity.

Since this is not a full-scale commentary of the Bible, I have had to limit my remarks to representative books and passages. You may not see your favorite book in the Table of Contents, but chances are that I mentioned it in passing – or at least dealt with other passages and books that are parallel to the ones you want to know more about. Now it's up to you to follow through and continue your studies. The principles that I've shown you should take you not only in the right direction, but "further on and further in."

I'm going to wish many times that I had withheld this book from publication – so that I could put in something new that I discovered about Christ in the Bible. Just about every time I open the Bible something new jumps out at me. But I am not the fount of information about Christ; the Spirit of God is the one who reveals Jesus to his people. He is your real Teacher. (John 14:26)

May the Lord Jesus answer your prayer and fill you with the knowledge of his glory.

Appendices

CHRIST IN EPHESIANS

I once read the book of Ephesians with the purpose of marking all the places where Paul mentions Christ in some way. I was getting the feeling that modern preachers didn't understand Jesus as much as they thought they did, because they never seemed to talk about Christ; it was always about duties of Christians, or our sins, or social issues. Sometimes they would drop his Name around in their sermons but without any purpose – only to sanctify, it would seem, what they were talking about. One could easily have taken Christ's Name out of their sermon and it would still make sense! What I wanted to see was if that held true of Paul's letter as well.

I found 100 places where Paul refers to Christ in some way. Examining each one I found that, far from simply using his Name to make the letter more "Christian," Paul was appealing to something in Christ to make his point. The letter would be nothing, in other words, if you took out the references to Christ. He *is* the argument of the letter.

This is all the more significant when one realizes that the letter to the Ephesians is the equivalent of a 20 minute sermon! For Paul to have used so many things about the Lord that many times in such a short span shows an amazing depth of knowledge of Jesus Christ. We simply are unequal to Paul's insight of the Lord; we are doing good when we form an entire sermon around one or two verses from his letter!

Here are the 100 occurrences of the references to Christ. I present them to show you that Jesus was constantly the theme for the Apostles when they wrote the other books of the New

Testament. Only if you get well-grounded in the Gospels will you begin to appreciate how the Apostles founded their Church letters on the doctrine of Christ.

Eph. 1:1	Paul was an apostle of *Christ Jesus*
Eph. 1:1	the letter was written to those who were faithful in *Christ Jesus*
Eph. 1:2	Paul blesses them with grace and peace from the *Lord Jesus Christ*
Eph. 1:3	Paul praises the Father of the *Lord Jesus Christ* ...
Eph. 1:3	... for the spiritual blessings he gave us in *Christ*
Eph. 1:4	the Father chose us in *him* before the world
Eph. 1:5	he predestined us to be adopted as his sons in *Christ Jesus*
Eph. 1:6	he has freely given us grace in the *One* he loves
Eph. 1:7	in *him* we have redemption through his blood
Eph. 1:9	the mystery of his will, purposed in *Christ*
Eph. 1:10	he will bring all things under one head, even *Christ*
Eph. 1:11	in *him* we were also chosen
Eph. 1:12	the apostles were the first to hope in *Christ*
Eph. 1:13	and we also were included in *Christ* when we heard the gospel
Eph. 1:13	we were marked in *him* with a seal, the promised Holy Spirit
Eph. 1:15	Paul heard about their faith in the *Lord Jesus*
Eph. 1:17	Paul prayed that the God of our *Lord Jesus Christ* might give the Spirit
Eph. 1:20	the mighty power which God exerted in *Christ*
Eph. 1:20	he raised *him* from the dead ...
Eph. 1:20	... and seated *him* at his right hand
Eph. 1:22	God placed all things under *his* feet ...
Eph. 1:22	... and appointed *him* to be head over everything for the church
Eph. 1:23	the church is *his* body ...
Eph. 1:23	... the fullness of *him* who fills everything in every way
Eph. 2:5	God made us alive with *Christ*
Eph. 2:6	God raised us up with *Christ* ...
Eph. 2:6	in the Heavenly realms in *Christ Jesus*
Eph. 2:7	his grace expressed in his kindness to us in *Christ Jesus*
Eph. 2:10	we were created in *Christ Jesus* to do good works
Eph. 2:12	once we were separate from *Christ*
Eph. 2:13	now in *Christ Jesus* we have been brought near ...
Eph. 2:13	... through the blood of *Christ*
Eph. 2:14	for *he himself* is our peace
Eph. 2:15	abolished the Law in *his* flesh
Eph. 2:15	*his* purpose was ...
Eph. 2:15	... to create in *himself* one new man out of the two
Eph. 2:16	*he* put to death their hostility
Eph. 2:17	*he* came and preached peace
Eph. 2:18	through *him* we both have access to the Father

Eph. 2:20   *Christ Jesus himself* is the chief cornerstone
Eph. 2:21   in *him* the whole building is joined together
Eph. 2:22   in *him* we too are being built together to become a dwelling

Eph. 3:1   Paul is a prisoner of *Christ Jesus* for the sake of the Gentiles
Eph. 3:4   Paul's insight into the mystery of *Christ*
Eph. 3:6   the Gentiles and Israel share in the promise in *Christ Jesus*
Eph. 3:8   Paul preaches to the Gentiles the unsearchable riches of *Christ*
Eph. 3:11   God accomplished his eternal purpose in *Christ Jesus our Lord*
Eph. 3:12   in *him* and ...
Eph. 3:12   ... through faith in *him* we may approach God
Eph. 3:17   that *Christ* may dwell in our hearts through faith
Eph. 3:18   how wide and long and high and deep is the love of *Christ*
Eph. 3:21   to him be glory in the Church and in *Christ Jesus*

Eph. 4:1   Paul is a prisoner for the *Lord*
Eph. 4:5   there is one *Lord*
Eph. 4:7   each one of us has grace as *Christ* apportioned it
Eph. 4:8   when *he* ascended on high ...
Eph. 4:8   ... *he* led captives in *his* train and gave gifts to men
Eph. 4:9   *he* also descended to the lower earthly regions
Eph. 4:10   *he* who descended is the very one who ascended higher than
             the heavens
Eph. 4:11   it was *he* who gave some to be apostles, etc.
Eph. 4:12   so that the body of *Christ* may be built up
Eph. 4:13   so that we reach unity in the knowledge of the *Son of God*
Eph. 4:13   attaining to the whole measure of the fullness of *Christ*
Eph. 4:15   we will grow up into the Head, that is, *Christ*
Eph. 4:16   from *him* the whole body grows and builds itself up
Eph. 4:17   Paul insists in the *Lord*
Eph. 4:20   we did not come to know *Christ* that way
Eph. 4:21   surely you heard of *him* and were taught in *him* ...
Eph. 4:21   ... in accordance with the truth that is in *Jesus*
Eph. 4:32   just as in *Christ* God forgave you

Eph. 5:2   just as *Christ* loved us and gave *himself* up for us
Eph. 5:5   no idolaters have any inheritance in the Kingdom of Christ and of God
Eph. 5:8   now we are light in the *Lord*
Eph. 5:10   find out what pleases the *Lord*
Eph. 5:14   wake up, O sleeper, and rise from the dead, and *Christ* will
             shine on you
Eph. 5:17   understand what the *Lord's* will is
Eph. 5:19   sing and make music in your heart to the *Lord*
Eph. 5:20   giving thanks for everything in the Name of our *Lord Jesus Christ*
Eph. 5:22   wives, submit to your husbands as to the *Lord*

Eph. 5:23	the husband is the head of the wife as *Christ* is the head of the Church
Eph. 5:24	the Church submits to *Christ*
Eph. 5:25	*Christ* loved the Church and ...
Eph. 5:25	... gave *himself* up for her
Eph. 5:27	*he* presented her to *himself* as a radiant Church
Eph. 5:29	*Christ* feeds and cares for the Church
Eph. 5:30	we are members of *his* body
Eph. 5:32	the union of *Christ* and the Church is a profound mystery
Eph. 6:1	children, obey your parents in the *Lord*
Eph. 6:4	bring your children up in the training and instruction of the *Lord*
Eph. 6:5	slaves, obey your masters just as you would obey *Christ*
Eph. 6:6	like slaves of *Christ*, doing the will of God from the heart
Eph. 6:7	serve wholeheartedly, as if you were serving the *Lord*
Eph. 6:8	the *Lord* will reward everyone for whatever good he does
Eph. 6:9	*he* who is both their Master and yours is in Heaven ...
Eph. 6:9	and there is no favoritism with *him*
Eph. 6:10	be strong in the *Lord* ...
Eph. 6:10	... and in *his* mighty power
Eph. 6:21	Tychicus, the faithful servant in the *Lord*
Eph. 6:23	Paul blesses with love and faith from the Father and the *Lord Jesus Christ*
Eph. 6:24	grace to all who love our *Lord Jesus Christ* with an undying love

THE NAMES OF CHRIST

Following are most of the Names of Christ that are distributed across the Old and New Testaments. Here is material for Bible studies and sermons for years!

Advocate	Job 16:19
All & in all	Colossians 3:11
Alpha & Omega	Revelation 21:6
Altar	Hebrews 13:10
Amen	Revelation 3:14
Apostle	Hebrews 3:1
Ark	Hebrews 11:7
Arm of the Lord	Isaiah 53:1
Atoning sacrifice	1 John 4:10
Author of our faith	Hebrews 12:2
Author of Life	Acts 3:15
Author of salvation	Hebrews 5:9
Banner	Isaiah 11:10
Beginning of Creation	Revelation 3:14
Beloved Son	Matthew 3:17
Blessed Ruler	1 Timothy 6:15
Branch	Isaiah 11:1
Bread	John 6:51
Bridegroom	Matthew 9:15
Bright morning star	Revelation 22:16
Brother	Hebrews 2:11
Carpenter's son	Mark 6:3
Chief Shepherd	1 Peter 5:4
Chosen One	Isaiah 42:1
Christ	Matthew 1:18
Clothing	Romans 13:14
Commander	Isaiah 55:4
Consolation of Israel	Luke 2:25

Cornerstone	1 Peter 2:6
Creator	Colossians 1:16
Desire of nations	Haggai 2:7
Dew	Hosea 14:5
Door	John 10:9
Everlasting Father	Isaiah 9:6
Example	John 13:15
Faithful witness	Revelation 1:5
Firstborn	Colossians 1:15
Foundation	1 Corinthians 3:11
Fountain	Zechariah 13:1
Freedom	John 8:36
Friend	Matthew 11:19
Good Shepherd	John 10:11,14
Head	Colossians 1:18
Heir of all things	Hebrews 1:2
High Priest	Hebrews 4:14
Holiness	1 Corinthians 1:30
Holy Child	Acts 4:27
Holy One of God	Mark 1:24
Hope	1 Timothy 1:1
Horn	Luke 1:68,69
Husband	Ephesians 5:25
I am	John 8:58
Image of God	2 Corinthians 4:4
Immanuel	Matthew 1:23
Jesus	Matthew 1:21
Judge	2 Timothy 4:8
Just One	Acts 7:52
Kernel	John 12:24
King Eternal	1 Timothy 1:17
King of the Jews	Matthew 2:2
King of kings	Revelation 19:16
Ladder	Genesis 28:12
Lamb of God	John 1:29
Last Adam	1 Corinthians 15:45

Lawgiver	Isaiah 33:22
Leader	Isaiah 55:4
Life	Colossians 3:4
Light	John 12:46
Lion of Judah	Revelation 5:5
Lord of All	Acts 10:36
Lord of Glory	1 Corinthians 2:8
Lord of Lords	Revelation 19:16
LORD	Exodus 34:6-7
Man of Sorrows	Isaiah 53:3
Master	Matthew 23:8
Mediator	1 Timothy 2:5
Messenger of Covenant	Malachi 3:1
Messiah	Psalm 2:2
Mighty God	Isaiah 9:6
Nazarene	Matthew 2:23
Only Begotten Son	John 3:16
Overseer of Souls	1 Peter 2:25
Passover	1 Corinthians 5:7,8
Peace	Ephesians 2:14
Physician	Luke 4:23
Portion	Lamentations 3:24
Power of God	1 Corinthians 1:24
Prince of Peace	Isaiah 9:6
Prophet	Deuteronomy 18:15
Radiance of God's glory	Hebrews 1:3
Ransom	1 Timothy 2:6
Redemption	1 Corinthians 1:30
Refuge	Joel 3:16
Resurrection	John 11:25-26
Reward	Genesis 15:1
Righteousness	Jeremiah 23:6
Rising Sun	Luke 1:78
Rock	1 Corinthians 10:14
Root of David	Revelation 22:16
Root of Jesse	Isaiah 11:10

Ruler	Matthew 2:6
Salvation	Psalm 118:14
Savior of the world	John 4:42
Seed	Galatians 3:16
Seed of Woman	Genesis 3:15
Servant	Matthew 12:18
Shield	Genesis 15:1
Shiloh	Genesis 49:10
Son of David	Matthew 12:23
Son of God	Matthew 16:16
Son of Man	Matthew 16:13
Son of Mary	Mark 6:3
Son of Most High	Luke 1:32
Song	Psalm 118:14
Strength	Philippians 4:13
Sun of righteousness	Malachi 4:2
Supply	Philippians 4:19
Teacher	Matthew 23:10
Temple	Revelation 21:22
Treasure	Matthew 13:44
Truth	John 1:17
Vine	John 15:5
Way	John 14:6
Wisdom	1 Corinthians 1:30
Wonderful Counselor	Isaiah 9:6
Word	John 1:1

SCRIPTURE INDEX

Mark 8:34-35	131
Mark 10:52	76
Luke 3:21-22	173
Luke 4:1-2	131
Luke 6:35-36	84
Luke 6:38	80
Luke 7:39-40	163
Luke 7:50	76
Luke 9:58	128
Luke 9:59-60	83
Luke 12:2-3	158
Luke 12:16-21	128
Luke 12:20-21	223
Luke 12:45-46	138
Luke 13:16	77
Luke 14:7-11	201
Luke 16:9	80, 128
Luke 16:27-31	102
Luke 16:29	35
Luke 17:19	76, 77
Luke 18:14	77
Luke 19:9	77, 242
Luke 20:26	163
Luke 24:27	5
John	115
John 1:1	134
John 1:1-5	53, 374
John 1:14	347
John 1:32	173
John 3:10	21
John 3:12-13	75
John 3:14-15	88
John 4:10	163
John 4:21-24	321
John 5:19	59
John 5:39	293
John 5:39-40	78
John 6:35	75, 234
John 6:39	89
John 6:63	89, 169
John 6:66	165
John 7:38-39	89
John 8	73
John 8:6-8	164
John 8:24	163
John 8:39-44	78
John 8:56	72, 183, 260, 334
John 10:10	88
John 10:16	242
John 11:25-26	88
John 13:2-4	79
John 13:34-35	86, 141
John 14:2-3	205
John 14:2-4	198
John 14:6	27, 75, 187
John 14:6-7	115
John 14:8-10	134
John 14:13-14	75
John 14:26	376
John 15:3-4	198
John 15:15	51
John 15:18	271
John 15:18-19	131
John 15:26	129
John 16:24	350
John 16:33	132
John 17:3	88, 109
John 17:4	347
John 17:5	85, 246
John 17:11,24	80
John 17:22-23	85
John 17:24	90, 198, 247
John 18:36	79, 127
Acts	263
Acts 1:8	169
Acts 2	265
Acts 2:27	171
Acts 2:29	171
Acts 2:40	165
Acts 3	266
Acts 3:22	146
Acts 4	268, 269
Acts 4:12	187
Acts 7	270
Acts 7:55-56	272
Acts 9	331
Acts 10	272
Acts 13	274
Acts 13:42	274
Acts 15	275

FOR FURTHER STUDY

The following books are available on **Amazon.com**

MYSTERY REVEALED: A BEGINNER'S BIBLE SURVEY

THE THRONE OF DAVID

WHERE THE PATHS MEET

A NEW MODEL FOR BIBLICAL STUDIES

TEN KEYS TO THE BIBLE

THE BIBLE EXPLAINS CREATION

KNOTS UNTIED

THE SECRET TO ANSWERED PRAYER

JESUS AND THE NEW TESTAMENT

A HOLY TEMPLE

REMOVING THE VEIL

THE CHURCH MILITANT

You can also find them by going to the following website:

www.Ravenbrook.org

NOTES

NOTES

www.ingramcontent.com/pod-product-compliance
Lightning Source LLC
Chambersburg PA
CBHW060238100426
42742CB00011B/1566